Threatening Others

This series of publications on Africa, Latin America, Southeast Asia, and Global and Comparative Studies is designed to present significant research, translation, and opinion to area specialists and to a wide community of persons interested in world affairs. The editor seeks manuscripts of quality on any subject and can usually make a decision regarding publication within three months of receipt of the original work. Production methods generally permit a work to appear within one year of acceptance. The editor works closely with authors to produce a high-quality book. The series appears in a paperback format and is distributed worldwide. For more information, contact the executive editor at Ohio University Press, Scott Quadrangle, University Terrace, Athens, Ohio 45701.

The Ohio University Research in International Studies series is published for the Center for International Studies by Ohio University Press. The views expressed in individual volumes are those of the authors and should not be considered to represent the policies or beliefs of the Center for International Studies, Ohio University Press, or Ohio University.

Threatening Others

Nicaraguans and the Formation of

National Identities in Costa Rica

Carlos Sandoval-García

Ohio University Research in International Studies
Latin America Series No. 42
Ohio University Press
Athens

12 11 10 09 08 07 06 05 04 5 4 3 2 1

The books in the Ohio University Research in International Studies Series
are printed on acid-free paper ∞ ™

Library of Congress Cataloging-in-Publication Data

Sandoval García, Carlos.

[Otros amenazantes. English]

Threatening others : Nicaraguans and the formation of national identities in Costa Rica / Carlos Sandoval García.

p. cm. — (Research in international studies. Latin America series ; no. 42)

Includes bibliographical references and index.

ISBN 0-89680-235-3 (pbk. : alk. paper)

1. Nicaraguans—Costa Rica—Public opinion. 2. Illegal aliens—Costa Rica—Public opinion. 3. Public opinion—Costa Rica. 4. Identity (Psychology)—Costa Rica. 5. Nationalism—Costa Rica. 6. Ethnicity—Costa Rica. 7. Discrimination—Costa Rica. 8. Costa Rica—Ethnic relations. I.Title. II. Series.

F1557.N5S26513 2004

305.868'728507286--dc22

2004000099

Contents

Tables

Abbreviations

Costa Rican Newspapers

Al Día (AD)
Diario Extra (DE)
La Gaceta (LG)
La Nación (LN)
El Norteño (EN)
El Pacífico (EP)
La Prensa Libre (LPL)
La República (LR)

Nicaraguan Newspapers

Barricada (B)
El Nuevo Diario (ND)
La Prensa (LP)
La Tribuna (LT)

Miscellaneous Abbreviations

CATS	Certificados de Abono Tributario (Tax payment certificate)
CENIDH	Comisión Nicaragüense de Derechos Humanos (Nicaraguan commission for human rights)
CPDH	Comisión Permanente de Derechos Humanos (Permanent commission for human rights)
EDSN	Ejército Defensor de la Soberanía Nacional (Army for the defense of national sovereignty)
EPS	Ejército Popular Sandinista (Sandinista popular army)

FSLN	Frente Sandinista para la Liberación Nacional (Sandinista national liberation front)
MCRL	Movimiento Costa Rica Libre (Movement for a free Costa Rica)
ODECA	Organización de Estados Centroamericanos (Organization of Central American states)
PC	Partido Comunista (Communist party)
UNOC	Unión Nicaragüense de Obreros y Campesinos (Nicaraguan union of workers and peasants)
USAID	U.S. Agency for International Development

Acknowledgments

IN 1993 I MET some Nicaraguan workers in the course of an ethnographic project in San José, Costa Rica. They had arrived in San José looking for jobs. Roberto, Benjamín, and Geovanny may not have been aware of it but, while we were building a house, they taught me what it can mean to be a foreigner in "my" country. Nine years have passed between that experience and the writing of this book, and diverse institutional and personal changes have taken place. This project was originally undertaken as a Ph.D. thesis in the Department of Cultural Studies and Sociology at the University of Birmingham, United Kingdom. My gratitude to John Gabriel and Jorge Larraín for offering me warm support and friendly criticism as my supervisors. I also thank Michael Green and Sue Wright, who read through some drafts and improved this project in various ways. Gargi Battacharyya and Sarah Radcliffe were stimulating examiners who encouraged me to reflect on my work. The participants in the Graduate Research Workshop also provided me with generous feedback between 1997 and 2000. Cali Coquet, Jane Barry, and Shana Hughes read the manuscript at different stages and improved my shaky English enormously. Lucila Espinoza helped me to work on the bibliography. My gratitude also goes to Thomas Walker, Latin American editor at Ohio University Press, for his interest in this project and to Lowell Gudmundson, the reader, who provided generous comments and insightful suggestions. Many thanks also to Gillian Berchowitz and Sharon Rose of Ohio University Press and to copy editor Bob Furnish for seeing this project through to completion.

I am grateful to many people who have contributed insights, information, and advice, including Ciska Raventós, Patricia Alvarenga, Iván Molina, Marielos Giralt, and Lucy Gutiérrez. Also my thanks to Frances Kinloch and Miguel Angel Herrera, researchers at the Instituto de Historia de Nicaragua y América Central at the Universidad Centroamericana, Managua, who advised me on diverse topics of Nicaraguan history.

A very big thank you to the authors of the testimonials: Juan Bautista Alvarado, Aleyda Blandino, Elmer Bustamante, Lissette Castillo, José

María Centeno, Michelle Delgado, Aracely Flores, José Tobías Galeano, Tomás Jirón, Daviana M. Guerrero, Verónica del Carmen Huerta, Nereyda Larios, Marta Lorena Martínez, July A. Martínez, Vicente P. Mondragón, Ever Rivera, Octavio Rivera, Manuel Rodríguez, Martín Rodríguez, Elí Sandoval, Guadalupe Sequeira, Freddy Silva, Pánfilo R. Sobalvarro, Alba A. Talavera, Leoncia Tellez, and Gary Alfonso Urbina. My thanks also to the staff and audiences of the following radio and television programs which allowed me to publicize this activity: *El nicaragüense* (radio Libertad), *Nicaragua y usted* (radio Emperador), *Sala V* (TV42), *La voz nica* (radio Cucú), *Buenos días* (TV7), and *Noti 14* (TV14). The United Nations Development Program and the Institute for Social Research at the University of Costa Rica supported the reproduction of a number of copies of the testimonials at two different stages of this project.

Students, teachers, and principals at the following primary and secondary schools were very kind in agreeing to participate in the writing of stories about Costa Rica as a nation and the Nicaraguans in Costa Rica: La Carpio, Colegio de Siquirres, Colegio Lincoln, Colegio Saint Clare, Conbi College, Dante Alighieri, Liceo de Pavas, Liceo de Poás, Liceo de San Carlos, Liceo de Sarapiquí, Liceo Vargas Calvo, Rincón Grande de Pavas, and Los Sitios. Thanks to all of them.

I also thank the University of Costa Rica and the Committee of Vice-Chancellors and Principals of the Universities of the United Kingdom for allowing me the opportunity to undertake postgraduate studies. Finally, I thank my mother, Marielos, and my sister María, who have encouraged and supported me all my life and especially during the illness and unexpected death of my father, Arnoldo. I wanted to show him the result of being away for three years, but the dreams that really matter are, most of the time, unattainable.

Introduction

In September 1997 the Costa Rican men's soccer team lost its match against the United States. This meant that Costa Rica failed to qualify for the World Cup Finals in France in 1998. After the match, the supporters—mostly men—could not believe the result. According to media reports, some boys even "renounced" their nationality: "With this team, I prefer to change my nationality," said one. In one newspaper photo posters state, I Am Nica and We Are Nicas (*LN* 9/8/97). To become a "nica" is the most degrading step a Costa Rican could take in extreme circumstances, such as defeat in soccer, one of the most nationalized and masculinized of all cultural practices. The disappointed fans did not want to be Sandinistas, rather they chose to be nicas. In Costa Rica this abbreviation is usually employed to underline the difference between Costa Ricans and the Nicaraguans who live in Costa Rica. Indeed, to be a nica has become an offense in itself. While *gringo* describes any white foreigner, regardless of nationality, and carries a positive connotation, *nica* signifies undesirable otherness.

This example illustrates the principal concerns of this research. It indicates ways in which national identities work through other identities, in this particular case through masculine traits, and also highlights how a sense of nationhood rests on everyday practices such as soccer. The links between the media and everyday practices in the formation of nationhood are also crucial in this example, since the fans employed racialized representations of Nicaraguans provided by the media in order to represent their disenchantment. Their reaction was, in turn, reworked as a sports news item in such a way that their own "national disillusionment" could be represented as public opinion. In other words, the sense of national belonging works through the media; without public diffusion, such reactions would become isolated.

National identities in Costa Rica have been characterized by essentialist representations that highlight an idyllic sense of the past, a "white" population and recently a prosperous middle class and stable democracy as key sources of belonging. Conversely, the Nicaraguan "other" is frequently associated with a turbulent political past, dark skin, poverty, and nondemocratic forms of government. In other words, similar categories are deployed to define the "true nationals" and the "other." This representation of Costa Rica as a unique nation has been constructed through contrast with other Central American nations, which have faced more economic injustice and political contradictions. Relations with Nicaragua have been of particular importance, given the dramatic economic crisis and political polarization there, which have driven thousands of Nicaraguan citizens out of their country. As of the 2000 census, 226,374 Nicaraguans were living in Costa Rica—nearly 6 percent of the population (INEC 2001, 5). If temporary workers are also considered, that number might reach three hundred thousand (7.8 percent) during harvest seasons.

The meaning of leaving Nicaragua and being badly paid in Costa Rica was summarized by a Nicaraguan woman who lives in a humble community located in Pavas (east of San José): "Here the *tugurios* [shanties] are made of wood and zinc sheets; furthermore, we've got a water supply and electricity. In Managua, we had neither wood, water, nor electricity; the houses were made of cardboard boxes" (Quesada 1998, 13). Nicaragua is, after Haiti, the poorest nation in Latin America. About 80 percent of the population live below the poverty line and 44 percent live in extreme poverty (in Costa Rica, approximately 20 percent of the population live below the poverty line). In 1997 over 40 percent of the total population survived on less than one dollar per day, according to research conducted by the United Nations Development Program. Throughout the 1990s unemployment was considered the main national problem (CENIDH 1998, 12, 26, 57; UCA 1999, 10; *LP* 9/20/01).

Mitch, the worst Caribbean hurricane in perhaps the last two hundred years, has made these indicators even more pessimistic. Approximately nine thousand people died and two and a half million were injured. The lost infrastructure was equivalent to 65 percent of GDP. If the Nicaraguan population grows by 2.5 percent per year, the GDP will have to increase by 6 percent annually during the next forty years for Nicaraguans to reach the average per capita income in Latin America (UCA 1999, 46, 49; *LN* 4/22/99). Besides being badly paid, the Nicaraguan community in Costa Rica is often racialized and criminalized. Some commentators have suggested that it is a result of their "immigration," blaming them for their own situation. In a way, the immigrant is becoming the communist of the twenty-first century.[1]

This book explores the extent to which recent processes of exclusion and racialization of Nicaraguans are related to the ways in which the Costa Rican national identity has been historically represented, through the accentuation of differences in relation to external others (neighbor nations) and internal others (indigenous people, peasants, and blacks). Of particular importance is to look at the formation of the sense of nationhood in Costa Rica and the representation of the Nicaraguan as other as long-term, mutually affected processes. This reciprocal interaction requires us to analyze not only current events but also historical developments, since "without the effort of reworking versions of the past there can be no change in the present" (Clare and Johnson 1998). In this sense, the arrival of Nicaraguans in Costa Rica began to be recognized in the nineteenth century, when political conflicts and the expansion of the coffee industry in Nicaragua caused peasants to be expelled from their lands; some went to Costa Rica looking for jobs, especially in the construction of the railroad to the Atlantic region and in the banana plantations that would be planted there. The Nicaraguan civil war that took place between 1927 and 1932 also activated immigration. On the other hand, since independence from Spain in 1821, there have been long-term disputes and conflicts associated with the definition of the borders between the two states. Nationalistic discourses have turned such borders into racialized boundaries. Hence, Nicaraguans have long been considered both internal and external others. They are perceived as immigrants, but also as members of a state that until some years ago was perceived as a communist threat. Currently, both internal and external representations are interwoven and are reworked in particular circumstances.

Meanwhile, the hegemonic sense of nationhood in Costa Rica seems to have been associated with three principal patterns of representation: an idyllic past that goes back to the colonial period, racialized representations that consider Costa Rica to be a nation inhabited by "white" people, and widespread notions of uniqueness based on cultural differences. The past, as a source of identity and difference, has been crucial. Liberal histories have argued that the deprivation suffered during the colonial period engendered equality among the inhabitants, which, in turn, was interpreted as a distinctive "rural democracy." Later, such rural democracy became a vital definition of current Costa Rican politics. Class-based, ethnic, and gendered inequalities have been replaced by images of a society defined by public consensus.

A second way of representing nationhood is related to racialized imagery. The small size of the indigenous population—in relation to other Central American provinces during the colonial period—was interpreted within hegemonic perspectives as a sign that the Costa Rican population is the "whitest" in Central America. This has been reinforced through the emphasis on *mestizaje*—descendants of mixed unions of Spanish and indigenous people—as a key explanation of the country's ethnic configuration. But, as William Rowe and Vivian Schelling have noted, "The difficulty with the concept of *mestizaje* is that, without an analysis of power structures, it becomes an ideology of racial harmony which obscures the actual holding of power by a particular group" (1991, 18). This selective ethnic representation has underlined the white character of the population, suppressing the settlements of indigenous people, blacks, and inhabitants of the coasts. Indeed, the regionalization of "races" and the racialization of certain regions have hardly been recognized in public discourse. In turn, this suppression of regions inhabited by these "internal others" made possible racialized comparisons between the dark-skinned Nicaraguan and the "white" Costa Rican.

A third form of belonging is a sense of uniqueness. The achievement of a stable electoral democracy has meant a strong sense of being different from the other Central American nations. Uniqueness emerges as a result of having a "different" culture that has engendered peculiar traditions. In the case of Costa Rica, these traditions have been associated, principally after the 1950s, with democracy and lately with peace, two scarce attributes in Central America. Thus culture became a new source of identity. The incompatibility of lifestyles between the true nationals and the "foreigners" constitutes a "differentialist racism" that is not a result of biological arguments but is a consequence of belonging to different cultures (Barker 1981).

This historical configuration of a timeless, racialized, and cultural national identity has been threatened in the current context, which is characterized by a sense of distrust in the Costa Rican democracy. Diverse surveys have illustrated the existence of a crisis in the representation of nationhood forged during the 1950s and 1960s in Costa Rica. For instance, nonparticipation in the general elections rose from 18.9 percent in 1994 to 30 percent in 1998. Despite the fact that the 2002 elections were probably the most hotly contested in many years, nonparticipation reached 31 percent.[2] Stuart Hall and his colleagues (1978, 146, 158) conceptualized this distrust as *dislocation,* which can be considered a decline in, and an undermining of, the patterns of material and social organization, the destabilization of its own complex internal system of social ordering. These processes generate *social anxiety* and a *sense of loss* perceived as a "crisis of moral values" and institutions. This sense of loss is also perceived as a loss of identity; what is threatened is "national pride" (Elias 1996, 358). These dislocations seem to have been projected onto the Nicaraguans, who are perceived as being responsible for a wide array of crimes, insecurity, and diseases. In turn, these forms of racialization and criminalization have interpellated the Nicaraguans, who have introjected a stigmatized representation of themselves. This is the main hypothesis of the following chapters.

In close relation to this main hypothesis, this project follows three theoretical and methodological aims. First, I inquire into the ways in which an "imagined community" (Anderson 1983) is made to conform through various ways of belonging but also, and perhaps more important, by means of exclusion and projection of undesired images onto outsiders. Nations are considered to be not so much communities as formations of difference and inequality (Clare and Johnson 1998). This complex constitutive interplay of belonging and difference will be explored through three key dimensions: representations, subject formation, and material inequalities.

Second, this project attempts to overcome the opposition between textual and ethnographic analyses, a strong disciplinary boundary in cultural studies and cultural theory (Hall 1980a; Johnson 1986). National identities are frequently constructed from above but that does not imply that their analysis should concentrate on those public and highly elaborated versions. Nations are represented as narration, but it is of the utmost importance to inquire into the decoding and contestation of these narratives in everyday life.

A third aim is to link spatiality and temporality as distinctive references in the configuration of national identities. Temporal and spatial locations have usually been considered independent dimensions. However, since time does not exist outside space and vice versa, these might be considered chronotopes (Bakhtin 1981, 84). Certain versions related to an idyllic past, for instance, are often located in certain geographic areas. Hence restricted versions of the past tend to be related to selective spatial locations.

This project is organized around a situated research problem: the role of the Nicaraguan other in the constitution of national identities in Costa Rica. It also seeks, however, to address more generally why the sense of national belonging constitutes a crucial identification in contemporary societies. I hope to interweave these empirical and theoretical aims in different ways to obliterate the distinction between area studies and theory. While the term *Latin American studies,* for instance, seems to deal with particular cases, *theory* is often associated with "general" debates, and implicitly refers to European and "American" developments.[3] It is not only a social division of labor—where prestige is proportional to the remoteness of theory from the mundane world, but also a (post)colonial issue that shows ways in which power and knowledge are institutionalized. Latin America, for instance, is known for its soccer players, dictators, Latin lovers, and even novelists, but science, either social or natural, does not belong to the regional folklore.

These theoretical and methodological concerns are closely related to personal experiences. In 1993 I met some Nicaraguan workers in the course of ethnographic fieldwork on housing construction and factories (Sandoval 1997, 130–40). They had worked previously in sugarcane plantations (paradoxically, the most bitter and arduous agricultural job because the plant's leaves cut the workers' hands and arms), but they were very badly paid and spent almost all their salaries on food and accommodation. So they traveled to the capital, San José, seeking jobs in construction. Besides their material poverty, my deepest sadness was provoked by their solitude. They were inside the country but outside the nation. Silence, fear, loneliness, and nightmares were common. One worker had lost one of his nails while excavating a ditch; later a small amount of lime had gotten into his eyes and caused painful irritation. However, he did not go to the hospital, as he thought he would be expelled for not having official immigration documents.

The exclusion of these workers has allowed me to think about my own sense of national belonging. Despite the powerful version of a Costa Ricanness grounded in the rural past, local peasants are considered plebeian. In doing this research, I was reminded of parts of my family that were rural and later working class. My arrival at the university was the time and place in which I recognized my own stigmatization.[4] This book has been written from this sense of exclusion, but it also seeks to refute forms of macho masculinities that are often highly valued in rural and working-class contexts. In this sense, this research is also a way to reflect on my own national belonging. After all, as feminist perspectives have highlighted, we locate our own autobiography inside the question we might want to ask (McRobbie 1982, 12).

It is not an easy task, since these national identities are embedded in one's own subjectivity. In this context, the permanent exercise of reflexivity has been useful. It has meant making strange the familiar and vice versa. Norbert Elias notes that "to become aware of the peculiarities of the habitus of one's own nation requires a specific effort of self-distancing" (1996, 2). The challenge seems to be how to make oneself other for oneself (Kristeva 1991; Bakhtin 1982). In this sense, Edward Said states, "The job facing the cultural intellectual is therefore not to accept the politics of identity as given, but to show how all representations are constructed, for what purpose, by whom, and with what components" (1994, 380).

Reflexivity also raises questions regarding the institutional location of this research. Questions such as "To what is research a 'contribution'?" (Green 1997, 206) are always complex challenges. In Central America uncertainties aroused by such questions include hyperpoliticized answers and various sorts of theoreticism, including postmodern prophecies. This book is published in the United States, but what about the Nicaraguans' future? How can one avoid transforming the subjects of this research into objects or, as Angela McRobbie puts it, "holidaying on other people's misery" (1982, 55)? How can this research contribute to the overcoming of processes of racialization and exclusion? These tensions are by no means absent from the motivation that informs the research. Indeed, there is a permanent effort to turn anger to reflexive accounts. In general, this project might contribute toward a more critical and reflexive understanding of national identities in Costa Rica as a long-term configuration. It is also my hope that the Spanish version of this book may both support the work that grassroots organizations are currently carrying out and elicit empowerment processes in members of Costa Rica's Nicaraguan community, for whom exclusion is, most of the time, a painful experience.

THE EXPOSITION OF the outcomes of this project has been organized according to the spatial and temporal sites explored throughout my research. The chapters follow a temporal sequence from present events—the center of most of the current disputes—to historical developments, and returning to current issues. This organization aims to show the social and historical determination of national identities without assuming a deterministic view. Determination has been a crucial problem in the research of national identities (e.g., top-to-bottom analyses are frequent) and is also a key element in the exposition of the material. This path of exposition emerged throughout my reading of *Policing the Crisis* (Hall et al. 1978), which begins with analysis of media representations of mugging and ends with the way British governments police a more structured crisis.

Similarly, the present book starts with an analysis of why and how the media have depicted the Nicaraguan community as a problem and explores the historical formation of the Nicaraguan as an other in Costa Rican imagery. This historical perspective emphasizes that criminalization and racialization of Nicaraguans in Costa Rica have been long-term processes that cannot be explained merely as consequences of immigration. This book also analyzes ways in which both conjunctural and historical developments of nationhood are experienced and contested from a more (auto)biographical perspective in everyday life.

In general, I inquire into three key sites of national identity: media discourse, historical and literary interpretations, and everyday life. Each aspect comprises different spatial and temporal locations (chronotopes) as well as diverse cultural forms. Although these chronotopes are closely connected, this does not suggest a linear or mechanical relationship between, for instance, everyday life events, conjunctures, and historical formations. Nor do the links between them constitute the existence of a single national identity. On the contrary, these are sites characterized by disputes over the power of representing nationhood.

Chapter 1 attempts a working definition of national identity, considering it a metanarrative that works through other identities, such as those constructed about "race," class, or gender. The chapter insists that national identities cannot be reduced to highly elaborated versions, such as literary or historical interpretations; everyday genres and practices produce and reproduce national identities in diverse forms. The deconstruction of discourses cannot avoid analysis of the ways in which such discourses intersect other texts and are contested in more biographical terms. Hence, the chapter seeks to outline a tentative framework of public and biographical sites through which a sense of national belonging is experienced.

Furthermore, this theoretical chapter distances itself from theories of nationalism that have paid little attention to the relationship between the creation of "imagined communities" (Anderson 1983) and "invention of traditions" (Hobsbawm 1983, 1), on the one hand, and the processes of exclusion present within nation-building projects, on the other. In other words, the exclusion of undesired others is a powerful way of constructing commonalities. The analysis of how "race," gender, or class identities are present in (or suppressed from) representations of nationhood offers a crucial opportunity to consider national identities simultaneously as formations of belonging and difference.

Chapter 2 explores media representations of Nicaraguans in Costa Rica between 1994 and 1996. Two key interrelated dimensions are considered. First, I attempt to show ways in which certain issues become media events. Here, concepts such as framing, labeling, and salience are crucial since they highlight how the media can define public debates, as well as spatial and temporal forms of remembering. A second dimension is the analysis of enunciation strategies through which the discourse of the nation is produced. The construction of the "we"—meaning *the* nation—has been of particular importance. Moreover, I have also studied how passive voices and nominalization are deployed to suppress certain social actors from the discourse.

In general, the text does not allow readers to establish relations between different issues. For instance, members of the counterrevolutionary groups that were organized from Costa Rica during the 1980s perpetrated most of the kidnappings that took place during the 1990s, the news of which occupied hundreds of front pages. However, such links did not gain salience; instead, the media replaced a political inscription, *contras,* by a racialized representation: the kidnappings were committed by "nicas." During the 1980s, the Contras were recognized as "freedom fighters," whereas in the 1990s the mainstream media did not acknowledge their former allies. Although social science and the humanities have emphasized that all knowledge is situated, the media still believe that their enunciations are made on behalf of collective interests.

Chapter 3 explores the historical formation of nationhood in Costa Rica and the Nicaraguan other as interrelated processes. The purpose of this chapter is twofold. First, it seeks to show that historical interpretations and literary narratives are in themselves key sites of dispute and contestation over legitimated versions of nationhood. Second, it looks at the relationship between processes of criminalization and racialization present, for instance, in the media discourse and the long-term formation of the Nicaraguan other in Costa Rica.

The chapter attempts to go beyond immigration perspectives, which blame Nicaraguans for the discrimination they experience. What is at stake is the analysis of a legitimated national identity that has taken as its foundation several highly selective traditions such as an idyllic past, a sense of geographic isolation, and representations of Costa Ricans as a "white" middle-class population, in sharp contrast with the violent, dark-skinned, deprived Nicaraguan other. Indeed the accentuation of differences regarding Nicaragua has played an important role in the representation of Costa Rican "exceptionalism." The definition of borders between Nicaragua and Costa Rica, as well as political issues during the nineteenth and twentieth centuries, has been interpreted by the political elites through nationalist frameworks. Both Nicaragua as a state and Nicaraguans as citizens became undesired others in Costa Rican imagery. In particular, the poor and dark-skinned Nicaraguan has been a crucial other in the constitution of the Costa Rican imagined community.

Chapter 4 examines processes of national identification in everyday life. Pupils from thirteen primary and secondary schools were asked to write two stories; one on Costa Rica as a nation and the other on Nicaraguans in Costa Rica. For both stories students were asked to use metaphors since these rhetorical devices are frequently used for representing the self and the other. These stories were contrasted with history textbooks employed in formal education, which provided an important mediation between historical interpretations elaborated by intellectuals and the reception of such discourses by primary and secondary students. Members of the Nicaraguan community were also invited to write about their lived experience as immigrants in Costa Rica. This offered an opportunity for the analysis of ways in which Nicaraguans themselves have contested racialized discourses like those discussed in chapter 2.

Chapter 5 explores the extent to which the dislocation of key foundations of the sense of nationhood in Costa Rica and the emergence of a racialized politics were interrelated processes during the 1980s and 1990s. The chapter includes, first, an analysis of the transition from an anti-communist opposition to the former Sandinista government to the racialization of Nicaraguan nationality. Second, the chapter seeks to analyze how the racialization of the Nicaraguan community seems to be an expression of the decline in public investment and the deterioration in public services such as education, health, and housing. It addresses the main questions often asked in everyday life: How did the communist Nicaraguans become "nicas"? How many Nicaraguans live in Costa Rica? How violent are Nicaraguans? Are Nicaraguans taking Costa Ricans' jobs? and Do immigrants collapse public services?

The conclusion revisits two tensions present throughout the research project: on the one hand, the links between representations, subject formation, and materialities; on the other hand, the interplay between historical formations, the media, and everyday life. This section also explores reflexively the personal, institutional, and conceptual location of this project. Finally, the project looks at ways in which images and practices of nationhood can be called into question not only as part of academic debate but also in the public sphere.

This project has involved many translations. Different cultural forms—including e-mails, jokes, graffiti, news reports, essays, and testimonials—have been translated from Spanish to English. The main aim has been to make these texts available to non–Spanish speakers, but it does not ignore the implications involved, especially when English has become the language of globalization. In the case of the testimonials, documentation has involved not only translation into English but also the transformation of oral conversations into written form, a new experience for most of the authors. Perhaps a major difference between this project and the debates about testimonials among literary experts, especially in the United States, is that in this case there has not been a division between the local production and circulation of the testimonials within the communities on the one hand, and their interpretation on the other; both stages have been part of the research experience, since I worked with the authors throughout the writing process.[5]

Chapter 1

Making Sense of National Identities

NATIONAL IDENTITIES ARE imagined communities but also, and perhaps more important, they are formations constructed on the basis of difference and inequality. The dynamic between belonging and difference is a mutually constitutive interplay of representations, subject formation, and materialities. Language is also central to the construction of national identities. I will introduce some contributions made by the Bakhtin Circle that consider language as a historical and social practice. Methodologically this chapter presents a tentative framework for the analysis of different temporal and spatial locations in which national identities are configured. In the temporal domain, there are multiple references to the past and links to the present, and such references are also located spatially, either in the public sphere or in other more private sites.

Rather than a systematic elucidation of theories and "schools," which "disable and disempower what was empowering and interesting about the original insights" (Said 1994, 387), this chapter discusses concepts as problems, as historical movements that are still unresolved, as Raymond Williams (1977, 11) suggests. This is especially difficult since Western languages tend to foreground substantives and objects at the expense of relations and to reduce processes to static conditions (Elias 1978, 113). A relational perspective requires us to explore national identities in "complex, shifting and contextual terms, rather than in abstract, absolutist formulations" (Gabriel 1994, 47).

National identities might be interpreted as different meanings of belonging and are often related to senses of origin, continuity, and destiny. These meanings are not natural but can be socially naturalized and taken for granted, since they are imagined by specific social groups through diverse cultural practices and rituals as a relatively unconscious activity. Nationhood is not constituted by permanent repertoires but can be considered as contingent identifications, which are reworked through diverse cultural forms and practices by specifically situated social agents. This diversity of cultural forms and locations confirms that there is not a single national identity but multiple and diverse versions under certain relations of subordination (Colley 1994, x). Certain events—border conflicts and soccer competitions, among others—activate a sense of national belonging in diverse ways, though not all citizens experience their sense of nationhood in the same way. An important observation about the narratives of nationhood is that most nations are portrayed as unique. Paradoxically, uniqueness seems to be a common self-attribute of nationhood in differing contexts, emphasizing those factors that can be favorably compared with other cases. Michael Billig stresses that "this mixture of universality and particularity enables nations to proclaim themselves as nations" (1995, 73). In a similar way, Roland Robertson maintains that nations are made through "the universalization of particularism and the particularization of universalism" (1991, 73).[1]

There are complex relations between national identities and other forms of identification, such as those constructed in relation to "race," class, or gender. According to Richard Johnson, national identities might be considered grand narratives that regulate and police other identifications: "Discourses of the nation act on other identifications by sorting through them in different ways, recognising some, refusing recognition to others. Recognition or non-recognition are not the only possibilities however: national discourses may systematically *misrecognise* previously formed identities" (1993a, 207–8; emphasis in original).

National identities seem to expel those attributes that do not fit into a desired nationhood. The hegemonic versions of nationhood in Costa Rica, for instance, have been constructed as a predominantly white—implicitly male—middle-class population, located in central geographic areas. In other words, national belonging involves not only recognition of certain identities but also misrecognition and nonrecognition of internal others, for instance, indigenous peoples, blacks and peasants, who do not belong to the city, which is the place of modernity par excellence. That said, this project does not intend an abstract evaluation of national identities in Costa Rica but an informed critique of diverse articulations of "race," class, and gender under the heading of Costa Ricanness.

Another important set of relations is constituted by the links between national identities and nationalism. Sarah Radcliffe and Sallie Westwood suggest a subtle distinction between them: "National identity can be seen as a wider and more multi-dimensional category than nationalism, as national identity can exist within subjects (collectively or individually) without there being a process of mobilisation around a specific goal" (1996, 16). Nationalism can be considered a political category, whereas national identities might be conceptualized as representations and subjectivities associated with a particular sense of belonging. Research on nationalism has emphasized the study of its origins either as a primordialist phenomenon grounded on ethnic and linguistic bases (Smith 1995) or as a modern, secular, and political process in which "imagined communities" and "invention of traditions" play a key role (Breuilly 1982; Anderson 1983; Gellner 1983; Hobsbawm 1983). Meanwhile, analyses of national identities have attempted to recognize ways in which belonging is produced and reproduced in various temporal and spatial sites through cultural forms, practices, and institutions. National identities and nationalisms can also be related through their similarities. Indeed, nationalist movements have configured and reinforced national identities, but the latter have also underpinned nationalist movements. Both might be considered Janus faced; sometimes they play an emancipatory role, but they can also be sources of exclusion and racialization.

The latter tendency is the subject of this project and, therefore, racialization, a concept that will be frequently employed throughout these pages, requires a brief introduction. Robert Miles notes that racialization "refers to the historical emergence of the idea of 'race' and its subsequent reproduction and application" (1991, 76). Racialization is a work of ideological representation under which biological or cultural characteristics are deployed to signify a sense of difference (Gilroy 1987, 38–39). Racialization might be also be understood as a way of associating certain groups with a particular "nature" or "essence" that identifies them despite the internal differences present in any group and the similarities between the racialized group and those who construct such categorizations. Racialization works by associating a certain nature with certain biological attributes (skin color, for instance), but also by defining some sort of essence (violence, for example) through cultural attributes, such those related to nationality. Sometimes "biological" and "cultural" categories are combined, since the meaning of "race" is unstable and politically contested, combining representational elements and institutional dimensions (Winant 2000, 182). The racialization of the other also has implications for representing the self, the most crucial of which is the invisibility of whiteness as a missing center from which other groups are represented. As Richard Dyer states, "Whites are not of a certain race, they're just the human race" (1997, 3). Their power lies in their invisibility. This emphasis on racialization does not suggest that it is the only way of constructing images of otherness. Its relevance in this context lies in the fact that often it has been argued that in Latin America issues regarding racial differences do not hold the same relevance as in the United States, where patterns of segregation are well known, obscuring the pervasive racialized inequalities in Latin American societies.[2] Nonetheless, racialization, as well as other concepts used in this project, are not considered abstract categories, which can be "applied" to different contexts; they are rather a "tool-kit" (Foucault 1980), instruments that relate closely to a particular research problem.

Subject Formation, Representations, and Materialities

Nations are considered not so much unities as formations of differences and inequalities. This complex interplay of belonging and difference may be explored through three key dimensions: subject formation, representations, and material inequalities.[3] This interplay is highly relevant for research into national identities, since most analysis has paid little attention to the processes of internalization and contestation of public discourses of nationhood. As Radcliffe and Westwood maintain, "Explaining the existence of internalized imaginings of the nation alongside the (official) externalized national imaginings remains to be done" (1996, 16).

Interest in subjectivity is frequently associated with psychoanalysis, whereas representations have been a matter of concern in cultural studies. Economic perspectives—sometimes identified with Marxism—have underlined material and institutional factors in the constitution of difference and inequality. Rather than making a distinction between these three perspectives, this section attempts to outline some of their multiple relationships. Sander Gilman (1985, 17, 18, 20; 1988, 5) notes that a sense of difference emerges when the child begins to feel that the external world is not a mere extension of his or her self. It produces anxiety since this discontinuity between the self and the world is perceived as a loss of control over external objects. When the sense of order and control is considered to be under threat, anxiety arises and is frequently projected onto the "other," which begins to signify the external reality beyond the self. Similarly, Julia Kristeva maintains that the sense of self is constituted through the expulsion of these undesired social attributes. This expulsion is called abjection (McClintock 1995, 71–72; Sibley 1995, 8).

A major difficulty arises when one considers the historical and material conditions under which these boundaries emerge. David Sibley (1995, 8–9), for instance, maintains that the urge to expel undesired attributes (clean/dirty, we/they) creates anxieties because such separations can never be finally achieved. Although abjection seems to be the key for the understanding of exclusion, he notes that "the social and spatial contexts of abjection need considerable elaboration" (11). From a similar perspective, Ann McClintock suggests a *situated psychoanalysis,* "a culturally conceptualized psychoanalysis that is simultaneously a psychoanalytically informed theory" (1995, 72). She states that "perhaps . . . there should be no material history without psychoanalysis and no psychoanalysis without a material history" (74).

The understanding of material and symbolic boundaries seems indeed to require the obliteration of boundaries between social sciences. That obliteration has been a long-term preoccupation. In 1936, Norbert Elias writes regretfully in a similar vein: "Those concerned with the history of society, like those concerned with the history of mind, perceive 'society,' on the one hand and the world of 'ideas' on the other as two different formations that can be meaningfully separated" (1982, 282). The alternative does not lie in the construction of another grand theory regarding these complex relations, but in addressing such links in the analysis of situated case studies; this is a central aim of the following chapters.

The subjective meanings of national identities seem to be constituted as diverse processes of introjection and projection of feelings, images, and values from and onto others in such a way that a sense of border is produced. This emergence of borders is not an exclusively subjective process; it takes place in historical circumstances. In particular, the translation of borders into boundaries has been characteristic of modern Western cultures (Sibley 1995, 7). Starting in the sixteenth century, the European bourgeoisie started expelling from their practices and institutions activities considered as constituting excess, especially those associated with the body: fairs, markets, and carnivals. At the same time, values regarding distinction, hierarchies, shame, order, and taste were internalized. Manners became a site of profound interconnection between ideology and subjectivity. All this suggests that the constitution of psychic and social boundaries have been mutually constitutive processes and not fixed and abstract ones (Elias 1982; Stallybrass and White 1986). Interestingly, this fixation of boundaries in Europe coincided with slavery and the projection of erotic desires onto colonized people in Latin America and other regions; a relation that Elias, for instance, did not examine (Fletcher 1997, 52; Crang 1998, 65). As Paul Gilroy argues, "This inside/outside relationship should be recognized as a more powerful, more complex, and more contested element in the historical, social and cultural memory of our glorious nation [England] than has previously been supposed" (1993, 11).

Those attributes that do not fulfill the desired national identity are projected onto excluded others. This kind of projection results, as Peter Stallybrass and Allon White (1986, 5) argue, in a conflictive fusion of power, fear, anxiety, and desire in the construction of subjectivity. Societies, under particular historical conditions, select a certain number of categories onto which they project their anxieties (Gilman 1988, 11). The subjective dimension of national identities, for instance, is frequently represented as a preservation of national frontiers, as a projection and protection of an internal collective personality. There are frequent icons that consider the nation as a home, as a place of security (Balibar 1991b, 95).

Nicaraguan citizens in Costa Rica, for example, are frequently depicted as a threat to public health, since some of them have entered the country suffering from cholera. There are also border disputes between the two governments in which each nation is menaced. In other words, the body and the nation are represented in similar ways; both are threatened by outsiders. The body becomes a place of mediation between political conflicts and subjective meanings in a way that personal and national borders are turned into boundaries, particularly through media discourse. Nicaraguans are also considered to be responsible for undermining the social order and for being the presumed authors of all sorts of crimes, even when there are no statistics supporting such arguments. Hence disease, as well as crime, should be policed. Although the formation of nationhood in Costa Rica is not exclusively related to Nicaraguans, what makes the latter crucial others is that, historically, their representation has articulated (Hall, 1980b, 338) racialized, class-based, and gendered abjections in various ways.

This enactment of boundaries around the human body and the body politic can be better interpreted following a typology suggested by Mary Douglas, who highlights four ways of representing fears of pollution: "The first is danger pressing on external boundaries; the second, danger from transgressing the internal lines of the system; the third, danger in the margins of the lines. The fourth is danger from internal contradiction" (1966, 123–24). Discourses about immigration illustrate the first case, since various metaphors represent Nicaraguans as a wave "swamping" the national body. The internal boundaries are considered to be under threat—for example, by criminal acts that are commonly associated with Nicaraguans. A third source of threat is identified in the undermining of external boundaries, as in the long-term disputes over the definition of borders. In the fourth source of threat, internal contradictions within the system, the decline in public services such as health, education, or housing has meant a serious problem in a country where standards of living are above the regional average. This material decline has put under threat Costa Rica's strong self-image as a middle-class nation. As such, it is not hard to imagine how Nicaraguans are blamed for this deterioration.

Psychic forms displayed around Nicaraguans include fear but also a desire to control them through immigration policies or stigmatization. Nicaraguans have been internalized under the categories of negation and disgust, which remain very active and have become indispensable, since it is through them that the "true" Costa Ricans can be identified. As Barbara Babcock maintains, "What is *socially* peripheral is so frequently *symbolically* central" (in Stallybrass and White 1986, 5; emphasis in original).

Thus an analysis of the ways in which Nicaraguans are racialized can allow us to gain a better understanding of the national identity in Costa Rica.

One of the most relevant similarities between subject formation and the constitution of national identities is that both are represented through the accentuation of differences regarding the other. Myths of internal homogeneity are created independently of the heterogeneities that define the nation (B. Williams 1989, 429–31). As Billig maintains, "Those differences between members of the same category are minimized and differences between categories are exaggerated" (1995, 130). In this particular case, modes and topics through which Nicaraguans are stigmatized express those aspects that Costa Ricans consider undesirable in their own society (Erdheim 1995, 22). Elias (1994, xxiv–xxv) suggests that these relations between outsiders and those who are established can be conceptualized as power differentials between groups without necessarily reducing the explanation to the psychological or biological dispositions and attributes of those involved. The "established" group associates itself with charisma, a specific virtue that is lacking in the others, who are identified as *anomics,* one of the most common patterns of cultural exclusion. As outsiders are felt to be anomic, close contact with them threatens any member of an established group with "anomic infection": she or he might be suspected of breaking the norms or taboos of her or his own group. Complex relations between social order, aesthetics, and morality are activated in such a way that outsider groups are not only perceived as unruly breakers of laws and norms but also as not particularly clean. However, such processes of exclusion do not produce shame or guilt, since stigmatization is reified and naturalized through ethnic markers.

Without an outside, what is inside would no make sense, and the opposite is certainly true. Thus, identity and difference are closely related. Gilman notes that "because the Other is the antithesis of the self, the definition of the Other must incorporate the basic categories by which the self is defined" (1985, 23). The self is constituted through its relationship to significant others, and in turn representations of the other are indirect images of the self. As Jan Pieterse (1992, 233) maintains, images of the other—which are contextual and historical—do not circulate because of their truthfulness but because they project the concerns of the image-producers and consumers (also see Crang 1998, 169; Said 1994, 60).

Representations of difference, another keyword of this section, might be contextualized as part of modern Eurocentric views. Peter Wagner (1994, 38–39) and Jorge Larraín (1996, 91) maintain that modernity has imagined the other in three interconnected dimensions: on the temporal axis, they are a sign of backwardness, which can be conceived as the opposite of modernity. The second dimension, the spatial, is outlined as the distinction between insiders as bearers of progress and outsiders as barbarians. A third form of exclusion takes place within modern societies by means of class-based, gendered, and health-related exclusions in such a way that the working class (primarily men), women, nonheterosexual, and disabled peoples are stigmatized in diverse forms and by a variety of means. "The distinction," Wagner argues, "between reason and unreason is at the roots of all modern attempts at boundary-setting" (1994, 40). These temporal and spatial boundaries have also meant, as McClintock notes, the distinction between the "natural" sphere of the family and the "political" sphere of civic society, which excluded women, slaves, servants, and the colonized from liberal individuality. Thus, "domesticity and empire merge as a necessary element in the formation of the liberal imagination" (1995, 178).

Debates about nation and nationalism in Europe have emerged in this modern context, especially as a consequence of the end of the absolutist state and the influence of doctrines of self-determination and sovereignty. Ernest Renan, for instance, concluded that nations cannot be established on the basis of ethnic or linguistic homogeneity since they are internally diverse. Instead, he argued that a nation might be conceived of as a political community. As John Breuilly (1982, 18) maintains, it is one of the classic examples of subjective definitions of a nation, where there are no "objective" sources—either language or "race"—but only a contingent definition of it. But modernity also underpinned the colonial expansion of Europe, in the course of which the range of human, cultural, and physiological variation became more widely known to a larger number of people (Miles 1991). Racism has had close ties with this expansion: the expulsion of the Moors and the Jews from Spain, for instance, was carried out on the basis of "purity of blood," one of the key processes in the emergence of race as a concept. Such internal expulsion of "internal others" was, on the other hand, an important reference in the processes of colonization and genocide in the so-called New World, which in turn became an external other, an important precedent in the constitution of the West (Todorov 1984; Balibar 1991c, 52–53).

Thus self-determination and sovereignty became a subject for debate among citizens, a feature that was not granted to "internal others" (working-class men and women) nor to the colonized others. Tzevetan Todorov (1991b, 134–38) shows indeed that in the case of Renan as well as other French thinkers of the eighteenth and nineteenth centuries, "race" and racism have had close ties with debates about nationhood: all citizens of France hold the same rights but not every human being could be considered to be citizen; indeed citizenship belonged to "white" people. While "yellow," "black," and indigenous "races," according to Renan, were unable to organize themselves, whites were identified with beauty and rationality (132–34). In short, as Robert Young has noted, "White skin therefore became both a marker of civilization and a product of it" (1995, 35). Thus it might be argued that racism constructs difference through biological or cultural attributes, whereas nationalism seems to construct a key opposition between citizens and noncitizens (Todorov 1991b, 286). The two are closely connected; Nicaraguans, for instance, are not only stigmatized through ethnic markers but are also labeled, in terms of citizenship, as illegal immigrants.

This historical relationship between nationalism and racism does not pretend to be an abstract generalization. It attempts to emphasize that both ideologies are intrinsically related in certain doctrines inspired by the philosophies of the French Enlightenment, which became key references for nation-building projects in Latin America (Stepan 1991, 72; Larraín 1996, 145). The liberal elite hoisted nationalist claims on the basis of exclusionary divisions within the new republics. Simón Bolívar, for example, known as the Liberator in narratives of the independence of Latin America, was not particularly sympathetic toward blacks during and after the wars of independence (W. Wright 1990, 28). As Radcliffe and Westwood note in the experiences of nationalism in Latin America, nation-building projects "privilege a specific construction of ethnicity as part of a racial project in which difference is subsumed" (1996, 38). The elite spoke (and still speak) "on behalf of the people," but only a few of the latter were considered citizens of the new states. The analysis of "imagined communities" has to specify, as Radcliffe and Westwood argue, "*who* imagines the community and *how* they do so, and what differences in communities consequently arise" (26; emphasis in original).

Citizen exclusion and racialized representations are also related to economic and material inequalities, the third dimension that seems to be crucial for an interpretation of national identities. Immanuel Wallerstein (1991, 80–83), for instance, has shown that material inequalities and racist representations have been linked historically. Endless capital accumulation occurred in the context of colonial expansion; hence those forms of economic exploitation and racialized representations of internal (working class) and external others (colonial people) have been closely interwoven phenomena. The crucial consequence of these links between material factors and representations of the other is the fusion of a socioeconomic category with an anthropological and moral category (Balibar 1991a, 209).

Racialization is inextricably related to class divisions but cannot be reduced to the latter. Following Peter Wade (1993, 338), it might be argued that while *race* is a signifier of physical difference, *class* refers to relations of production. Thus, rather than emphasizing their autonomy or the determinacy of any of them, what is relevant is to explore some of the ways in which class and "race" are related in particular contexts. In this sense, the racialization of the other not only is a matter of representation but plays a key role in the formation of social inequality. As Stuart Hall and his associates (1978, 347; Hall 1980b, 316) argue, "race" is the modality in which class is lived. Indeed, most of the Nicaraguan citizens in Costa Rica, as well as most of the blacks and indigenous people, belong to the most deprived sectors of the population.

Materialities are organized in institutions that constrain or enable practices and cultural forms under defined sets of power relations. This emphasis on institutional dimensions does not necessarily mean adopting a deterministic perspective, but as Errol Lawrence argues, "Whilst we should not forget that these dominant definitions are contested we must also remember that they are embodied within the dominant institutional order and inscribed within the social relations of everyday life" (1982, 50). Policy-making regarding "immigration," jobs, health, housing, and education (see chapter 5) illustrates precisely how, despite contestation, institutional decisions contribute to processes of exclusion and inequality. Thus, certain problems resulting from a decline in public investment have been associated instead with the Nicaraguan community.

These links between subject formation, representations, and material exclusions have meant rethinking the opposition "we-they," as was formulated originally in the first drafts of this project. A critique of this binary opposition is advanced by Aijaz Ahmad (1992, 90, 182–83), who stresses that the word *difference*—with lowercase *d*—is local and empirically verifiable, not denoting any epistemological category or perennial ontological condition. Otherwise, such an opposition might turn into another "celebration of the difference," evading analysis of the ways in which identities are embedded within inequalities. Furthermore, the Nicaraguan other is not external to the sense of nationhood in Costa Rica. As Johnson (1997, 12) maintains, outsiders remain indispensable; they are inside the self, since identities carry, in their inner configurations, some version of the other that partially constitutes them. The Nicaraguan other is not an abstract and binary representation (we/they) either. It might be considered a historically situated formation based on racialized, class-based, and gendered inequalities.

Overcoming the Boundary between Textual and Ethnographic Approaches

Research on national identities and nationalisms has often considered the public and most articulated cultural forms (e.g., novels, poetry, essays) in which such identifications are present. More ambiguous identifications are often embedded in less structured and more private and personal sites, as has been noted from varying perspectives (Alter 1983; Hobsbawm 1990; Johnson 1993a, 1993b; Larraín 1996). National identities are frequently constructed "from above," but that fact does not imply that their analysis should concentrate on those public and highly articulated versions. On the contrary, as Johnson argues, "No public version will acquire ideological life at all unless it connects itself to common sense meanings. No ideological form can succeed in the public sphere unless individuals and groups invest in it, translating it into their inner speech" (1993a, 113).

The preeminence of highly articulated cultural forms as sites of analysis of national identification can also be understood in the context of the "linguistic turn" that has meant an "overwhelming textualization of cultural studies' own discourses," as Hall (1996, 274) has characterized certain debates. It has meant a disciplinary boundary between textually oriented approaches and those that focus on cultural practices.[4] John Clark summarizes the problem:

> This tension, emerging from the attempt to synthesize the literary and anthropological senses of culture, has been a formative and highly productive one for the field. There has been a constant temptation to fragment the problem of culture, separating the study of discourses or texts from the practices of cultural subjects, precisely because the task of holding onto both elements is so difficult. On the textual wing, there has been a tendency to dissolve the tension by dealing with subject positions rather than subjects. This leaves to one side the difficult question of the actual efficacy or productivity of the text-discourse and reads only the intended effect on the ideal subject projected within the text-discourse. In some instances, this has involved an elision between the subject position and the subject, as if texts do produce their subjects in a vacuum, separated from either other texts or other social relations. On the other wing, that of lived experience, there is a temptation to homogenize the situated culture of subjects and treat text-discourses as the external impositions of an alien culture such that the situated culture provides the raw materials of resistance. This reconstructs the separation of dominant and subordinate cultures and the danger of essentialist or expressive views of culture. (1991, 16–17)

Both perspectives have been subject to various critiques. Scholars have challenged the concept of experience, whose formulation rests on positivist premises and which contains implicit notions of authenticity which seldom recognize that any experience is always selective and organized from the present situation (Pickering 1997, 14). Meanwhile, textual perspectives, with their fixed and frozen conception of language, have also been questioned. Power works through language, but the former is *not* reduced to the latter; "Textuality is never enough," Hall (1996, 271) argues. Christine Gledhill formulated an early critique in which she considered that "the evidence that language has a determining effect on society is a different matter from saying that society is nothing but languages and signifying practices" (in Morley 1992, 179).

The dichotomy between public discourses and everyday life present in the debates on national identities might be interpreted as part of these broad debates in cultural studies and cultural theory. Since language seems to be a key concept, I will explore the extent to which it is possible to recognize its crucial location in cultural practices, avoiding either the possibility of "dissolving the social into discourse" (Wood 1986, 62; see also Larraín 1994, 88) or the assumption that considers experience outside a given language as "conceptually autoevident" (Pickering 1997, 176).

It is striking that these debates were advanced by Mikhail Bakhtin, Valentin Voloshinov, and Pavel Medvedev as early as the 1920s, when formalist linguistics and orthodox Marxist perspectives isolated language as a "structure" or as a "reflection of reality," respectively.[5] I do not suggest that their insights are not debatable, nor do I claim that their perspectives have no internal differences, but they did attempt to overcome such crucial structuralist oppositions as langue/parole, diachrony/synchrony, and discourse/experience. They conceptualized language beyond the dichotomy structuralism/culturalism, showing that there is no experience outside language but there is no language outside history either. However, the translation of their books into Western languages did not take place until the 1960s, when these dichotomies had been assimilated by several human sciences.

Language is not reified nor considered sufficient; on the contrary, two concepts, utterance and chronotope, are highly relevant. The concept of utterance seeks to overcome the public/private opposition, since a separation of this kind seems to be based on the dichotomy between langue (public) and parole (private). The concept of chronotope suggests that meanings are constructed through various temporal and spatial locations. Both concepts are discussed in the next few pages. The Bakhtin Circle addressed a bold critique of orthodox Marxist perspectives and formalist interpretations on language. In the first case, they questioned the assumption that language is a reflection of reality, and in the second their appraisal challenged those perspectives that considered language as a system. Their critique argued that the signs are neither the reflection of material conditions nor a formal and arbitrary unity. Languages are considered multiaccentuated; meanings are social actions in certain social relations, and different groups attempt to accent language in such a way that their voices, experiences, and values may be recognized as the most legitimate ones. "The sign becomes an arena of class struggle" (Voloshinov 1973, 23). Any word is inhabited by diverse meanings; language is no longer transparent (Voloshinov 1973; Medvedev 1985, 48, 121; R. Williams, 1977). Language is not just content either; characters, plots, scripts should be considered as part of an artistic creation and not just as an empirical reality reflected onto content. This conception of language as reflection and content has fallen somewhat out of favor at present. However, those perspectives that considered language as a system have had a strong influence. Indeed, langue and synchrony have been key concepts of formalist and structuralist perspectives. Language became a reified system, and it has even been argued that there is nothing outside the text.

These latter arguments have had a strong influence on the debates on identity. Margaret Sommers, for instance, argues that "all of us come to *be* who we *are* by being located or locating ourselves in social narratives *rarely of our own making*" (1994, 606; emphasis in original). Some pages later, she maintains that "narratives are not incorporated into the self in any direct way, rather they are mediated through the enormous spectrum of social and political institutions and practices that constitute our social world" (625). This concept of narrative presents some difficulties mainly because it seldom clarifies the historical formation of such narratives, nor the processes of appropriation and internalization of them by different social groups; indeed, how such mediation takes place is an unexplored matter. While in former perspectives, ideology or language constituted individuals as subjects, now ideology and language seem to be replaced by narratives. The main argument and the problems associated with it remain.

Borrowing Larraín's critique of post-Althusserian perspectives, one might argue that to consider narratives as constitutive of subjects inflates the role and autonomy of narratives and obscures their own determinacy (1994, 88; 1996, 214–15). To insist on the social construction of identities does not deny historical determination; antiessentialism does not mean indeterminacy. In turn, indeterminacy also restrains possible ways of contestation and resistance. As Andrew Parker and associates argue, a "further challenge, perhaps, would be to move beyond this reverse logic of anti-essentialism, to acknowledge that, by working politically and philosophically through the implication of the particular, new kinds of solidarities might be forged" (1994, 3).

This overextended role of language as constitutive of subjects through narratives as well as the split between literary discourses and everyday life seem to be related to the presence of formalist conceptions of language. As an alternative, the concept of utterance approaches language as a historical and communicative practice. Rather than the sign understood as an arbitrary relation between signified and signifier, the concept utterance is considered to be the minimal unit of communication (Medvedev 1985, 8, 120; Bakhtin 1982, 265). The utterance is unfinished and daily communication is in permanent generation. The utterance is constituted in dialogue with other utterances to which it is a response or from which it seeks to solicit a response (Bennett 1979, 76). It also questions the dichotomy between synchrony and diachrony, since "the relation between the speakers changes even a little bit. . . . In this generation, the speech lives an intensive life, though different than in literary creation" (Medvedev 1985, 95). As Gary Morson and Caryl Emerson maintain, "Meaning is never entirely located *in* the text nor is it identical with the author's intentions. . . . [Neither is it] completely the product of interpreters" (1990, 284–85; emphasis in original).

The splitting between langue and parole is no longer present since "the reality of language is, in fact, its generation" (Voloshinov 1973, 28, 56). Language is not a structure but a lived and social practice: *"Language acquires life and historically evolves precisely here, in concrete verbal communication, and not in the abstract linguistic system of language forms, nor in the individual psyche of speakers"* (95; emphasis in original). Sense and meaning are generated as a process of communication between voices socially and historically situated, most of the time amidst unequal resources of material and symbolic power. Disputes over meanings—present, for instance, in the ways in which belonging and difference are shaped—are intrinsically linked to material inequalities.

The dictionary's sense of a word is technical, but any concrete utterance is social. Language takes place as a permanent process of generation within valuable (and variable) horizons (Medvedev 1985, 121). Michael Holquist puts the problem in the following terms: "What is the *particular* feature in language that serves as the threshold between selves and others? Bakhtin finds an answer in language's capacity to model addressivity and dialogue" (1990, 57; emphasis in original). Any word is written to be read; it is unfinished and oriented toward the process of communication. There is no meaning outside the social communication (Bakhtin 1982, 277).

The social generation of meaning takes place as relations between authorial speech and reported speech (Voloshinov 1973, 115). Sometimes, the authorial speech quotes the reported speech without major transformations; this is called direct discourse. For instance, the media employ the police definitions of criminality in such a way that various forms of stigma are usually taken for granted in crime news. Another possibility is the mixing of voices that is called indirect discourse. Although Voloshinov and Bakhtin are optimistic about the obliteration of boundaries between discourses, the mixing of voices does not always challenge authority. A common example is the *we* construction in discourse about the nation: *we* frequently signifies the conjunction of the media with certain political views. By employing the word *we,* the media speak "on behalf of" the nation, order, and democracy. Norman Fairclough underlines how such a translation gives "a populist force to official voices, but at the same time preserves the legitimacy of official discourse" (1995, 71). I will explore these enunciation strategies in detail in chapter 2.

The concept of utterance also addresses the concept of experience. Voloshinov argues that there is no experience outside language: *"Experience exists even for the person undergoing it only in the material of signs"* (1973, 28; emphasis in original). Experience is no longer a site of "authenticity" since it is possible only when felt or thought through language. The concept of utterance also enables us to identify multiple links between public and inner speech located in more private sites. Genres are not reduced to literary ones such as novel, poetry, or essay. There are what Voloshinov calls everyday genres: "Each situation, fixed and sustained by social custom, commands a particular kind of organisation of audience and, hence, a particular repertoire of little everyday genres" (1973, 97). Such genres show positions and dis-positions, which are present as common sense in verbal utterances but also in forms of address, intonations, "twitches and winks." Common sense is a "half-way" and an "uncoordinated" space of ambiguity and contradiction, a "philosophy of the non-philosophers," as Antonio Gramsci (1973, 326) proposes.[6] There is not just one common sense nor is it something rigid and immobile. Sayings, proverbs, intonations, and modes of address can be "valid and effective but within determined limits: the farmer 'knows' his seasons, the sailor 'knows' his seas, but both may remain mystified about kingship and cosmology" (Thompson 1978, 199). My fieldwork, reported in chapter 4, explores these processes of national identification. It means refusing essentialist perspectives of belonging that usually consider the nation as nature, but it also challenges those trends that assume national identities exclusively as narratives. An ethnographic perspective might show that national meanings are also embedded in practices, routines, and rituals that are crucial in the formation of nationhood.

Time, Space, and Cultural Forms

Senses of belonging—such as origin, continuity, or destiny—are complex sets of time and space references. Past hegemonic formations leave traces that are activated under certain conditions and similar processes may be present in the spatial dimension. Most historical narratives of nationhood in Costa Rica, for instance, consider only the Central Valley, excluding the coastal regions, where ethnic diversity is greater. In other words, selective versions of the past are intrinsically related to restrictive geographical boundaries. Time and space are clues of belonging and, in turn, ways of exclusion. In other words, both time and space are constructed socially and are highly selective.

Temporal references to the past, present, future, or any combination thereof have become crucial sites for the representation of national belonging; indeed, "lived situations . . . are three-dimensional" (Elias 1996, 355). The sense of the past in particular has provided salient materials for the invention of national identities and nationalism. Edward Said (1994, 1) argues that "appeals to the past are among the commonest of strategies in interpretations of the present." The past is sometimes interpreted as the origin of a national identity deeply rooted in colonial times, ignoring that nations are only one, relatively recent, historically contingent form of organizing space (Gupta 1997, 179). But the past is also portrayed as threatened by current developments. And the past is represented through those suppressed issues that constitute "structuring absences" (Johnson 1993b, 195), which determine how the present is configured. Homi Bhabha argues that "being obliged to forget becomes the basis for remembering" (1994, 161). Forgetting is as important as remembering. "Part of the struggle against cultural power is the challenge to forgetting posed by memory," as Roger Bromley (1988, 12) also notes. While the past is a precondition in order to imagine the nation, the nation has also been the frame in which the past is generally evoked. As Patrick Wright maintains: "The nation is the modern integration par excellence, and it is in the service of the nation that public images and interpretations of the past circulate" (1986, 24). Perhaps the strongest implication of the idea of a nation having its location in the past has been precisely its naturalization as a "timeless polity," even though Latin American nations did not exist before the nineteenth century.

Spatial dimensions can be recognized as a continuum between public and private sites. Such distinctions are not "natural" but are the result of specific power relations, which can be observed in practices and institutions. Space is just as important as time; both are socially produced. Phil Cohen (1980, 85) noted early in the 1970s that territoriality is the process through which environmental boundaries are used to signify group boundaries. Indeed, the moral panic articulated around outsiders is closely connected to ideas of the sanctity of territory and the fear of transgression (Sibley 1995, 39, 43). Some spaces become nationalized under specific circumstances; perhaps the most common example is borders, transgression of which becomes a national shame. In general, as Wade notes, "The inscription of difference in landscape is fundamentally important not only because this constitutes certain social relations . . . in racialized ways, but also because difference is experienced in a spatially embodied fashion" (1993, 64).

However, research on national identities and nationalism has given more emphasis to the temporal dimension (Radcliffe and Westwood 1996, 80). According to Said, "Most cultural historians and literary scholars have failed to remark the *geographical* notation that underlies Western fiction, historical writing, and philosophical discourse of the time" (1994, 69; emphasis in original). Indeed the interplay of time and space is a key element in the representation of nationhood. Whereas spatial boundaries are crucial in the representation of national uniqueness through the demarcation of differences, temporal notations are usually deployed to signify the nation as a perennial form of political organization. As Radcliffe and Westwood maintain, "Official discourses of nationhood re-present the nation as historically continuous and geographically discontinuous, by interweaving space and time" (1996, 79). But also certain nationalist discourses seek to integrate the national territory through internal migration and colonization. As Wade points out, "In this version, as the nation becomes one territorially, it also becomes one racially and culturally" (1993,

59). Overall, the representation of the sense of national space is a shifting one, one that goes from selective images of certain regions to inclusive portrayals that attempt to integrate "marginalized" areas within nation-building projects.

Analyses of nationhood have usually considered temporal and spatial locations as independent dimensions (see Schlesinger 1991, 173–74). However, time does not exist outside space and vice versa. This relationship requires space-time and time-space, which implies the recognition of the historicity of territory and the territorialization of history (Poulantzas 1980, 114–16). Mikhail Bakhtin (1981, 84) conceptualized the interplay of space and time as chronotopes.[7] The concept of chronotope was initially developed for the analysis of literature but it might be adapted for the study of other cultural forms. A common feature of chronotopes is their evaluating aspect, through which hierarchical configurations of meanings are represented (Bakhtin 1981, 243; Sandywell 1998, 196, 207; Allan 1994, 194). This evaluative character of chronotopes can be seen in the celebrations of the new millennium. A temporal change, according to a particular narrative of time, was represented on a universal scale. In turn, this temporal transition acquired spatial dimensions, since the Greenwich meridian was considered, at least in England, as a "world-wide standard of calculation." Even Channel 4, a British TV company characterized by fairly critical programming, showed a series in which journalists visited various "non-Western" communities situated along *the* meridian line, asking the people there if they knew that they were located on the same meridian as London. This temporal and spatial inscription of power would be impossible without the imperial expansion that meant the opportunity of being *the* center. In other words, despite postmodern claims, Eurocentric narratives of time and space are still alive. In a more general view, Gilroy (1993, 4–5) has noted how the spatial expansion to both sides of the Atlantic, known as modernity—a temporal category—can be understood both as enlightenment and also as a period of enslavement.

Genres and cultural forms are highly defined by their representation of time and space. Literature or historical accounts, for instance, are characterized by long-term and public references, but (auto)biographies and oral stories are frequently related to more personal dimensions. Meanwhile, media discourse provides the predominant public versions about current developments, and everyday-life genres express ongoing issues in more local or communal dimensions. While this project attempts to recognize the peculiarities of each of these cultural forms, it also endeavors to show some of the multiple links and articulations among and within them; finally any spatial location is constituted by a multiplicity of social times (Braudel 1980). It is necessary to grasp both public and more local moments, as well as historical and conjunctural dimensions, researching and theorizing the variant relationships among them. The easiest alternative is to explore only public narratives but, as Johnson argues, "To work only on public narratives, even critically, is to recycle the dominant images, and a characteristically topdown point of view. It is the *combination* of a knowledge of everyday differences, whether produced autobiographically or through ethnographies of different kinds, *and* the critique of public versions, that provides the new opportunities" (1993a, 109; emphasis in original).

A methodological alternative might be to identify key spatial and temporal sites, and those cultural forms through which these chronotopic sites are represented. It refuses both images of the social as an "organic whole" or as a sum of "fragments." Sites are conceived as strategic locations through which national identities can be explored empirically. Figure 1.1 illustrates "where" and "when" national belonging is articulated through particular cultural forms. It is neither static nor a bounded representation. Public and personal locations, for instance, are "unstable and the product of power relations; they are shifting, mobile, uneven, contradictorily defined and fought over" (Epstein and Johnson, 1997, 21; see also Yuval-Davis 1997). The temporal axis is also a shifting and diverse continuum. This figure is envisaged as an open-ended process in which the agency is conceptualized in terms of cultural practices that configure and are configured in defined institutional settings (R. Williams 1977).

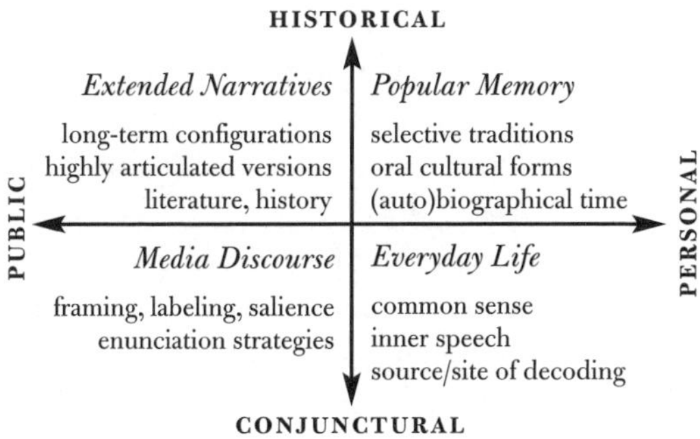

Figure 1.1 Temporal and Spatial Dimensions of National Identity

The overlap between historical and public dimensions includes articulated narratives present in literature and history. Thus, an important task of my research is to deconstruct ways in which nations have been narrated. Throughout these narratives, the emergence of the "riotous" Nicaraguan and the "white" and "peaceful" Costa Rican have been mutually affected processes, showing that exclusion and racialization are not just the consequence of recent "immigration" of Nicaraguans into Costa Rica, as especially the media have argued, but a long-term process in which the nation has been constructed as unique and exceptional. But the historical dimension is not only public since there are also private versions of history, most of the time embedded in biographic experiences. I will attempt to recognize these more personal versions by analyzing testimonial pieces written by Nicaraguans and Costa Ricans in which they represent different forms of belonging and difference.

Biographic writing has been considered an example of self-exalted narratives that arise in the context of bourgeois possessive individualism and nation-building projects (McClintock 1995, 313; Steedman 1997, 109). In this context, Doris Sommer (1988, 111) provides a subtle distinction between autobiography and testimonial, a common genre in Latin America. She notes that testimonials are written through a collective voice that might be considered a "translation of a hegemonic autobiographical pose into a colonized language that does not equate identity with individuality." While the traditional autobiography is written about the author's own sense of "uniqueness," testimonials are characterized by an "implied and often explicit 'plural subject,' rather than the singular subject associated with traditional autobiography" (Sommer 1991, 38; McClintock 1995, 326; Linkogle 1996, 35–36).[8]

Neither are testimonials written in essentialist terms; rather their enunciation is constituted of collective voices. McClintock notes that "the plural voice is plural not in the sense of speaking for, or being representative of, the whole but in the sense that it cannot be heard outside its relation to communities" (1995, 326).

Another set of relations emerges from the intersection between public versions and current events. The media are the main institutions for the construction of the public sphere, especially through the use of framing to classify social actors and issues. Todd Gitlin defines framing as *"persistent patterns of cognition, and presentation, of selection, emphasis, and exclu-*

sion, by which symbol-handlers routinely organize discourse, whether verbal or visual" (1980, 7; emphasis in original). Framing does not imply a monolithic perspective on media discourses nor a conspiratorial perspective, but it does suggest the capacity of the media to define public debate and public visibility. The media have framed, for instance, the immigration of Nicaraguans in Costa Rica as a national threat, racializing and criminalizing it on the basis of particular cases. Paradoxically, framing seems to work through fragmentation.

Everyday life is, in turn, a site where more personal views and feelings on current issues emerge. It can be considered as "those cultural moments in which meaning is not so readily separable as a text because it is so intimately connected to the other practices which surround and accompany it" (Johnson 1993a, 110). The fieldwork undertaken as part of this project explored these moments in which meanings are not yet narratives but fragments that emerge in the context of ongoing experiences.

Everyday life as a site of analysis has been full of all sorts of criticisms. Some analyses underline the colonial character of anthropology—the discipline that has been extensively based on fieldwork—as a predominantly male activity in foreign cultures. The field seems to be reified as a "source" and the people as "informants." "With the rise of ethnography," Said notes, "there is a codification of difference" (1994, 130). The various ways the researcher and the research are implicated within contexts of cultural subordination have frequently been debated (Willis 1997; Marcus 1998). A crucial outcome of these debates has been the concept of reflexivity (Davies 1999, 10; Bourdieu 2000, 119). Pierre Bourdieu and Loic Wacquant point out, "To adopt the point of view of reflexivity is not to renounce objectivity but, on the contrary, to give it its full generality by questioning the privilege of the knowing subject, arbitrarily freed, as purely noetic, from the work of objectivation" (1992, 214).

Reflexivity refers then to the search for a more explicit debate on the ways in which research is undertaken. Bourdieu and Wacquant suggest three crucial sites of objectivation: social location (class, gender, ethnicity, age), position in the academic field, which despite postmodernity "has its peculiarity that its verdicts and pronouncements are among the most powerful socially," and concepts and categories that "delimit the thinkable and predetermine the thought" (1992, 38).

A crucial challenge seems to be how to recognize empiricist limitations present in ethnography without renouncing analyses of everyday life as a site of dispute for legitimated meanings of the social world. Indeed, the opposite direction, based on textual deconstruction, also envisages risks, since a deconstruction abstracted from more social processes cannot properly estimate the power and limits of cultural forms in the social world (Johnson 1993b, 182; Willis 1997; Green 1997, 201). Overall, the analysis of everyday life attempts to make appear strange one's "own" nation, calling into question assumptions not only present in political and intellectual debates, the most frequent source of inquiry (in the case of Costa Rica, see Solís and González 1998), but also naturalized in everyday representations, practices, and rituals.

Up to this point some peculiarities of cultural forms and chronotopic references have been emphasized, but another aim of my research is to explore borrowings between these different chronotopes. Everyday life, for instance, offers repertories turned into "national" icons above all by the media, which in turn are decoded in everyday life. It is crucial to explore which everyday life practices become "nationalized" and how such nationalized practices and representations are, in turn, socially read (Johnson 1993a, 191). There is also considerable overlap between the media, literature, and history. The media discourse usually goes back to history, looking for key references, especially during celebrations or conflicts. Similarly, everyday representations sometimes reproduce celebrated versions of national history, which have become widespread, especially through educational institutions. However, these official versions might be critically contrasted with lived experiences, as some pieces written by students will show (chapter 4).

These relations do not take place only among preconfigured representations of belonging and difference; there are also new national identifications emerging in the interplay of cultural forms and practices. Raymond Williams (1977) outlines these new identifications as "structures of feeling," which are social experiences in solution and in process that have not emerged as public versions, but are in process of constitution. They are a set within specific internal relations, at once interlocking and in tension, which "provide a descriptive term for cultural practices which are in the process of active formation as part of ongoing social life" (Pickering 1997, 36). The following chapters empirically explore these sites and some of their relationships. Throughout the research process, several methodological decisions were made and each is discussed in the appropriate chapter, since it is in close relation to empirical material that methodological debates make sense. This path of exposition aims to avoid the split between theory and methodology, on the one hand, and empirical material on the other.

Chapter 2

Media Representations of Nicaraguans in Costa Rica

Central America has practically disappeared from the agenda of news agencies and, therefore, from the North American and Western European media. This stands in stark contrast to the 1980s, when the geopolitical location of Central America, as well as the participation of the United States in the region, especially through its support to the Contras in Nicaragua, attracted international attention. As Said notes, "The history of other cultures is non-existent until it erupts in confrontation with the United States" (1993, 391). Now there is no war, so there is no news. Other regional conflicts have eclipsed the newsworthiness of Central America. Hurricane Mitch and the earthquake in El Salvador were exceptions to this trend.

Unfortunately, in this case and surely in others as well, no news in this case does not mean good news. The military conflicts and the political polarization in Central America have left deep, sad traces among the populace. The absence of news about Costa Rica cannot be interpreted as a promising indicator either. The deterioration of public social services as well as growing public insecurity has threatened the self-identity of a nation considered democratic, egalitarian, and unique. These internal processes demand to condense and elaborate possible causes, and Nicaraguans, according to hegemonic views, emerge as responsible for some of these crucial problems.

It might be argued that the representation of the Nicaraguan other as a threat and a problem has been carried out with special emphasis by the printed media, which in turn seem to affect the agenda of other media, especially radio and television. This chapter explores ways in which conjunctural issues about the Nicaraguan community in Costa Rica have been represented by Costa Rican newspapers, in particular *La Nación* (*LN*) and *La República* (*LR*). *La Nación,* the major Costa Rican newspaper and media group, has played a decisive role in the constitution of a sense of nationhood during the second half of the twentieth century. Its ideological discourse combines neoliberal economic perspectives with political conservatism. It has attempted to represent its particular political interests beyond political parties; it "speaks on behalf of the nation." Its name, *La Nación,* sums up its agenda very well. Unfortunately, media studies have paid little attention to the relationship between *La Nación*'s discourse and its institutional location in the constitution of the political culture in Costa Rica. During the past twenty years, *La Nación* has been a major voice in favor of neoliberal perspectives. In this context, the Costa Rican welfare state has vacated its paradigmatic role and the new agenda emphasizes privatization, commercial openness, and competitiveness. This chapter attempts to fill this gap.

This political-economic transition has been accompanied by a strong disenchantment with politics among many people. In 1995 José María Figueres, president of Costa Rica (1994–98), was the second least popular president in Latin America, after Argentina's Carlos Menem. Figueres received a 73 percent disapproval rating, Menem 79 percent (*LT* 12/27/96). In a 1996 survey 75 percent disapproved of Figueres. In contrast to Nicaragua, the media in Costa Rica are not linked with political distrust. In a 1995 poll 65 percent maintained that the Costa Rican media performed well or very well.[1] In 1999, 42 percent named *La Nación* the preferred printed medium (Cordero 1999, 9). Moreover, in Costa Rica the similarities among newspapers are more significant than the differences. Perhaps the most important distinction between, for instance, *La Nación* and *La República* is that the former has more institutional resources and a more overt interest in defining nation-building projects. The analysis of these two Costa Rican newspapers will be complemented by looking also at the Nicaraguan press—in particular *Barricada* (*B*), *El Nuevo Diario* (*ND*), *La Prensa* (*LP*), and *La Tribuna* (*LT*).[2] This comparison shows that certain views published by newspapers in one country have been contested by the media in the other, and it aims to facilitate a more reflexive interpretation, since particular views or absences can be made explicit.

The period under consideration, 1994–96, is characterized by an increase in the arrival of Nicaraguans in Costa Rica and virulent border conflicts between the two states. Furthermore, during this period kidnappings—committed especially by former Contras—were used to criminalize the whole Nicaraguan community in Costa Rica. While some topics, such as immigration, disease, or kidnapping, associate certain attributes with Nicaraguan citizens, other frames, such as border conflicts and the general election of 1996, emphasize political or institutional characteristics regarding the Nicaraguan state. The former category defines Nicaraguans as foreigners, whereas the latter characterizes the Nicaraguan government in a more institutionally oriented perspective.

Conflicts are a common pattern in both frames and, indeed, Nicaraguans are commonly represented as troublemakers. Exclusion and racialization are media hyperframes that are seldom discussed. In this context, media narratives are dominated by key oppositions: law versus illegality is the narrative context of immigration; cleanliness versus contamination is predominant when diseases are the main topic; kidnappings are framed as a conflict between peace and insecurity. These patterns of exclusion obscure the diversity of news items within a limited number of cognitive paths. Besides, news items are ritualized on certain pages, especially those devoted to crime news reports. Thus mystification and ritualization fix normative and institutional procedures, but perhaps their more important consequence is the organization of the collective memory through processes of accumulation, consonance, and omnipresence (Martín 1986; Wolf 1992) that place issues and social actors in certain temporal and spatial locations. This chapter is organized around these key oppositions, exploring the implications of these media representations in the configuration of social actors and chronotopes.

Table 2.1 presents a detailed quantification of the frames through which Nicaraguans became a media event. All news items regarding the Nicaraguan community in Costa Rica published during 1995 and 1996 have been analyzed (see also appendix 1). This analysis of framing and labeling has been combined with case studies of those news items, reports, or editorials that are particularly relevant in the context of this research.

Both strategies attempt to highlight general patterns of media representation and, at the same time, to inquire into particular forms of discourse. The analysis of general frames and particular cases also aims to work from concrete problems instead of abstract formulations (Gabriel 1994, 7, 47). Overall, the key theoretical assumption of this chapter is that discourses are not a mirror of reality, nor are they an isolated structure or code. The sense of national belonging is not produced elsewhere and then expressed in words; on the contrary, it is produced discursively and the media are crucial institutions for this configuration. But the word is not an encapsulated world either. Instead of a structuralist reading of news, recognizing minimal units, this chapter attempts to link the study of representations and those textual procedures through which such representations are produced. If meaning is a social action in particular social relations, it is of the utmost importance to locate such meanings in lived experience, where they acquire and make sense (see chapter 4). As Mikhail Bakhtin and his colleagues have argued, language is a space for dispute among social actors (Voloshinov 1973).

In Latin America there have been interesting polemics regarding the analysis of media discourse (Fuentes 1990). During the 1970s, for example, semiotic and sociological perspectives criticized each other's accounts. While semiotic analyses emphasized the study of those internal discursive operations through which meanings are produced, sociological perspectives looked at the links between such meanings and wider social contexts. According to semiotic perspectives, identified especially with Eliseo Verón's work, sociological analyses look at the text as a source, but they do not analyze its internal dynamics. On the other hand, the principal criticism of semiotic perspectives, made mainly by Armand Mattelart and his colleagues, is their "immanent" approach to language as an independent world, without relation to social processes. In a way, the strength of the former is the weakness of the latter and vice versa. This chapter seeks to overcome this antinomy. Thus, some discursive patterns, which are crucial to the construction of a sense of national belonging, have been carefully explored. These are, for instance, the "we" as collective voice (Billig 1995, 71, 73), the suppression of the agency through impersonal or passive voices and "nominalization" (Fairclough 1995, 26, 112–13), forms of ex-nomination (Barthes 1972; Fiske 1996), and the links between authorial and reported speech (Voloshinov 1973).

Table 2.1

Framing in News about Nicaraguans in Costa Rica,
La Nación *and* La República, *1995–96*

Framing	*La Nación*				*La República*				Total	
	1995		1996		1995		1996			
	N	%	*N*	%	*N*	%	*N*	%	*N*	%
IMMIGRATION	11	15%	6	2%	21	45%	13	8%	51	9%
Unidentified	-		-		-		3		3	
Illegal Nicaraguans	5		-		9		1		15	
Social services	1		-		-		2		3	
Disease	-		1		4		1		6	
Economic impact	-		-		-		1		1	
Human rights violations	-		2		3		2		7	
Governmental actions	4		1		5		-		10	
Other	1		2		-		3		6	
CRIME NEWS	41	58%	260	97%	13	28%	142	90%	456	84%
Kidnapping	4		247		1		128		380	
Assault	4		3		2		5		14	
Sexual violation	1		3		-		2		6	
Murder	26		6		8		3		43	
Nicaraguan victim	4		1		1		-		6	
Nicaraguan suspect	14		-		4		2		20	
Nic. victim & suspect	8		5		3		1		17	
Other	6		1		2		4		13	
BORDERS	19	27%	3	1%	11	23%	1	1%	34	6%
Limits	2		-		2		-		4	
Duties	-		-		-		-		-	
Incidents	15		-		9		1		25	
Mines	1		3		-		-		4	
Other	1		-		-		-		1	
MISCELLANEOUS	-	-	-	-	2	4%	1	1%	3	1%
TOTAL	71	100%	269	100%	47	100%	157	100%	544	100%

Sources: La Nación and *La República,* 1994–96.

In a more institutional domain, a number of perspectives have highlighted the links between the media and the constitution of nations and national identities (Anderson 1983; Giddens 1991). The media are an institutional precondition in the constitution of the modern sense of national identity. The ability for imagining the nation is closely tied to print capitalism, in the case of Western Europe, and to radio and cinema in Latin America. The sense of national belonging is created through the wide dissemination of news; different people in different places read similar stories, with similar heroes and villains. More recently, the media have reinforced the "time/space compression" (Harvey 1989) that shapes modernity as a post-traditional order, connecting the local and the global in new and varied forms.

Despite their centrality in modern societies, a major feature of the media is, paradoxically, their invisibility in terms of public debate. Controversies about media effects, for instance, discuss particular effects without noticing that their institutional presence in everyday life is a major effect in itself. *La Nación,* for instance, has rarely been related to the hegemonic representations of nationhood in Costa Rica throughout the second half of the twentieth century. In the field of journalism, newsworthiness or news values, for instance, are still regarded as attributes of certain issues, subjects, or institutions. News values are hardly recognized as produced through complex institutional processes in which ideologies become professional practices (Tuchman 1978). The analysis of newsmaking and professional cultures of journalism and media institutions has provided a better understanding of media performance. In the professional routines, diverse events and issues are typified and framed in such a way that only some of them are objects of journalistic attention. The consideration of the newest as the most important seems to be a key rule (Bourdieu 1998, 6).

The professional cultures of journalism experience diverse processes of naturalization. Generally, there is a lack of self-reflexivity and objectivation of professional practices and discourses. The naturalization takes place in close relation to the configuration of self-centered identities: the public appearance in the media as well as close contact with the political elite diminish possibilities for self-criticism, very often extinguished by daily job constraints. One of the most condensed expressions of this naturalization and self-centered identities is the word *coverage,* a common expression in the journalistic vocabulary that is sometimes also employed in academic and critical analyses. Closely related to positivist ideologies, "covering" seems to include at least two preconditions: first, the event is independent from journalistic institutions, and, second, journalism is a neutral enterprise. On the contrary, media institutions through typification, framing, and hierarchization configure crucial dimensions of the public sphere. Thus the media do not "cover,"[3] but they do strongly define the public visibility of issues, events, and social actors in certain spatial and temporal settings (Sandoval 1996, 97). The media seem to blur the distinction between a "real" event and its mediated representation (Fiske 1996, 2). Thus those social actors or issues that do not get media visibility do not seem to be recognized beyond their immediate locality. Topical events are typified according to professional ideologies and institutional networks. As Stuart Hall and his associates argue,

> The social identification, classification and contextualization of news events in terms of these background frames is the fundamental process by which the media make the world they report on intelligible to readers and viewers. This process of 'making an event intelligible' is a social process—constituted by a number of specific journalistic practices, which embody (often only implicitly) crucial assumptions about what society is and how it works. . . . Arguments *against* a primary interpretation are forced to insert themselves into *its* definition of 'what is at issue.' . . . Effectively, then, the primary definition *sets the limit* of all subsequent discussion by *framing what the problem is.* (1978, 54–55, 58–59; emphasis in original)

The media often establish the initial definition or primary interpretation of the topic in question. Despite minor differences, the main media frame regarding the Nicaraguan community in Costa Rica portrayed them as a problem, either in terms of "immigration," disease, border conflicts, or criminality. Even critical perspectives of media representations have to recognize such framing in order to challenge it. The next pages explore these framings in detail.

Water-Related Tropes: A Radicalization of Labeling

A complex interplay of economic, political, and military factors has generated the arrival of Nicaraguans into Costa Rica during the 1990s. The flight of capital, economic boycotts, and hyperinflation generated a deep economic crisis characterized, among other features, by unemployment, poverty, and scarcity of basic goods. Meanwhile, Nicaraguan society has also faced strong political polarization. In 1991, 40 percent of those polled in Managua considered Nicaragua a stable democracy; by 1995 that had fallen to 21. In another 1995 survey 46.9 percent said they did not place any trust in politicians (Córdova and Seligson 1995, 12, 36). Politics in Nicaragua is represented most of the time as crime news; disputes among a few—male—political actors define the political. Civil society appears most of the time as a "recipient" or "patient" affected by the actions of recognized political actors. Women, for instance, are seldom actors of political discourse. These tendencies are present in newspapers with various political persuasions.

The war of aggression against Nicaragua that was taking place from Honduras and Costa Rica implied complex diplomatic conflicts. Most of these conflicts were framed by media institutions, which, rather than offering options for dialogue between different social actors, became sounding boards for the conflict. Thus, both Costa Rica and Nicaragua were exposed to nationalist claims made by media institutions. Frequently, the Costa Rican media contested the Nicaraguan and vice versa. Media representations about the arrival of Nicaraguans in Costa Rica have usually been framed under these nationalist discourses.

The change of government in Nicaragua in 1990 did not imply economic reactivation; on the contrary, difficulties have increased and around 60 percent of the national labor force is currently unemployed. The arrival of Nicaraguans gets more visible during the agricultural seasons, when workers try to find jobs in coffee picking and sugarcane cutting as well as on banana plantations. Private security and construction are the most frequent jobs in the cities. For women, domestic work and work in factories are the principal alternatives. Those arriving in Costa Rica without official documents often do not receive the legal minimum salaries.

The representations of the Nicaraguan community in Costa Rica have experienced a change in labeling from unidentified Nicaraguans (*nicas indocumentados*) to illegal Nicaraguans (*nicas ilegales*). There has been an increase in immigration but there is also a more radical labeling. During 1994, Nicaraguans were recognized as immigrants (*LN* 7/23, 7/27, 7/29, 7/30, 9/12/94) and also as unidentified (*LN* 9/12/94; *LR* 6/22/94). The label *illegal* began to be employed in the context of the introduction of the

Provisional Job Card in 1995, an initiative designed not only to register "immigrants" and provide them with health services but to prevent job discrimination. In this context, however, the governmental discourse emphasized their illegal status. The first time *La Nación* used the term *illegal* to describe a Nicaraguan immigrant was in 1994 (9/3/94). During 1995 the term *illegal* underlined the paradox of being inside the country yet outside the nation; so-called illegals were inhabitants but not citizens.

Water-related tropes, which appeared during 1995 and 1996, meant another form of radicalization of labeling. A common feature is the use of the impersonal *wave* to describe "immigrants": "The Nicaraguans seem to come out of nowhere. They are a big, irrepressible human wave" (*LN* 1/6/95). Surprisingly, it was a news item, but contrary to the notions of impartiality and objectivity—the "essence" of journalism—its narrative is closer to a fairy tale (Langer 1998), in which the news is constructed around conflicts defined by the opposition between "villains" and "heroes." Considering Nicaraguans as a wave seems to carry at least two implications. First, it rationalizes the threat, since there is previous knowledge of the risks associated with the sea; second, it naturalizes Nicaraguans in such a way that strong measures against them do not represent any guilt among those "lifeguards" in charge of implementing immigration policies.

Being "swamped" by Nicaraguan immigrants is another familiar water-related trope present in media discourse. In 1999, a day after the beginning of the amnesty (see chapter 5), the front-page headline of *Al Día* (2/2/99), a newspaper owned by *La Nación* media group, read, "Nicas Invade Immigration [Office]," and the biggest internal headline read, "Nicas Swamp Immigration." The accompanying photos illustrated the same metaphor: an anomic group is presented as a mass, out of control. In turn, this racialized representation has interpellated Nicaraguans, as the testimonials written by members of the Nicaraguan community make clear. Aracely, for example, writes, "They say we are swamping their country, as if we were a contagious disease." And Leoncia states:

> I believe that in all countries there is racist hate, because nobody wants to know anything about foreigners. We are "things," not "different" faces; they even push us away, avoid rubbing elbows with us. They don't notice that we need to feel well, that we need help, because the problems we are facing are bigger than what is usually thought. But

> many say, "Ah, it is not my family, nor my social circle, nor my political party." We are nothing more than strange beings.[4]

The concept of a wave seems to represent an obliteration of fixed limits, distinctions, and differences. This undermines physical but, above all, symbolic boundaries. Employed in diverse contexts such as Germany (Linke 1999), England (Lawrence 1982; Gabriel 1998), Australia (Hage 1998), the United States (Chaves 2000), Austria (*Daily Telegraph* [London], 2/9/00), or Costa Rica, water-related tropes are symbols of fear. Since limits cannot be distinguished anymore, efforts are made to reinstall boundaries, which enables us to localize the sources of fears and anxieties (Gilman 1988, 1).[5]

This threat posed to boundaries illustrates how important space becomes as a signifier of national identities. As David Sibley argues, "Separation is a part of the process of purification but to separate presumes a categorization of things as pure or defiled" (1995, 37). There is a crucial link here between transgression of boundaries and racialization. Those who transgress certain sacred territories are categorized as belonging to some "inferior race" or having the same, delinquent "nature" and are considered responsible for crimes and other undesirable acts.

Nominalization: Erasing the Subject's Agency

While Nicaraguans were represented by more radical labels during the 1990s, Costa Rican responsibility in presumed human rights violations was erased from news items. Nominalization (Fairclough 1995) transforms nouns—violence, for instance—into subjects in such a way that it seems that violence is self-produced. In 1994, for instance, a group of landless peasants, including some Nicaraguan families (*precaristas* in Spanish), had a confrontation with the police. One headline was a typical example of nominalization: "Violence without Truce in Sarapiquí" (*LR* 6/1/94). Violence has no explicit agency; there are no explanations of events, they just take place. Nominalization becomes a discursive device through which the "naturalization" of events is made possible. The worst consequence of such incident was the death of a minor, who took no part in the conflict. His distressed mother reflected on the relation between being poor and being a foreigner: "I just want justice for my son. That is not possible because we are poor and foreigners; we are treated like animals, we have a right to live too."

This blurring of agency is also termed exnomination (Barthes 1972). John Fiske notes that exnomination is the means by which a subject "avoids being named and thus keeps itself out of the field of interrogation and therefore off the agenda for change" (1996, 42). Perhaps the principal consequence of exnomination is that such absences prevent any possibility of self-criticism. Neither the police nor the media discourse can be subjects of critique because they do not overtly take part in the stories. Teun van Dijk argues that "such an attitude is not difficult to explain: the press is a unique institution that controls all that is published about itself" (1994, 81).

Meanwhile, the Nicaraguan press reported several critical periods of human rights violations between 1994 and 1996. At the beginning of 1995, for example, forty-five Nicaraguans were deported (*LT* 2/23/95). The Permanent Commission for Human Rights (CPDH) denounced the fact that the expelled workers had been cheated: they had traveled one hour by bus from the community of Juan Viñas (Cartago Province), where they had left their families and provisions, to San José because they had been told that their situation was going to be legalized. However, it was a lie (*LT* 2/24/95; *LP* 2/24/95).[6]

The deportees were working in a sugarcane plantation, the property of some of the principal owners of *La Nación*, which scarcely mentioned the issue (*LN* 2/25/95). *La República* published several news items during this time. The first paragraph of each story presents a very similar structure:

> Although the Nicaraguan Union of Workers and Peasants (UNOC) denounced the xenophobic treatment of the "Nicas" who enter the country [Costa Rica], the official version [of Costa Rica] denies that abuse or mistreatment takes place when they are expelled. (*LR* 1/19/95)

> In spite of the excessive number of Nicaraguans, the authorities remain conservative in their calculations. (1/20/95)

> In spite of the friction between Costa Rica and Nicaragua caused by the deportation of forty-five Nicaraguans who claimed they have been victims of aggression, the massive influx of illegal Nicaraguans continues. (2/5/95)

Each of these three examples is constructed through two statements: the first is the viewpoint of the workers (or about them) and the second is the authorities' version, which has been assimilated by the newspaper as its own. In the first case, the statement of the UNOC is written in the past tense ("denounced"), but the "official" version is given in the present tense, a more convincing form of enunciation since it implies that the action is currently taking place.

An opposition is established between the outsiders' versions (UNOC, victims of aggression) and an assimilated police discourse by the newspaper. This incorporation of the reported speech, as noted in chapter 1, is frequently present in crime news. The authorial view, in this case the newspaper's narrative, assumes the police institutional voice as its own. This discursive pattern reveals that journalists usually produce crime news almost exclusively based on official versions, with hardly any other source. And precisely because crime stories are not recognized as serious or "hard" news, they are taken-for-granted discourses through which notions of law and order are represented. These media representations also express a denial of racism, since the authorial speech belies the aggression and shows that immigration has not diminished. A step forward takes place when the presumed perpetrator is victimized. A news item stressed this common reversal of roles: "All recognize that the situation is critical, all claim that a solution is urgent, but until now nobody has put forward any suggestions to limit the immigration problem that Costa Rica suffers" (*LR* 1/5/?). Those presumed responsible are suppressed; instead the "threat" posed by the immigrants has acquired newsworthiness. Thus, a violation of human rights has become a news item about the excessive number of immigrants. As van Dijk notes in the cases of England and the Netherlands: "The journalist or columnist believes that his or her own group or country is essentially 'tolerant' toward minorities or immigrants" (1992, 103). Unfortunately, blaming the victims for their own situation is a common denial of racism in a variety of contexts (Fiske 1996, 106).

In 1996 the expulsion of two hundred Nicaraguans, who were working in banana plantations, marked a new critical juncture (*LP* 7/8/96; *ND* 7/9/96). The issue acquired salience after priests from two Nicaraguan communities denounced it (*ND* 8/22/96; *LT* 8/23/96; *LP* 8/23/96). A national commission was formed in Nicaragua by the Ministry of Foreign Affairs, the Nicaraguan Commission for Human Rights (CENIDH), and the Catholic church of Juigalpa (*B* 8/24/96).[7] *La República* (*LR* 8/23/96) did not give salience to these denunciations; on the contrary, the labeling was defined by the police response. The headline—"Police Refute Aggression against Nicas"—presents another typical inversion of roles: an instance where the police were suspected of having committed human rights violations is constructed from the police's viewpoint; thus the suspected actor is exonerated from any responsibility. The inversion of actors works, again, through the identification of the authorial speech—the newspaper's voice—with the reported speech—the police version. The latter becomes the subject of the news item in such a way that the disciplinary power of the police acquires discursive dimensions. Conversely, Nicaraguans do not constitute subjects of their own enunciation, they are "patients," affected by the actions of others (Fairclough 1995, 112). A similar pattern occurs in an editorial published by *La Nación* (*LN* 8/26/96), which was reproduced in turn by *La Prensa* in Nicaragua. It presents the "we" as a collective voice that speaks "on behalf of the nation," a frequent device that will be discussed below: "Our system of values is founded on the basis of the dignity of the human person and the rule of law is cosubstantial with democracy. Democracy has been our best authority. We must distinguish, therefore, between the deviant behavior of certain authorities—which, in this case, has not been proved yet—and the attitude of the Costa Rican people and the Costa Rican state" (*LP* 8/28/96).

The norm is democracy; any deviant behavior is an exception. The editorial then links contemporary issues with "our common history"; looking to the past is a way of making sense of the present: "Second, it is necessary to invoke our common history: the Nicaraguan people have suffered many decades of persecution, natural calamities, and poverty. Costa Rica has always offered them its hand in a fraternal and generous manner. The number of Nicaraguan immigrants has considerably overtaken the economic possibilities of our country" (ibid.).

In her own eyes, Costa Rica does not need self-criticism; she is a model. The collective voice ("we") not only is a configuration of collective identity, it also signifies a form of mobilization since it is able to address a variety of people that surely belong to different regions and social backgrounds. The "we," constructed in opposition to Nicaraguans and the Nicaraguan government, articulates diverse aspects under a single heading: Costa Rica is a "democracy," is "generous," and is a "model country." Any mistakes that might have been made had been the result of individual failings.[8] The editorial continues: "In this regard, Costa Rica has been a model country. . . . Costa Rica needs Nicaraguan labor and the investments of Nicaraguan citizens in our country have been very positive, not to mention their cultural contribution" (*LN* 8/26/96).

Costa Rica is a model not only for Nicaragua but also for the world. The established group, in this case the Costa Rican nation, is associated with charisma, a virtue lacked by "outsiders." But at the same time there is a precise differentiation among Nicaraguans, since some are "workers" and others are "investors." Whereas the former are needed, the latter are welcomed. These systematic forms of stigmatization have interpellated the Nicaraguan community in Costa Rica. In a letter to the editor, a Nicaraguan reader argues,

> In a society such as yours, which values its own traditions of democracy and freedom, it is self-defeating to encourage xenophobia and outrage against those whose only crime is to sell their labor in order to send something to their beloved relatives. . . . We must remember that in disasters such as the one that took place in Limón [Province, Costa Rica], we [Nicaraguans] were the first to give our blood and our effort to help the wounded. It is ironic that, being brothers, we look at each other with rancor. (*LR* 8/15/96)

Two weeks later another Nicaraguan reader wrote, "We are a humble people, but with a noble heart; we are neither tall nor blond nor white foreigners [*machillos*], but we are human beings. We seek jobs in order to feed our families" (*LR* 9/3/96).

This case shows ways in which ethnic markers are internalized by Nicaraguans. Their identity is constructed through the stigmatized representation of them by hegemonic voices. They perceive themselves through their physical differences with Costa Ricans. The centrality of the body as a mediation between representations and subjectivities is clear in these letters.[9]

Cholera and Fears of Pollution

Immigration has coincided with the reemergence of epidemics such as cholera, dengue fever, and malaria in Central America and elsewhere in Latin America. *La República* highlighted the relationship between

Nicaraguans and the incidence of cholera in November and December 1994, when thousands of Nicaraguans traveled to Costa Rica looking for jobs. However, the percentage of cholera among Nicaraguans is low if one considers their living conditions and their lack of health services. According to the Ministry of Health, between 1992 and 1998 there were 124 cases of cholera in Costa Rica, 66 percent of them in nonnationals, most of them Nicaraguans. Most of these cases (sixty) were diagnosed between 1994 and 1995 (MS 1998, 2). A simple comparison between Nicaraguans who suffered from cholera and the estimated number of the Nicaraguan community can offer a more precise assessment. From January to June 1994 authorities in northern Costa Rica "detected" fifty thousand "undocumented" Nicaraguans (*LN* 7/24/94). During the same period twelve Nicaraguans became ill with cholera (*LR* 12/12/94). The importance and implications of this very low number were exaggerated by the media, which reported the cases as the most serious public health problem in Costa Rica during that period. Meanwhile, 17,677 cases of dengue fever had been reported in 1994 (ibid.), but this did not receive similar labeling.

The health panic created around cholera has to be interpreted as a result of the lack of epidemiological knowledge among health authorities during the presidential administration of 1990–94. The case of Peru, where twenty thousand cases were diagnosed weekly, prompted an overestimation of the possible impact in Costa Rica, according to an interview with Leonardo Maranghello (1/21/99), an epidemiologist at the Ministry of Health.[10] But cholera is not merely a health issue; it masks cultural and social exclusions. The mainstream concern was not solely that the ill people were "foreigners" but that they were poor Nicaraguans. What defines their illness is not their nationality but their poor living conditions. Cholera is a fear of pollution within Costa Rican society that threatens the nation as a body. Peter Stallybrass and Allon White (1986, 145) argue that the body becomes a "transcoding" between public references to the nation and subjectivity. The nation is threatened through the undermining of the health of the body. The "outsiders" are associated with dirtiness and infection.

Additionally, the institutional relations between the media and health "sources" must be taken into account. Health authorities frame these issues in such a way that cholera and dengue fever are depicted as the result of the presence of "foreigners" and not as a result of a decline in sanitary facilities. In turn, media institutions locate such issues within a pretypified crime-news framing about stigmatized people. Time and again the authorial speech assumes the reported speech as its own. There is no debate about the salience of the cases of cholera, nor is the absence of weekly reports of cases of dengue fever surprising, since most of the patients are Costa Ricans. The people with cholera were never interviewed. They are victims of cholera but also revictimized as "carriers of pollution" by the journalistic discourse. The absence of the interview as journalistic genre is relevant in this context, because it is a cultural form in which people can be recognized not only as objects but also as subjects. The news "talks" *of* them but not *with* them, as is typical in monological thinking (Bakhtin 1982, 333). Thus, immigration and health are framed under similar criteria.

A news item in *La República* is typical: "The principal problem in the northern region is that people don't report the illegal Nicaraguans they receive in their houses, who could be ill" (*LR* 12/14/94). Such a point of view presupposes a relation between *ill*egality and *ill*ness; however, a person sick with cholera does not "pollute" other persons as a consequence of face-to-face interaction. The contagion is possible only if his or her excrement contaminates food or water. Furthermore, since the cholera bacillus is vulnerable to acids, contamination depends on a high concentration of bacilli (Maranghello, interview). Although the media panics regarding cholera cannot be sustained by epidemiological facts, the fact that cholera can be transmitted by excrement might have played a key role in the symbolic construction of fears of contagion. Excrement remains a taboo in most Western cultures and a strong signifier of otherness. As the information is framed, it seems to imply that, again, Nicaraguans are going to "pollute" the Costa Rican nation.

In 1995 *La República* reported that health authorities in Nicaragua and Costa Rica had agreed to coordinate the prevention of cholera, dengue fever, and malaria: "The aim is to avoid more ill people entering the national territory [of Costa Rica]." Even more surprising is the caption under the accompanying photograph: "In the border areas, it has been ordered that those with suspected symptoms be reported" (*LR* 5/23/95). While the meeting between the health authorities responsible for the two countries attempted to improve coordination, the core news promoted a sort of policing of "polluted" people. And in 1996 it was reported that, according to the Costa Rican minister of health, the cholera bacillus had acquired a resistance to the medicines employed up to that date. However, the accompanying headline suggested something completely different: "Nicas Are Immune in Fight against Cholera" (*LR* 7/23/96). Bacteria have been replaced by "Nicas" in such a way that an epidemic problem is racialized.

These fears of pollution have a long history that shows, in a broad sense, ways in which racialization works through other discourses. Cholera in particular has long been a signifier of defilement, especially after a cholera epidemic struck the Costa Rican army during the War of 1856 (see chapter 3). Throughout the transition between the nineteenth and twentieth centuries, Nicaragua has been represented as a nation where fever and dysentery were common (Víquez 1887, 14; Dana Gardner Munro, quoted in Molina and Fumero 1997, 10). Furthermore, cholera epidemics in the United States and England during the nineteenth century were also associated with fears of pollution (Stallybrass and White 1986, 142; Rosenberg, quoted in Lancaster 1992, 256; Sibley 1995, 25).

Overall, disease has been used to signify difference and pathology; outsiders—working-class people, homosexuals, and immigrants—are commonly associated with disease. They represent what a hegemonic sense of nationhood fears to become, especially if the disease is contagious (Sibley 1995, 25). Outsiders have been felt as anomic; close contact with them threatens the established group with "anomic infection" (Elias 1994, xxiv). In turn, order and control are the antithesis of pathology and policing the body becomes synonymous with policing the nation-state (Gilman 1988, 1; Gabriel 1998, 99).

From Border to Boundaries: Tailoring Nationalism

Disputes over border limits, immigration policies, and navigation taxes through the San Juan River have been frequent sources of disagreement between the Costa Rican and Nicaraguan governments since independence from Spain in the nineteenth century. During the 1980s, these disagreements took place in a polarized political environment period that characterized relations between the two governments (León and Ovares 1983, 68). These conflicts were framed as a national threat on both sides of the border. Although Nicaraguan and Costa Rican newspapers emphasized different views, they exhibited similar nationalistic claims and tabloid narrative patterns.

In this context, two case studies are highly relevant. The first came out as a consequence of a distribution of lands made by the Costa Rican government among Costa Rican and Nicaraguan families in a region that belongs to the Nicaraguan state. It was framed as a threat to the national territory by Nicaraguan newspapers. The second case was the capture of thirteen Costa Rican policemen by the National Army of Nicaragua. According to Costa Rican authorities, the capture took place in Costa Rica, but Nicaraguan officials disagreed.

The dispute concerning the distribution of lands appeared in *Barricada* in March 1994. The headlines demanded the expulsion of Costa Ricans: "Ticos Will Be Expelled" (3/8/94). Meanwhile, the peasants, quoted in *Barricada,* were more reflective: "If these lands belong to Nicaragua, we will leave them immediately" (3/8/94). Different reported voices emphasized these nationalistic claims. Even *Barricada* and *Nuevo Diario* quoted Cardinal Obando, a strong adversary of the political forces represented by both newspapers, as a supporter of this new "national crusade":

> "We must fight for the sovereignty of our country; we have seen Nicaragua crucified from all four sides and we have seen our neighboring countries entering our territorial seas, taking our fauna and especially our fish." . . . Obando employed the same Sandinista slogan in the last decade but in a different context. He said, "The motherland should be loved and we should defend her and also her communities along the borders in order to prevent them [the peasants] asking for a change of nationality." (*ND* 3/15/94)

In Nicaragua the hierarchy of the Catholic Church and the Sandinista government had been divided by political and ideological struggles but by this time were united by nationalistic commitments. The next reference made by *Nuevo Diario* linked this conflict to the past, when in 1824 the inhabitants of Nicoya, now part of the province of Guanacaste, decided to belong to Costa Rica, because of internal political problems in Nicaragua (see next chapter). "*Guanacastización* Must Be Avoided," warned the headline (*ND* 3/15/94). Media representations reworked historical developments in order to make sense of present issues. History provided justifications for present decisions; the past was interpreted as a key for the resolution of present conflicts in such a way that past and present were organized as a continuum. Meanwhile, *La Tribuna* offered the most convincing news: the government of Costa Rica bought the disputed property called Jumusa at the end of the 1970s. The former owner did not explain, nor did the government of Costa Rica confirm, that the property was part of Nicaraguan territory. It then was distributed among thirty-six families, six of which were Nicaraguan (*LT* 3/17/94, 6/26/95).

The same topic reappeared in 1995 when some Costa Ricans decided to found a new republic, Airrecú, with an extension of 213 kilometers, actually in Jumusa, on the border between Costa Rica and Nicaragua. *Barricada* suggested the existence of a conspiracy: "Other sources asked by *Barricada* don't discount the possibility that this initiative could be hiding the omnipresent Costa Rican zeal to take possession of Nicaraguan lands" (*B* 6/27/95). The nationalistic campaign had thus been restarted. Some front-page headlines were especially confrontational: "We Will Eject Them by Force" (*ND* 6/27/95), "EPS [Army] to Airrecú" (*B* 6/28/95), "Sovereignty Defended" (*ND* 6/29/95). There was also a certain celebration of a possible dislodging: "Major Membreño added that until now they hadn't received the order to dislodge the settlers, even when the decision that they had to leave our territory was made last May 5. But he remarked that they are ready to execute the order as soon as is necessary" (*ND* 6/29/95).

Until, even, and *but* acted to contrast what had been ordered and what was executed: "until now" they had not received the order, "even" when the decision was made, "but" they are ready to act. The reported speech was encapsulated in the authorial and forced to say what the authorial wanted to underline. *La Prensa* provided the most convincing explanation, emphasizing investment in tourism and the smuggling of timber and livestock as the possible motivations of the new republic (*LP* 6/29/95). A handful of regional business leaders had decided to found the new republic, and in fact its hypothetical inhabitants ignored "the separatist plan" (*ND* 6/29/95). *Barricada* recognized the importance of the commercial interests, but the news items were framed within a polarized and nationalistic perspective (*B* 6/29/95). The same problem reappeared yet again in 1996. Again *Barricada* published the strongest headline: "Costa Rican Invasion Returns" (*B* 11/22/96; *ND* 11/22/96). However, the media attention diminished, especially as a consequence of the kidnappings that became the major focus of the media agenda. Although the main concern of this chapter are the media representations published by newspapers in Costa Rica, the above case illustrates how border disputes acquired salience in both countries and how the newspapers in one country were contesting "official" versions in the other. Paradoxically, they were divided by nationalistic goals but united by similar discursive strategies.

In turn, the Costa Rican case shows how border conflicts have been represented by Costa Rican newspapers. In March 1995 the Nicaraguan army captured thirteen policemen. It is not clear whether the capture took place in Nicaragua or in Costa Rica; the last news published by *La Nación* regarding this issue seemed to confirm that it occurred in Nicaragua (*LN* 3/10, 3/11/95). But more than being an issue of truthfulness, this narrative shows the transformation of the policemen into heroes. A dramatic chronicle dramatized a phone call:

> He [one of the captured policemen] took four minutes to complete the route. He was conducted from the office that has given him shelter for two days, during his detention, to the telephone of the commander's headquarters. . . . On the telephone the sound of an opened door could be heard, and the policeman entered. Without waiting for an answer to his hello, the [Nicaraguan] commander's guest asked, "Is it true that you are calling from Costa Rica?" (*LN* 3/5/95)

The reactions of their relatives were also depicted. The mother of one of them asked, "What happened to my boy?"

> "Why aren't they [the policemen] freed? Come back, please." Entreaties mixed with tears, after four days without sleep and the dozens of questions that had emerged with the last image of the boys . . . mothers, wives, fathers, sons, and relatives of the thirteen policemen captured received messages from Rivas [Nicaragua]. The messages were delivered, at the request of the policemen, by a team from *La Nación* who was in that city. . . . Despair and uncertainty reign in thirteen Costa Rican homes, most of them in La Cruz, Guanacaste [Province]. All of them urged the [Costa Rican] national authorities to make the greatest effort in demanding the return of the captured policemen to Costa

> Rica. . . . They are interested neither in land, boundary stones, nor borders. (*LN* 3/6/95)

The policemen were transformed from victims into heroes; they became *the* men of the nation. Ordinary people lived and suffered unique experiences that turned them into heroes. In this context, John Langer offers a telling contrast between media representations of elites and ordinary people. While elites in the "nonserious news" reports seem to be represented as "being-as-they-are," ordinary people appear to be "acting-as-they-do," "displaying their virtuosity or revealing the results of their personal accomplishments" (1998, 69). The policemen, who were depicted as national heroes, might fit into the latter category, and crime news, usually considered a lowly genre, became the center of nationalist narratives. As in the tales analyzed by Vladimir Propp (1968), *La Nación's* team, as well as the relatives of the policemen, effectively became supporters of the national heroes. But this news item was not the only nationalist tale. The editorial commenting on the issue produced a masterpiece of how the authorial voice becomes the voice of *the* nation. First, *La Nación* "speaks on behalf of" the people: "Fortunately, the people of Costa Rica, cured of these evils and more politically mature and freed of the tricks to which the Sandinista Popular Army [EPS] is accustomed, observe and analyze the facts with prudence and, sometimes, even with humor."

La Nación takes for granted its authority to "speak on behalf of the nation"; it is never discussed. In a second step, *La Nación* and the nation are fused by the narrative. "Speaking on behalf of" goes further and is replaced by the "we": "We know how to distinguish between the actual violence of the International Law that has sometimes put our border in mourning and the defeated tactics of the EPS, which are like those that used to be employed by the Somocista Guard."

Who the "we" is never is considered. The newspaper's voice does not appear explicitly but it does not lose its presence; on the contrary, it is present without being named; it has become the voice of the nation. The third sequence of the editorial takes place when the authorial voice distances itself from the Costa Rican nation but emerges speaking on behalf of the Nicaraguan and Costa Rican peoples: "The governments of Costa Rica and Nicaragua suffer serious political, economic, and social problems. Those of Nicaragua are immeasurable. It is an offense to common sense and to the dignity of our people that time and resources have been wasted" (*LN* 3/6/95).

The editorial is constructed in such a way that the subject of enunciation does not appear. It is not located as a particular and defined institution; its voice has been generalized, naturalized. This invisibility locates the newspaper voice beyond the disputes between the two governments. In this context, a common pattern in editorials is the construction of "we" as a collective subject: "we know," "we consider," and "we have said many times" are common expressions. An individual voice has become a collective voice; it is *the* public opinion. "We" overcomes the opposition between the newspaper voice and other voices. As Michael Billig points out, "The 'we' is a universal code for the naming of particulars" (1995, 73). The collective voice constructed around the "we" speaks on behalf of the people, the law, the tradition, the nation. This self-attribution is constructed through an interesting semiotic process in which the newspaper represents a sort of national will. These textual practices are crucial for the processes of the construction of hegemony since the newspaper is no longer a particular voice. In turn, the "enemies" are not only opposed to the "we" but also to "the very moral order which 'we' can claim to represent" (Billig 1995, 88).

But where does the newspaper's authority come from? It could be argued that *La Nación*'s *symbolic* power has had a long process of legitimization—approximately fifty years—since the foundation of the newspaper. It was in 1946 that the first editorial defined its aims and it is one of the few cases in which the "we" has been depicted as a particular "group of Costa Ricans" (reproduced in *LN* 10/12/96). A key issue in this context has been to present the interests of the newspaper's owners as national aims through relatively autonomous journalistic practices. The name of the newspaper, *La Nación,* has been, until now, a self-fulfilling promise.[11]

An important difference between *La Nación* and other newspapers in Costa Rica has been its ability to be located institutionally beyond political parties. This does not mean that *La Nación* is not engaged in politics, as some commentators claim, yet it is another way of doing politics. A similar contrast can be drawn in the case of Nicaraguan newspapers. While *Barricada* and *Nuevo Diario,* for instance, mobilize nationalist claims through the threat of an "invasion" (a narrative heritage from the confrontation against U.S. aggression during the 1980s?), *La Nación* elaborates its national calls through the victimization of actors, who are in turn transmuted into heroes.

Overall, these cases make explicit ways in which borders are a key element in national identities; official discourses of nationhood are closely related to notions of space. As Radcliffe and Westwood argue, the history of limits is a "key component in geopolitical imaginations" (1996, 56–57). Identities are purified through the purification of space, through the racialization of boundaries (Morley and Robins 1994, 122). Borders are turned into boundaries.

New Elections, Old Framing

While the news about the Nicaraguan community in Costa Rica has been characterized by the duality racialization/criminalization, reports about Nicaragua as a state continue reproducing cold war politics, constructed around the opposition between the Sandinista National Liberation Front (FSLN) and democracy. It was the prevalent framing throughout the 1980s and was reworked during the Nicaraguan general elections of 1996. The media representation of Nicaragua has been a crucial issue in Costa Rica, especially since the end of the 1970s. The triumph of the Sandinistas was followed by strong political polarization. The war of aggression supported by the Reagan administration was depicted as a "fight for freedom" and the opponent was portrayed as the "Soviet devil" and its "regional satellite," Cuba. Media institutions started a "ritualization" of issues and actors: "freedom versus communism," "peace versus war," "democrats versus communists," to mention just a few. The government and Nicaraguan society were the "communists"—"enemies of democracy and freedom," two bastions of the hegemonic Costa Rican national identity.

Appendixes 2 and 3 offer a general perspective of the international news published by *La Nación*. The foreign news agenda has been defined by the internal disputes within the FSLN during 1994, the conflicts between former president Chamorro and the parliament regarding the electoral reforms throughout 1995 and the national general elections in 1996. In particular, the elections of 1996 were framed in a "new old fashion." Few actors take part in politics; civil society was an object of discussion, yet it was not an actor. Again, "to speak on behalf of" is the narrative pattern. There was no recognition of other sites from which to analyze politics. Just weeks before the Nicaraguan general elections of 1996, *La Nación* published several news reports that are highly relevant in this context. A journalist was sent to Managua so, more than secondhand reports from news agencies, these materials made explicit how the newspaper represented the elections. The reports were written and published at the beginning of October 1996, two weeks before the elections, in the context of a sudden increase in the FSLN's acceptability to the voters.

The elections were depicted as the opposition between two political actors: Arnoldo Alemán (of Alianza Liberal) and Daniel Ortega (FSLN). The reports started with a chronicle of demonstrations organized by both candidates. Alemán was characterized as a "fat man, like a bear." Ortega was the "new Daniel with a white shirt and black trousers" (*LN* 10/6/96). The second piece was an interview with Alemán, who "is not worried when some people call him *somocista*. Nor when it is said that he is an ally of the Cuban exiles" (*LN* 10/7/96). Ortega was not interviewed; instead of talking with him, the journalist wrote about him. Ortega has been made over; this is the central concern of the piece. A photograph shows the change: Ortega during the 1970s and Ortega in 1996. The headline of the article asks: "Will the voters swallow the hook?" (*LN* 10/8/96). The next subject of the reports was Tomás Borge, head of state security in the 1980s, "one of the worst phases of violation of human rights" in Nicaragua. He was a member of a "regime that attempted to 'Cubanize' Nicaragua" (*LN* 10/9/96). The last but by no means least important interview was with Cardinal Obando, who is considered "more powerful than any other military commander." He was asked about the most "suitable candidate" (*LN* 10/10/96).

While news reports about the Nicaraguan community in Costa Rica call them Nicas—a group within which there are no political differences—these reports show social actors in an old polarized political framing: the FSLN is a "communist threat" with a new look, and Alemán is depicted as a bear. These metaphors reworked old representations. In 1983, for example, Ortega was a "wolf in sheep's clothing" (*LN* 4/25/83, in León and Ovares 1983, 60). Polarized politics was reproduced through polarized journalism. The explicit support for Alemán is not surprising. What is even more relevant perhaps are the ways in which politics is conceptualized in these journalistic pieces. The campaign was a masculine universe:

two men fighting for an election, which was defined as a childbirth in the headlines of the first piece (*LN* 10/6/98). The "object" of the fight is a feminized prize: the victory of the elections was meant as the control of the "motherland."

The rest of the people are "the masses." The relations between the politicians—either Alemán or Ortega—and the masses were defined as vote hunting (*LN* 10/8/96). The journalist in that piece was worried by the growth of the FSLN; he even suggested a cause: the Alemán campaign had started too late to "hammer" past mistakes, especially scarcity of goods and compulsory military service (*LN* 10/6/96). Hammering the masses over the head with certain issues will make sense of the past. The emergence of this symbolic violence is taken for granted: to hammer them does not seem to be perceived as violence; after all, they are the masses. Alemán provides another image: the people must not divide their votes so as to support him as presidential candidate as well as his eventual deputies to the parliament. Alemán calls the people to vote for his party's candidates "in Indian file" (*LN* 10/6/96), a common expression in Latin America, which refers to the image of the "indigenous people" walking one after the other. In this context, calling citizens to vote "in Indian file" means calling them to vote in a disciplined way for all candidates proposed by Alemán's party. Meanwhile, the term *masses* appears a total of seven times in two reports; and in three photographs the "masses" are represented as an anomic "crowd." Conversely, *citizenship* is employed only once. Although the journalist is strongly present within the reports through the employed nouns ("masses"), verbs ("to hammer"), and adjectives ("Indian file"), he represents himself as a collective witness in Jinotega: "where *we* arrived to follow the last period of the Nicaraguan electoral campaign" (*LN* 10/6/96; emphasis added).

Despite promises of democratization and elections, political culture reworks old ideologies within new scenarios and characters. Unfortunately, the processes of democratization have not implied new forms of representation and political practices. There are no young people, women, or representatives from different ethnic or economic backgrounds. They are going to be "hammered" with propaganda; they are "voters," not citizens. Overall, there are similar images between and within racialized and "cold war" politics: while the "immigrants" are an "irrepressible human wave" and their illegal status is closely related to illness, the voters are "masses." Beyond differences in content, the ideological matrix is a deeply authoritarian monologue. The "other," either an immigrant or a voter, is an object of consciousness; she or he does not represent a separate consciousness (Bakhtin 1982, 334).

From Freedom Fighters to Kidnappers

Although pacification initiatives in Nicaragua included demobilization of military groups, a culture of violence does not change by decree. On the contrary, former participants in the military conflict have been involved in assaults, murders, and kidnappings in the north and south of Nicaragua. According to religious authorities, at least two thousand people have been murdered by former Contras in the northern and central regions of Nicaragua during the 1990s (*LN* 2/23–25/96). Meanwhile, the media attention in Costa Rica was most closely focused on kidnappings. They were framed as "developing news" (Tuchman 1978, 54–55), maintaining the public's attention through expectation, mystery, and melodramatic narratives. The kidnappings became the most important news items during 1996, not only because of the involvement of Nicaraguans, but also because these items were typified as crime news. Certain divisions of labor take place: journalists visit different places; witnesses and experts are consulted; the predominant information sources are the police and judicial authorities.

Recycled news items filled information gaps when editors wanted to keep an issue in the public eye and no new elements were available. Melodramatic pieces were produced, especially around the victims; they were transformed into heroes through testimonies (*LN* 3/14, 4/18–21, 9/18–19/96). Ordinary people were presented as extraordinary and vice versa. Rather than being an example of insignificant or superfluous journalism, crime news items offer a strategic location of analysis. John Langer points out the relevance of these "non-serious" news items: "Crucially, rather than locating these types of stories as merely tangential to questions of communicative power due to their ostensible non-political or non-serious inflection, it will be maintained that it is precisely these characteristics which render such stories so 'political,' investing them with a particular, even unique, capacity to do ideological work, perhaps in ways which are unavailable to the more conventionally defined serious, significant news" (1998, 8).

In 1993 several members of the Nicaraguan embassy in San José were kidnapped. The deed was carried out by former Contras, and some of them would organize other kidnappings during the 1990s (see appendix 4). The second kidnapping that achieved media salience took place in 1994 and involved two executives of the company Cabo Marzo, located in Costa Rica's northern region, near the Nicaraguan border.

In 1996 kidnappings were permanent media events. The most important was the capture of a German tourist and her guide in the community of Boca Tapada on January 1. Many items were written, and eight months later the story was still on the front pages of Costa Rican newspapers. Its salience was motivated by the eventual implications for tourism, which attracts tens of thousands of people every year.

The resolution of the kidnapping in Boca Tapada reactivated the kidnapping of the members of the Nicaraguan embassy in Costa Rica, since a suspected kidnapper participated in both crimes. Moreover, the trial of the chief suspect in the kidnapping of the Cabo Marzo executives took place in March 1996. In August of the same year two Dutch investors were kidnapped. These incidents show a broad pattern: most of the crimes were committed by a small group of former Contras. The group also attempted to kidnap a former Costa Rican deputy and the former Costa Rican ambassador to Nicaragua, and they committed other criminal offenses in the border region between Nicaragua and Costa Rica. Overall, as in a nightmare, the "freedom fighters," as Ronald Reagan liked to call the Contras during the 1980s, turned into the kidnappers of the 1990s.

The kidnapping in Boca Tapada was not only typified as crime news but as the main national news for at least three months. The first strategy of resolution employed by the government was to track the kidnappers. This offered more possibilities for a typical crime-news framing, concentrated on the suspected perpetrators. *La República* called the event "subversion" (*LR* 1/3/96). Later, the action of the police was depicted as "hunting" (*LR* 1/8–13/96), a characterization that was repeated when the victims were liberated and the police sought to capture the kidnappers. *Hunting* was also employed in relation to the kidnapping of the Dutch citizens (*LR* 9/18/96; see also *ND* 3/3/96). *La Nación* was less sensationalist in its labeling. Interestingly, most of the news about kidnappings in the Nicaraguan newspapers took *La Nación* as a source (*ND* 1/5/96; *LP* 8/26/96). It employed a similar framing and, above all, lacked analytical discussion about the ways in which violence was fomented in Costa Rica's northern region. Headlines in *El Nuevo Diario* were sensationalist and nationalist: "Wave of Terror against [Tourism], the Principal Economic Activity: Costa Rica: Another Attack against Tourists" (*ND* 1/8/96), "Ticos Almost Throwing in the Towel" (1/10/96), "In Nicaragua They Would Be Caught" (1/5/96). *La Prensa* sometimes lost its serious style and presented front-page headlines such as: "Fears Grow for the Lives of the Kidnapped" (*LP* 1/22/96), "Have the Kidnapped Died?" (2/10/96), "The Kidnapped Will Die of Hunger" (3/2/96).

A kidnapping, like any tale, requires a villain (Propp 1968), so the first suspect was presented a week later (*LR* 1/4/96). After his capture, he was depicted as an aggressive person, but the causes of his violence were not clear. His description sought to transform social processes into an individual essence: "He is a man with a penetrating and inquisitive glance. It has been said that he wears close-fitting jeans [belted] above his waist. Generally, few of his friends are known" (*LN* 1/12/96). The connection between the fit of his trousers and his presumed violence is an unanswerable point! In fact, at the end of January, it was confirmed that he was not linked to the kidnapping (*LR* 1/30/96). The authorities of the Judicial Police recognized that his presumed responsibility had been promoted by the media and criticized the sensationalist media reports of the kidnapping (*LR* 2/1/96; *LN* 3/19/96).

A second phase of the story of the Boca Tapada kidnapping was defined by the lack of new information and the decline in media attention. During February the focus was on the negotiations between the kidnappers and the relatives of the victims. A third period started in March with the liberation of the victims. *La Nación* published several chronicles of the kidnappings; by this time the victims had been transformed into heroines. In April the principal suspect, a former Contra, was arrested (*LR* 4/28/96). Interestingly, only two items of news published by *La Nación* emphasized the relationship between the rise of criminality and the Contras. The first reported a statement by the Commander in Chief of the Nicaraguan army: "The former government of President Oscar Arias always pretended not to see [*se hizo de la "vista gorda"*] the Contras' presence in Costa Rica, and this is the result" (*ND* 1/11/96). This declaration provoked the only news item about the kidnappings, the headline of which overtly blamed the Contras for these issues (*LN* 1/14/96). However, this link never became the topic of editorials. Indeed, an editorial blamed immigrants as a whole group for such crimes: "Costa Ricans and Nicaraguans have participated in many of these criminal actions [kidnappings], though, as is obvious, the military experience of many Nicaraguan immigrants has contributed to the organization of the most audacious operations" (*LN* 1/8/96).

The chief of the Nicaraguan police also recognized that both Nicaragua and Costa Rica were paying the consequences of the solution adopted in the Nicaraguan embassy kidnapping in 1993 (*LR* 6/30/96), when the kidnappers were allowed to leave Costa Rica before they could be brought to trial. The kidnapping of the Dutch citizens generated similar comments (*ND* 9/19/96). Unfortunately, such declarations were analyzed by the Nicaraguan press as part of a tabloid style of journalism, which conceives crime news as raw material for nationalist crusades. The second explicit link between the kidnappings and the military conflict in Nicaragua was reported in an interview with a former member of the FSLN and later chief of a Contra group, Edén Pastora, who was operating on the border between Costa Rica and Nicaragua (*LN* ?/7/96).

Interestingly, the views of the chief of the Costa Rican Judicial Police in the northern region, Fernando Sánchez, were not considered either. Sánchez argued that former Contras committed most of the crimes that attracted the media's attention, especially kidnappings, in a context characterized by easy access to guns used previously in the military conflict. The media, he noted, bear a strong responsibility in the criminalization of Nicaraguans, since the prominence given to crime news did not reflect the regional situation (interview by author, 3/16/99). Delinquency is considered an issue of nationality, not a consequence of a particular political culture. In this context, crime stories have been a crucial cultural form for the transition from a so-called cold war framing, in which the Sandinistas were a "communist threat," to media representations in which Nicaraguans frequently became criminalized and racialized. This relatively long-term process took place throughout the 1990s without major notice, since crime reports are not generally perceived as political or serious items.

The media attempted to mobilize collective opinion against the kidnappings: "If we are able to catch the kidnappers, an exemplary punishment would be important; a punishment that scares them" (*LN* 1/9/96).

As in former cases, it is unknown who "we" is. In any case, the slogan is punishment; there was no attempt to analyze causes. Importantly, the "we" fuses the views of nation, law, and newspaper; law versus chaos appears in its narrowest form. In this context, a demonstration was organized in order to repudiate the kidnapping of Boca Tapada and an editorial sought to mobilize "public opinion": "The Government has not stinted in its efforts—some of which weaken our juridical order—in order to free the victims, and the Costa Rican people have offered to them and their families constant moral and spiritual support. . . . In these conditions of inhumanity, the reaction of the Costa Rican people must be neither silence nor stoic endorsement of the facts." The editorial was also meant as a claim to the world's views on that situation: "Second, this march must be a message to the world. Costa Rica is not the country the kidnappers have wanted to depict in front of the world, with [their] clear antipatriotic intentions of discrediting the social and economic order" (*LN* 2/29/96).

The editorial addresses the government, the Costa Rican people, and world opinion not from a particular viewpoint but "on behalf of the nation's best interests." Thus, this kidnapping became an articulating issue around which the best interests of the country were made explicit and it became an everyday concern of a wide range of people. Although *La Nación* and the Figueres administration (1994–98) had strong disagreements over economic or internal affairs, the kidnappings reconciled them. Criminality, the "enemy within," achieved what "official" politics could not.

In August, *La Nación* published photographs in which one of the victims and a kidnapper were embracing (*LN* 8/7–8/96). While some commentators indicated that this image could be interpreted as an example of the Stockholm syndrome, a series of moral discourses took place. "Was it a real kidnapping?" was a common question (*LR* 8/9/96). The publicity generated by such photos ended any possibility of political analysis; the crime-news frame was substituted by a moral crusade against the victims. A column published by *La Nación* provided a bold interpretation:

> An eruption of violent emotions was provoked by the publication of a series of photographs in which the German Nicola Fleuchaus appeared to be kissing and resting her head on the shoulder of Julio Vega, one of the kidnappers. The surprising images provoked a catharsis, or rather a national exorcism, through which public opinion vilified the actions

> of both women and heaped on them feelings of frustration experienced in the face of a cruel and unusual reality in Costa Rican history, which has overwhelmed Costa Ricans' patience. The 1990s have been hard times and have given no respite to Costa Ricans: several successive kidnappings (the Embassy of Nicaragua, the Supreme Court, the executives of Cabo Marzo), the misfortunes of Banco Anglo Costarricense, the siege of the car robbers, murders like that of the couple and their son in the Fletcher quarter, and, even more, the economic recession that burdens, above all, the middle and lower social strata. So this feeling of impotence was turned without mercy against the two kidnapped women, that's the limit, are foreigners. . . . The government has taken advantage of this "external threat" to forge cohesion in a stunned society, and as a way of exorcising national frustrations. (*LN* 8/21/96)

This piece suggested a possible link between "national frustration" and the depiction of "external threats," a relationship scarcely mentioned by the media. It is worth noting that a female journalist wrote this column in *La Nación,* the newspaper that began the "moral crusade." Unfortunately, this column has been an exception during the 1990s. The Costa Rican media have been especially unaware of the criminalized and racialized representations of the Nicaraguan community in news reports. Another notable exception to this trend was published in 1999:

> If you want to dress a lie in the clothing of truth, begin to repeat it time after time. Appeal above all to the emotions of those who read or listen to you. Even more important: do not worry about documenting your claims, and if you manage data, manipulate them according to your own aims. . . . In Costa Rica, where an important segment of the Nicaraguan population has been obliged to immigrate, there are frequent voices that feed myths and falsehoods regarding this economic problem. Against them (some with access to the media) we must be vigilant. (*LN* 12/8/99)

This has been practically the only critical assessment published by the mainstream media in which there is an explicit reference to the media themselves. Interestingly, that reference was enclosed in parentheses, which seems to indicate the institutional constraints faced by journalists when they want to address the media themselves. However, it also shows that the media are complex institutions that enable and constrain professional practices. It demands to go beyond conspiracy assumptions that reduce that media to transmitters of ruling-class ideology.

Mining the Memory

The suspected authors of the kidnappings were first depicted as Nicaraguans, then recognized as former members of the guerrillas; the last alternative was to consider them Contras, even when their participation in the Contra organizations was underscored in the news items themselves. A specific political description, *Contras,* has been replaced by *Nicas,* a racialized representation.

The presumed participation of former "Contras" in the kidnappings was mentioned but it did not achieve prominence in media representations. The label is neither absent nor used exclusively. Fairclough (1995, 106) suggests that the media representations locate actors and issues within a scale of presence which includes absent, presupposed, backgrounded, and foregrounded elements. In this context, the depiction of kidnappers goes from presuppositions to seldom foregrounded explanations. This scale of presence results from tensions between professional imperatives related to objectivity and the ideologies supported by the media institutions. Most crimes have been committed by former Contras, there is no question about that, but at the same time the media did not renounce their broad ideological agreement with the Contras throughout the 1980s. Thus the imperatives of objectivity—the self-definition of journalism—are subordinated to cold war ideologies.

The absence of journalistic genres such as news analysis in the Costa Rican newspapers—as well as in other media—also constrains more contextual perspectives. News items frequently frame events as facts—not as processes. There is a strong positivist assumption that considers that "facts" are objective, whereas processes are subjective. This definition of newsworthiness is taken for granted and it is not recognized that "facts" are preconstituted typifications. But as Fiske points out, "Words work through categories, so putting an event into words involves categorizing it" (1996, 134).

This scale of presence has direct implications in the framing of time and memory. Crime news items suppressed any analysis about the culture of violence that has made possible kidnappings and other crimes. There are no critical analyses of the ways in which the military conflict during the 1980s has led to criminal violence during the 1990s. Such absences do not disappear completely from the media discourse. Johnson argues, "De-selection, however, is by no means the end of the story. To follow a well-worn argument in cultural theory, apparently unselected categories are never simply absent; they are 'structuring absences.' Their 'difference' defines those identities which are too insistently present" (1993b, 195).

Such structuring absences frame actors, temporalities, and locations. Those who were the freedom fighters, as Reagan called them twenty years ago, are now the enemies of order, peace, and democracy. However, there is no relation between kidnappings and the freedom fighters in the news reports. They belong to different stories; processes of memory and neglecting work together, illustrating how structuring absences define discourses. The suppression of debates about the causes of criminality among former Contras and members of the Sandinista army led to the racialization of Nicaraguans.

A similar process took place during the 1980s, when the "mission" of the media was to split the relations between the Somocista guard and the Contras. In 1983, in the context of the emergence of the Contra warfare in Nicaragua, *La Nación* offered master portraits of the nowadays forgotten Contras: "Any outsider to the group [Contras] can observe how, in the evening, each insurgent forms a circle with his mates and they say the rosary. It is easy to listen to how the fighters as a chorus repeats with devotion: 'Lord, give us good life and a good death.' . . . It is impossible to say that one of them looks like a soldier."

Faith has converted them into "renewed" freedom fighters: "It is true that among the extensive jungle of the region, a significant percentage of former Somocista guards undertake fierce combats against the Sandinistas. . . . However, they are not alone nor do their eyes light up for blood or revenge: they believe that the guard that protected Somoza died in July 1979 and now they consider themselves a military corps without a boss but completely renewed" (*LN* 5/14/83, in León and Ovares 1983, 55).

Throughout the 1990s the kidnappers are "nicas" but are never identified with Reagan's former "freedom fighters." These links are hardly recognizable, mainly because the political violence was framed as national news, whereas the kidnappings were labeled crime news. This split is also crucial in that it distances the media from acknowledging their support to military groups during the 1980s.

The undermining of memories not only takes place in temporal terms, it also implies geographical disruptions. In this context, it is useful to recognize how the violence in the northern and southern Nicaraguan borders is represented as an independent issue, even though both conflicts are fueled by the U.S. government's support for the Contras. An editorial published by *La Nación* is a case in point: "The violence gets new wings in the north of Nicaragua, where almost a hundred military bands operate. It is in the same surroundings where the so-called Contras were active. The Sandinista army and the government, presided over by Violeta Chamorro, watch with impotence as the annihilation of an armed band leads other new insurgents to take its place, killing or kidnapping farmers from the region and even fighting against the regular forces, though they don't have external support" (*LN* 9/18/94).

Here, the "so-called Contras" (in the past) and "the military bands" (present) in the north of Nicaragua are different tales, just as the Contras and "kidnappers" were split in the previous examples. The violence is worked out through nominalization; where its "new wings" come from is an unanswered question. The above editorial does not assume the labeling of Contras; the expression *so-called* distances the editorial itself from such categorization.

Another editorial, written two years later, refers to a similar topic. It was motivated by a message delivered by the bishop of Estelí—a Nicaraguan province—to the former president of Nicaragua, calling her attention to the violence in both northern and southern Nicaragua. The editorial claims, "In the northern region of Nicaragua two thousand people have died to date, and recently irregular military groups assaulted a European Union car and three occupants perished" (*LN* 2/25/96). Nominalization is complemented by impersonal speech forms. People died but it is not clear how or why. Time and again grammatical devices are deployed as a way of avoiding the issue of agency. At the end of 1996 an editorial drew attention to the situation on the border between Nicaragua and Costa Rica: "The inhabitants of the northern zone of the country [Costa Rica] have many reasons to feel threatened as a result of the insecurity in this border region with Nicaragua, which has been, for a long time, their daily bread. Three kidnappings in recent months, a cluster of different crimes over several years in the northern region, and the emotive state of the population are strong factors that demand a new strategy" (*LN* 9/9/96).

Although it is possible to reconstruct patterns and links between both sites, that is not precisely the "preferred reading" suggested by the media (Hall 1980b). This temporal and spatial splitting contributes enormously to the suppression of any attempt to explore the relationships between the presumed authors of these crimes along both borders of the Nicaraguan state.

During the 1980s the Contras might have installed thousands of antipersonnel mines in some areas along the border between Costa Rica and Nicaragua. An initiative of the Organization of American States sought to remove them in order to prevent more accidents and make such areas fit for agriculture. The news published around these issues went back to the 1980s and also provided an opportunity for the analysis of the construction of time, space, and social actors. In fact, only one case explicitly recognized the responsibility of the Contras (called guerrillas in the following news item): "Important parts of Costa Rican soil that are close to Nicaragua are really deadly traps, as the result of thousands of explosive mines that the guerrillas of the northern country [Nicaragua] buried during the military conflict with the Sandinista National Liberation Front" (*LN* 6/15/96).

The principal feature of these news items is the ways in which the Contras are avoided as the social actor responsible for the mines' installation. Two strategies, nominalization and the use of impersonal voices, are again crucial in the framing of absences. The war, for instance, is "nominative": "As a consequence of a war of almost ten years . . ." (*LT* 12/2/96). The phrase suggests that the war has been self-produced, that there is no human or institutional agency, and thus no possibility of establishing responsibility.

Another device is employed when the authorial speech recognizes the agency of Contras, but again it distances itself from them: "The territory was mined by rebels known as 'Contras' and by Nicaraguan troops" (*LN* 2/26/95). The authorial voice does not assume *Contras* as its own label, it has thus been attributed to an unidentified voice. The same newspaper that gave partisan support to the Contras sees them now as *so-called* Contras. At the same time, it is not clear who the "Nicaraguan troops" were. The mystery continues because the "military source" that has provided the information was not identified either.

In Costa Rican news items related to mines the passive voice is usually used: "It seems that the mines were laid during the war" (*LN* 10/31/96); "Five thousand mines could have been laid" (*LN* 12/1/96). The Nicaraguan newspaper *La Prensa* offers a similar pattern: "At least five thousand mines were planted in the northern region of the country [Costa Rica]" (*LP* 11/2/96). Who installed these mines is another "mystery." These news items about mines could have been an opportunity to recognize links between the war of aggression and the kidnappings. However, journalists and media institutions did not highlight such relations; on the contrary, they offer very fragmented stories.

In Costa Rica the media have represented Nicaraguans as a national threat. They are generally related to four main media frames: disease, "immigration," border conflicts, and criminality—often described by metaphor. These images have been particularly persuasive in the projection of fears onto Nicaraguans, since news reports can be considered objective but at the same time are narrated as fairy tales. The metaphors "transcode" representations of nationhood into subjectivity through the mediation of body images. As John Gabriel notes, "Paranoias around the body *and* the nation state have freely exchanged metaphors to the mutual enhancement of both" (1998, 98; emphasis in original). It is the articulation of such rhetorical devices (e.g., constructing collectives such as the "we," metaphors of otherness, among others) that makes media representations strongly persuasive.

Although some of the most revealing images of nationhood combine (or suppress) spatial and temporal references in different ways, the politics of space and politics of memory are generally autonomous domains. The concept of chronotope might provide a useful tool for looking at the interplay of temporal and spatial representations. While this chapter has explored conjunctural representations of actors in certain spatial and temporal settings, the next seeks to show that long-lived images present in historical, literary, and philosophical works are also highly selective.

Chapter 3

Costa Rican Exceptionalism and the Nicaraguan Other in Historical Perspective

THROUGHOUT THE NINETEENTH and twentieth centuries, representations of nationhood made by politicians and intellectuals have emphasized the uniqueness of Costa Rica, characterized by political values such as democracy, peace, and social equality. Moreover, Costa Ricans are considered the "whitest" population in Central America as well as the best Spanish speakers. Simultaneously, Nicaraguans have become an "other" in Costa Rican imagery. After independence, conflicts with the Nicaraguan state originating in the definition of borders inaugurated a tension that continues today. Furthermore, Nicaraguans have been historically represented by their "different" Spanish accent and dark skin. This critical perspective does not deny that overall the postcolonial period in Costa Rica has been less violent and plagued by inequality than in other Central or Latin American nations, but the emphasis on the country's uniqueness may have activated various forms of exclusion and racialization.

Not only was this chapter conceived as a historical framework aiming to contribute to an understanding of current issues, it also attempts to show that historical interpretation itself is a crucial raw material for constructing nationhood, since the "past" is a key reference for nationalist imaginations. Said points out that "authoritatively national and institutional versions of history tend principally to freeze provisional and highly contestable versions of history into official identities" (1993, 378). In a similar vein, Eric Hobsbawm notes that historians frequently provide the "raw materials for the market of nationalism, . . . what makes a nation is the past, what justifies one nation against others is the past, and the historians are the people who produce it" (1992, 1; 1998b, 22). In the case of Costa Rica, the constitution of a sense of nationhood and the emergence of history as an academic discipline have been interrelated processes (A. Quesada 1988, 56, 77). The definition of borders between Costa Rica and Nicaragua, for instance, was one of the first topics of historical interpretation. Historical interpretations encoded certain versions that were circulating among the political elite. These historical interpretations were in turn reworked by new generations of politicians as a legacy they must preserve.

The retreat of the social sciences into the present (Elias 1987b) seems to exclude historical analyses from cultural studies and cultural theory in general (Pickering 1997). However, the analysis of long-term processes can contribute to an understanding of how the sense of Costa Rica's uniqueness and the representation of the Nicaraguan other have been configured. These links between historical and present developments can show, moreover, that the current process of racialization of Nicaraguans is not a simple consequence of "immigration," as the media has often argued, but a process closely related to the ways in which nation and race have been interlinked in Costa Rica.

Contested historical versions of nationhood and otherness in Costa Rica have been written in diverse genres, especially essays, novels, and autobiographies.[1] In turn, these narratives of national identity refer to a variety of historical nation-building projects. The colonial period, the "national war" of 1856, and the civil war of 1948 have been the main topics of representation. Given the relationship between these three dimensions—versions of national identity, genres, and historical developments—this chapter does not always follow a chronological sequence nor is it an exhaustive analysis of primary sources. Examples discussed in the footnotes illustrate how certain historical developments have been reactivated in recent years.

Rural Democracy and the Freeborn Peasant

Most of the references to Costa Rican national identity construct lines of continuity that go back to the colonial period, which has been characterized as a long-term experience of geographical isolation, economic weakness, and a small indigenous population. These three issues were addressed after Costa Rican independence in different historical interpretations. One early study, *Bosquejo de la república de Costa Rica* (Brief sketch of the Republic of Costa Rica), published by Felipe Molina (1851) in several languages—including English, French, German, and Spanish—summarizes certain distinctions that would have strong repercussions. Costa Rica, he stressed, had an industrious and mostly white population, who lived in relative isolation due to the geographical characteristics of the country. Molina (1851, 28) estimated that the Costa Rican population consisted of about a hundred thousand "white" people and ten thousand "Indians." *Brief Sketch* was written in order to promote Costa Rica in Britain and the United States and became compulsory reading in formal education after 1862, introducing these representations among the social sectors who participated in formal education at that time (Taracena 1995b, 55; Palmer 1995, 77).

In 1909, Ricardo Fernández Guardia published *La cartilla histórica de Costa Rica* (Introduction to Costa Rican history), which emphasized the poverty of Costa Rica during the colonial period as a result of the absence of commerce. Such poverty was in turn interpreted by Fernández Guardia (1984, 72) as a source of a distinctive national identity characterized by "moderation." In 1941 another key book, *Historia de Costa Rica* (Monge-Alfaro 1982) was published. Carlos Monge-Alfaro not only outlined a chronology of presidents and military coups, as Fernández Guardia had, but advanced a durable interpretation of the colonial period: "The historical synthesis of the eighteenth century was the development of what we would doubtless call rural democracy." The peasant is the "crucial figure in our political, social, and cultural history" underpinning "the psychological basis of the Costa Rican people" (1982, 158, 160). This "rural democracy," forged in the eighteenth century, has been considered a symbol of Costa Rican nationhood. Further political developments were interpreted as part of this "democratic will," which also has its origins in the colonial period. Monge-Alfaro (160–61) traced a line of continuity between contemporary developments and the "freeborn peasant," whom he considered "the axis, the spinal column of our history: the nucleus around which the Costa Rican people will be structured." Nevertheless, Monge-Alfaro noticed that "rural democracy" was represented by counterexamples in the nineteenth century, when "[t]he only way in which the alternation of presidents could be guaranteed was by military coups" (215). Indeed, political violence has been frequent. Fabrice Lehoucq (1995, 151) maintains that on six occasions between 1882 and 1948 presidents imposed their successors on the people. During the same period, oppositional forces organized twenty-three rebellions against the governments and three of them were successful.

However, this evidence did not diminish the representation of rural democracy as the crucial outcome of the colonial period. Rodrigo Facio, in another very well known book, argues that "all Costa Ricans, in general, were landowners and the lack of a pronounced division of labor made the formation of opposed interests impossible." This social landscape promoted a "democratic tone" among Costa Ricans (1975, 42).

These historical interpretations have had a wide circulation through many reprints, remarkable for a small book market like that in Costa Rica. *La cartilla histórica,* for example, originally published in 1909, had been reprinted forty-nine times by 1975. Monge-Alfaro's book had been reprinted sixteen times by 1980 (I. Molina 1986, 3). The apparent absence of alternative views regarding the colonial period left the interpretations offered by Fernández Guardia and Monge-Alfaro without rival explanations and has contributed to the celebrated idyllic past as a key ingredient in narratives of nationhood. Sociological studies asserted that the introduction of the coffee industry, and later capitalist relations of production, had modified the colonial heritage, but the Costa Rica that existed before the coffee boom remained unexplored until the late 1970s (I. Molina 1984).

Colonial poverty as a source of a distinctive national psychology has been reproduced insistently in history textbooks used in primary and secondary schools (see Ferreto and Sáenz 1980, 130; Ferreto and Meléndez 1981, 74, 141, 143, 162–63, 209, 239; see also chapter 4). The presence of these interpretations in history texts is especially relevant, given the rise of formal education in Costa Rica during the twentieth century. Between 1927 and 1950, illiteracy among nine-year-olds decreased from 34.3 to 21.2 percent. By 1984 this percentage had diminished to 6.9 (I. Molina 1999, 8, 22).

A sense of the past has been a matter of interest not only among historians; it has become a crucial component of Costa Rican national identity within a wider setting. The attributes surrounding the concept of rural democracy crystallized in a metaphor that poses Costa Rica as the Switzerland of Central America, and even of Latin America. The cultural circulation of this metaphor, perhaps the most consistent icon of isolation and uniqueness, illustrates ways in which intellectual and political claims have been entrenched in everyday life. In 1863, Wilhelm Marr, a German traveler reporting his expedition through Central America, described Costa Rica as "an Eden comparable with Switzerland." He described the weather as "eternal spring" and said that "the fresh mountain air resembles the Swiss Alps. . . . One might imagine oneself in one of the loveliest of the Swiss valleys." Marr was attracted by natural landscapes but also by "young female peasants who seduced at first sight." Nature and nation were fused through sexuality and the nation was represented as a feminized landscape. Interestingly, Marr's idyllic depiction of Costa Rica was constructed by comparison with Nicaragua: "Costa Rica offers a pleasing contrast with Nicaragua, the land of the lost race" (in Fernández 1970, 137; see also 150, 157, 165, 185, 192, 222).[2]

The first Spanish translation of this traveler's literature seems to have circulated in Costa Rica for the first time in 1929. Historians of the day, given the scarcity of written documentation, used to quote traveler's accounts as one of the most important sources for characterizing the colonial past. And in the first decades of the twentieth century the Switzerland of Central America, through an advertisement by the former Office of Tourism, became a common representation among newspapers and politicians (Facio 1975, 192). Moreover, the popular song "Mi linda Costa Rica" (My beautiful Costa Rica) brought this metaphor into popular culture.

This metaphor condenses the complexity of national identities as long-term configurations. It establishes an identification with Europe as a source of modernity and progress and, at the same time, underlines the differences between Costa Rica and the rest of Central America. The gaze of the other—the European traveler as bearer of a modern mode of seeing—was the starting point encoded by historians; it then was institutionalized as the image of the country and as a media hit.[3] This identification with Europe and detachment from Central America has had a wide circulation, which illustrates ways in which a national representation became not only a matter of intellectual debate but also a form of popular identification (Rowe and Schelling 1991, 25). This interplay of institutions, practices, and cultural forms also makes it evident that there is a relative autonomy in the formation of nationhood.

Perhaps the main implication of the Switzerland metaphor has been the reinforcement of a sense of uniqueness.[4] In the nineteenth century, for instance, Costa Rica did not refuse to form part of the Central American Federation, but the priority was the creation of the hegemony of San José as capital of the new state and the control of the territory beyond the Central Valley (Taracena 1995a, 160). In 1934 the Costa Rican government rejected a Guatemalan initiative oriented toward regional economic integration. In the 1950s the Common Central American Market project, was termed the Central Americanization of Costa Rica (Solís 1992, 348). But Costa Rican "exceptionalism" has not been free of critique. Recently, El Guato, a ska band, parodied "Mi linda Costa Rica" in a new version that is popular among youth. The original song says, "So beautiful is Costa Rica that the Virgin of the Angels descended, and when she saw it to be as pretty as Heaven, decided never to return [to Heaven]." The new version is pessimistic: "So beautiful is Costa Rica that the Virgin of the Angels descended, and when she saw how different it was from Heaven, decided to go back."[5]

Seeking Costa Rica's Essence

In the 1950s and 1960s a new generation of intellectuals reworked previous versions of the concepts of rural democracy and the freeborn peasant. Rather than historical interpretations, these are philosophical essays, most of them written by university lecturers, who exerted an important influence in public debates (Ferrero 1971). These essays continue some of the concerns of the historical interpretations but now as an abstract enterprise, since they contain images of rural democracy and the Switzerland of Central America as a sort of "philosophy of history," which sought Costa Rica's essence. Time and again, the past provides an "origin" of identity. This idealization of the past is related to a strong identification between nature and nation. Thus, the colonial insulation of Costa Rica engendered individualism and shyness. In other words, the "nature" of the nation reinforces the country's essence.

El costarricense (Láscaris 1994), first published in 1962, is the most celebrated version of this philosophy of history.[6] Its starting point is a "factual truth that is undemonstrable": "The Costa Rican has developed a sociopolitical polity on the basis of individualism, freedom, and conviviality" (9). Some natural and geographical features are considered sources of national identity: mountains surround its territory, and its geography is a key for understanding the ways of life of the Costa Rican people. The broken landscape that characterized the Central Valley has created an isolated population, which pursues a desire for nature's calm. From this geographical context, Constantino Láscaris (1994, 21) finds that the Costa Rican is taciturn, peaceful, cautious, and respectful of human life. Again, nature becomes destiny.[7]

While the explanation for the Costa Rican being lies in the natural, the interpretation of Costa Rican democracy is in the rational. Láscaris states that democracy in Costa Rica was possible because there had existed a rational conception of the state. Without previous philosophical ideas about how to structure the state, the latter would have not been feasible (in Mora 1997, 135). After independence Costa Rica avoided the conflicts other Central American nations suffered and adopted a "modern" line. This philosophical conception has made "Costa Rica a different country, not to say unique" (Mora 1997, 134, 135). But was this rationality present before nation building or has it been projected afterward onto historical developments? These images associated with rural democracy, the freeborn peasant, and geographic isolation seem to repeat what Mikhail Bakhtin (1981, 147) calls *historical inversion*—the projection onto the past of highly appreciated political attributes such as justice, equality, and democracy. This historical inversion seeks to translate idealized representations into actual facts and into part of the national heritage. The strong presence of democracy and uniqueness is a relatively recent representation and it is precisely this philosophical speculation that contributed to this image of uniqueness, depicting desires about the nation as empirical explanations. In short, one might borrow Marx's lampoon and argue that this philosophy of poverty exhibits the poverty of an essentialist philosophy.

This philosophical search for the Costa Rican "being" led philosophers to the suspicious terrain of sexuality. The nation is identified with the family, but also with virginity and rape, representations also present in other cultural settings (Innes 1994; Laliotou 1994; Mackey 1996). The rape of the earth becomes a metaphor for the rape of the woman. The freeborn peasant cleared the land and turned it into a rural democracy. The machete is an "instrument of the daring struggle of clearing the virgin land making it fecund for men. Costa Ricans violated the virginity of the tropical forests with the machete and have made them a fertile womb" (Láscaris and Malavassi 1975, 17).

Agriculture is depicted as a male (and antiecological) enterprise, more precisely as a violation: the peasant rapes the virgin woman and makes her fertile. But that violation does not produce any guilt; on the contrary, it is a remarkable act. The tropical forests are the womb of the woman called Costa Rica, a woman that has become the motherland by the action of the *man.* The machete is the instrument of the violation, and the nation its product. Both narrator and addressee inscribed in this story seem to be men. An extraordinary issue, a rape, becomes an ordinary and naturalized event. Ann McClintock (1995, 30–31) notes that tales of "virgin lands" proceed *forward* in geographical space (e.g., "clearing the mountain") but going *backward* in historical time, since it is assumed that such areas were empty before the arrival of peasants.

Women and nature are related in diverse ways: the disruptive character of nature is sometimes identified with the irrationality associated with women, but nature is also represented as a feminized site of procreation (Jervis 1999, 138). While the former is close to the image of a desired woman, the latter is a metaphor of a protective mother(land). Both images are transformed by the action of men, who in turn experience interesting shifts: they are the procreators of the nation, but these "fighters" become the nation's sons when they look for shelter. This shifting representation of the nation, in which women become mothers and men turn into sons, shows also an intimate relationship between social processes and subjectivity. These images seem to project onto the nation those childhood feelings that were once felt toward the family.

After long philosophical journeys, the Costa Rican being has been found in the most patriarchal images: the rape of a feminized land, which engenders the nation. These essentialist narratives locate the national being in a biological certainty. Even more striking, this image is considered "exemplary" in a recent inquiry into the philosophical debates about "Costa Ricanness" (Mora 1997, 166). However, these gendered and violent representations have not been exempted from critique. Yolanda Oreamuno

(1994), for instance, questioned these representations of the nation early in the 1940s. However, the concept of gender has been generally missing from the current debates on nation and national identities in Central and Latin America. Nira Yuval-Davis also stresses that links between gender and nation are virtually absent in most perspectives on nationalism: "As nationalism and nation have usually been discussed as part of the public political sphere, the exclusion of women from that arena has affected their exclusion from that discourse as well" (1997, 2). Feminist research, as Uma Narayan notes, needs to include "not only contestation of *particular practices and institutions* detrimental to women but also to include challenges to the larger pictures of Nation, National History, and Cultural Traditions that serve to sustain and justify these practices and institutions" (1997, 21; emphasis in original). This gendered representation of nationhood has not been, until very recently, a matter of concern among historians. Most of the research has questioned those national representations associated with rural democracy, the freeborn peasant, and geographical isolation, as we shall see.

Rural Democracy in Question

During the 1940s, when historians had encoded a representation of the nation tied to a golden age located in the eighteenth century, realist novels began to question this idyllic portrayal.[8] Most of these novels are set in rural areas, where injustice dominates the landscape. Peasants are no longer a piece of folklore; they face multiple and diverse injustices, but they are also active and able to fight for better living conditions. These novels brought an expansion of chronotopes. The country is no longer reduced to the Central Valley, where most of the cities are located, and the rural areas are no longer a paradise.

Carlos Monge-Alfaro coined the concept of rural democracy in the early 1940s, but almost simultaneously, in 1939, Adolfo Herrera published his novel *Juan Varela* (1981), in which the principal character, Juan, seeks to establish his farm and after a succession of failures ends up in jail. He dreams, thinks, feels; finally he fails, but he fights to the last. The injustices Juan experiences are no longer the consequence of "natural" episodes but the result of social contradictions. Oreamuno notes how *Juan Varela* challenged the idealized "rural past": "*Juan Varela* cannot be shown to foreigners. *Juan Varela* is a problem. . . . [it] is the first break with this religious myth of the rural democracy, the rural house painted in white and blue and the peasant owner of pigs and hens" (1961, 77).

Mamita Yunai (Fallas 1986), the classic Costa Rican novel about everyday life in the banana plantations, was published in 1941. *Yunai* is a Spanish pronunciation of *United,* and *mamita* means "mom." Thus, the title seems sarcastic, since the injustices represented in the novel have no relation to the sense of protection associated with motherhood. The principal characters dream of possible worlds and weep in the face of structural constraints imposed by poverty and class exploitation. *Gentes y gentecillas* (Fallas 1981 [1947]) also addresses social injustices in rural areas, particularly in the context of the construction of the railway to the Atlantic region. Carlos Luis Fallas, the author, presents two ways of life: one characterized by power and moral authority and the other associated with the "plebeians," who represent a "fear of pollution" and "lack of culture." As with *Mamita Yunai,* the title *Gentes y gentecillas* is meant as a paradox: who the decent people (*gentes*) are and who constitute the rabble (*gentecillas*) is not clear. Through inversions of moral attributes, those who seem decent people can now become rabble and vice versa.

Toward the end of the 1940s other novels and short tales also insist that peasants do not belong to an idealized and monolithic past. In *Cuentos de angustias y paisajes* (Tales of heartaches and landscapes) (Salazar 1978 [1947]), peasants are no longer freeborn but are subject to diverse constraints. Similarly, *El sitio de las abras* (The site of the clearings) (Dobles 1979 [1947]) portrays a group of peasants attempting to establish a farm in an empty land, only to be frustrated by a landowner. Meanwhile, also in 1947, Oreamuno offered a gendered critique of the emerging urban middle-class family in *La ruta de su evasión* (The escape route), in which the patriarchal representation of the family and the nation is challenged and the characters display their own subjectivity.

Overall, these examples illustrate the lack of a definitive and unchallenged representation of nation. Historical accounts and fictional writing have frequently been considered separate domains and that boundary has sometimes impeded the recognition of how Costa Rica's rural democracy has been always under contestation. Nonetheless, analysis of contested nationhood has to take into account that both history and fiction have had asymmetric circuits of cultural circulation. While historical accounts of rural democracy became the "objective" and official interpretation of the past offered in formal education, novels, however "real," were dismissed as fiction.

Mikhail Bakhtin drew an interesting distinction between the epic and the novel that is of interest in this context. The novel-ty of the novel, he notes, is its heteroglossia and unfinalizability, in which different voices and chronotopes are present. In the novel the past becomes historical, whereas the epic, of which most of the historical and philosophical accounts discussed above are examples, is defined by heroic times characterized by a lack of reflection and criticism. Most of the historical accounts and philosophical speculation discussed above are examples of epic narratives:

> The world of the epic is the national heroic past: it is a world of "beginnings" and "peak times" in the national history, a world of fathers and of founders of families, a world of "firsts" and "bests." The important point here is not that the past constitutes the content of the epic. The formally constitutive feature of the epic as a genre is rather the transferal of a represented world into the past, and the degree to which this world participates in the past. (Bakhtin 1981, 13, 30)

This sort of idyllic history has produced what several academics call national narcissism (Azofeifa 1971, 115; Cersósimo 1978, 61; Solís 1995, 4). Self-centered identities impose political controls, limiting dissent, and, in turn, represent certain "others" as a threat to a timeless and "unique" democracy.

The interpretations of rural democracy and the freeborn peasant, isolated in his little farm, began to be questioned by historical research in the late 1970s. A case study undertaken by Lowell Gudmundson (1978) revealed, for instance, how the village of Barva, a small community in Costa Rica's Central Valley, did not coincide with the main attributes of rural democracy. Despite the imagery of an isolated peasant with no significant social relations, about three-quarters of the population there lived in communities, according to the information provided by the census of 1838. Furthermore, more than two-fifths of the peasants did not work their own land but were paid workers. This undermined widespread representations of a colonial time characterized by social equality.[9] The presence of commercial activities also showed that colonial poverty was not generalized to the degree previously believed and that commercial exchange was not completely absent. Overall, the notion of a freeborn peasant, owner of a small area of land and without major social and commercial relationships, could not be sustained by empirical evidence. Prior to the expansion of coffee, there certainly was social differentiation and capital accumulation (Gudmundson 1978, 132, 148, 154, 161).

These commercial activities were crucial in the extraction of surplus since the eighteenth century. The unequal exchange between the mercantile class, who also occupied political, military, and ecclesiastical positions, and the peasantry allowed the former the appropriation of any surplus produced in agriculture (Molina 1984, 28, 232; Acuña Ortega 1986, 64). The investment in coffee meant an emergence of the articulation of the local finances with the world economy and the emergence of capitalism in Costa Rica (Molina 1986, 9, 51). Moreover, an elite controlled political power, enabling them to lead the small amount of commercial exchange and the beginning of coffee cultivation during the nineteenth century. Samuel Stone (1985) concludes that until 1976, thirty-three of the forty-four presidents of Costa Rica had been descendants of only three *conquistadores*.[10]

This critique of celebrated interpretations of a rural democracy cannot underestimate some peculiarities of the capitalist development in Costa Rica either. An important distinction between Costa Rica and other Central American nations lies in the fact that while the indigenous inhabitants of other nations suffered the generalization of violence and expropriation of lands during the liberal period—as Jeffrey Gould (1997) concludes in the case of Nicaragua—the power of the emerging ruling class in Costa Rica was not restricted to the control of land or to imposition of a generalized serfdom but resided in dominance over the modest circulation of capital and commodities. During the coffee expansion, the oligarchy secured its power by controlling credit and exports (Acuña Ortega 1986, 51, 84). Rather than an accumulation of land, the priority was maximization of profits (Solís 1992, 394).

The liberal period (1870–1934) meant major processes of nation building, and representations of nationhood became an important concern. Between 1883 and 1920, for example, the number of provinces went from five to seven and counties increased from twenty-nine to fifty-six. The number of police stations rose from 61 in 1890 to 102 in 1900, and to 257 in 1920. The development of the telegraph and post offices also favored integration. Between 1885 and 1910, the number of communities linked by mail services rose from twenty-seven to forty-three. Meanwhile, the number of locations connected by telegraph increased from 28 in 1887 to 102 in 1910 (Gil 1996, 13–21). The reforms in the educational system, the increase in newspapers as well as the foundation of other public institutions and monuments such as the National Archive, the National Library, the National Park, and the National Monument were other important processes of nation building during the liberal period (Palmer 1995, 77). This period was also characterized by the loss of power of the Catholic Church and processes of secularization.

These institutional developments were closely related to the emergence of a sense of nationhood. Víctor Hugo Acuña Ortega (1995, 68) notes that in 1859, President Mora introduced for the first time in presidential discourses equality among citizens as well as the particular situation of Costa Rica in the region as distinctive national attributes. Peace would be another crucial representation during the liberal period. Democracy, on the other hand, entered into the political vocabulary only in the second part of the twentieth century but it became a keyword in presidential speeches that defined not only the political system but also attributes of the national identity (69). In general, toward the beginning of the twentieth century, liberal intellectuals had resolved several important aspects regarding nationhood. There was an agreement about the uniqueness of Costa Rica both in terms of political attributes and of ethnic homogeneity, and it was felt that the nation needed active state intervention in order to guarantee its prosperity (Palmer 1995, 75). Overall, the sense of nationhood was constructed culturally, but also institutionally. Being a colonial province over four centuries was a political precondition for the emergence of a sense of nationhood. Cultural and political dimensions of the nation affected each other and should be considered a mutually constitutive set of cultural forms, practices, and institutions.

From Rural Democracy to Middle-Class Nation

The representations of nationhood during the second half of the twentieth century were under the leadership of the triumphant forces in the civil war of 1948, which took place over five weeks and in which approximately two thousand people died. The new government banned the Communist Party (PC), nationalized banking, and abolished the army, which could turn against it. In particular, the abolition of the army was enormously useful, since representations of a peaceful and democratic nation were reinforced with notions of a civic and unarmed police (Solís 1992, 284–85, 298–99). These winning forces were later transformed into Liberación Nacional, the most consistent political party in voter turnout during the second half of the twentieth century.

The emergent political forces characterized the crisis of the 1940s as "a conspiracy against the republic and the family"; the liberal order had been threatened by corruption and electoral fraud. The oligarchy had undermined the national values and this decline was going to be resisted on the basis of "progress with order," a reference indebted to the positivism present in liberal ideologies (Solís 1992, 143, 263). The civil war was represented as a breaking point in the political history of Costa Rica, and the revolutionary government defined its actions as the foundation of a Second Republic, since it was in 1848 that Costa Rica was declared a republic for the first time.

This emphasis on ruptures over continuities has had important consequences in the configuration of national identities. The ruptures between "before" and "after" the war were depicted as a return to the traditions of equality, democracy, and uniqueness, values threatened by the alliances between the oligarchy and the PC during the 1940s. During the conflict, the PC—banned after the war and until 1970—supported the oligarchy, since the latter had approved the social legislation actually promoted by the PC and the Catholic Church.

The new political forces who came into power after 1953 undertook processes of modernization of the state and the economy during the following twenty-five years, including the expansion of infrastructure, public services, and jobs. Urbanization began to transform the national landscape and, currently, half the population lives in cities. Meanwhile television programming has meant the introduction of new "structures of feeling" (R. Williams 1977) during the twenty-five years that followed the civil war of 1948. Between 1963 and 1973 the number of families with television sets rose from 6.6 percent to 86.4 percent (Molina 2002, 102).

In this context, national identity grounded on rural democracy seems to have been superseded by the image of Costa Rica as a middle-class nation. Modernity has been replacing tradition. An early statement on this direction was provided by Eugenio Rodríguez in the 1950s: "The Costa Rican people are formed by a big middle class that constitutes the nucleus of our nationality. This society includes at its extremes working-class and peasant groups as well as a smaller sector of rich people" (1979, 99).[11] Although recent studies show that the middle class does not exceed 30 percent of the total population (C. Rodríguez et al. 1998), being middle class has become a key national identification. Rural democracy and the middle class as the "nucleus of our nationality" have not been just academic debates. Rural democracy became "national folklore" through painting, cookery, clothing, and music. Primary-school celebrations translated such iconography into institutional practices and children were able to recognize their nationality even before they began to read history texts. The middle-class icons did not enter into folklore, but attained prominence through the media and advertising: cars (especially 4x4s!), houses, and electronic appliances became signifiers of being middle class. Memory of words, as stressed by Raphael Samuel (1994, 36), becomes memory refracted through the iconography of things.

This transition in national representation from imagery of rural democracy to the middle class imagery has been characterized by contradictions and tensions. It is not a simple linear replacement but a dispute over the power of representing nationhood, showing that there is not a single hegemonic national identity but different versions struggling for the legitimacy of representing a sense of nationhood. Indeed, attributes associated with the freeborn peasant, such as tradition and isolation, have been perceived as synonymous with backwardness. Peasants are represented as the nation's soul but at the same time are discriminated against for being what they are. They have been stigmatized as *conchos* or *polos,* terms for those who, according to the hegemonic sense of distinction, do not have proper manners and do not follow rules of urbanity and sociability.[12] Thus, around the stigma of conchos or polos there is a profound interconnection of ideology and subjectivity.

Aquileo Echeverría encodes an interpretation of the peasant world "from above" in his book *Concherías* (1976 [1905]). Since the 1950s, the concho has been represented through female radio characters in which women who did not speak Spanish "properly" tried to understand urban customs—while other characters laughed at their troubles. Carmen Granados, an actress who interpreted such plebeian characters, has been considered the "national soul" (*LN* 8/16/98, 12/1/99). In the 1990s, the concho has been redesigned as a character who plays soccer in a popular radio program called *La Patada* (The kick).[13] His language is again the main motive of laughter. The link between fictional writing and the media has been crucial in this ambivalent representation of the peasant. It made it possible for intellectual representations made "from above" to become widely recognized. As Radcliffe and Westwood note, "Popular culture contributes to the ways in which individuals are able to place their biographies within the larger stage of the nation state" (1996, 83). Even now when certain people want to indicate that some action or comment is not proper or polite, they say, "This is a *conchada*" or "This is a *polada.*" Representations of rural backgrounds were naturalized as a place of exclusion and the polo was assimilated by the hegemonic "common sense" as an internal "other."[14]

This stigmatization of the peasant is closely related to the processes of modernization. Indeed, it could have not taken place without the spread of international commercial relations and the emergence of cities and the media. The opposition between city and countryside is a crucial axis in the construction of national identities. José María Perceval (1995, 119) notes how in Spanish (and probably in English as well) *villano* (villain) comes from *villa* (village, rural town). Similarly, citizenship seems to have the city as its location. It is not hard to imagine that in Latin America being both peasant and citizen is not easy.

Polo has been reworked on the Internet. A complex scale (*polómetro*) has been developed to measure the extent to which a person can be considered polo. Ninety-four questions examine the aesthetic preferences of respondents for clothes, cars, home decor, and "accent" (see table 3.1).

The topics suggest that the questionnaire was written by a group of urban men who are quite close to people considered polo, since they know private as well as public tastes. What is perhaps more striking is the obsessive desire to draw a line between those considered polo and those "distinguished" by good taste, accent, and manners. At the beginning of 2002, at least four additional versions of polómetro were circulating on the Internet. A tentative interpretation of these "tests" would suggest that there is a certain correspondence between an undermining of social divisions in terms of consumption and leisure (certain clothing, leisure places, and cars are relatively accessible to broad social layers), and the need to reinstall social hierarchies through assessing taste. The scale even includes a set of criteria by which to evaluate the answers. For instance, the response for those with more than twenty positive answers is: "Shit, polo, how did you get access to the Internet?" The list and the possibility of distributing it via the Internet were thought of as a joke about certain Costa Ricans, who could be considered internal "others" who do not fit into a desired national style. As in the case of representations regarding Nicaraguans in Costa Rica, "polómetros" play a key role in the normalization of exclusion, translating it into common sense and representations of everyday life. The crucial link between humor and the acceptance of exclusion will be revisited in chapter 5.

Table 3.1

Polómetro: An Online Questionnaire about Taste in Costa Rica

Factor	Number of Questions
Clothing	19
Car rituals	14
Home decor	12
Spanish accent	10
Media preferences	8
Consumption	7
Entertainment	7
Body language	7
Attitude to celebrities	2
Work	2
Other	6
TOTAL	94

Source: I thank Giselle Bustos-Mora for forwarding me the first version of this survey on taste. See also <http://www.ticopage.com/polometro.htm>

Meanwhile, the emergence of a middle-class nation has also created an urban version of the polo, the *pachuco,* who is usually considered a part of the "urban mob."[15] The pachuco could be regarded as a way of national purification. There are "true" Costa Ricans—peasants, teachers, intellectuals—and a new category of internal "others," the pachucos. In a way, a pachuco is not a Costa Rican. This representation seems to express the crisis generated by the transition from a patriarchal society to a modern, secular, capitalist, urban, and now "global" one. While the concho has been present in radio programs for many years, the pachuco has become a familiar character in television comedies. The pachuco's accent and clothing are again common sources of derision.

Overall, both the rural democracy and the middle class engender their own ways of belonging and difference. These stigmatized archetypes—concho, polo, pachuco—are characterized by their essentialist character, which aims to encapsulate those attributes that do not fit into an idealized national representation and in turn project them onto internal "others." Indeed, they are generally identified with bad taste and bad customs, illustrating ways in which class-based exclusions work through aesthetic criteria.

Tensions between an idealized rural past and the stigmatization of the peasantry are mobilized according to particular situations. "Rural democracy," for instance, is not a point of reference for national identity among young, urban middle-class people since they have spent most of their lives in towns; on the contrary they usually represent themselves as having overcome a backward rural past. However, their parents probably were born in rural areas and they feel nostalgia about their past and the values associated with it. Borrowing Raymond Williams's (1977) categories, one might argue that rural democracy can be interpreted as a residual configuration, whereas representations of the middle class are a dominant reference located within the context of the modernization of Costa Rican society. Rural democracy seems to be a reference to origin, whereas the values associated with middle class and modernity indicate a sense of destiny in a world economy. These contrasts make clear once again that there is no single, hegemonic, national identity; instead diverse projects compete and are activated according to specific issues and conjunctures.

From the Text to the Reader of National Narratives

Recent critiques have emphasized that national identities are not preexistent notions "reflected" onto narratives; references to national origin, belonging, continuity, and destiny are rather constructed in literature itself (Ovares et al. 1993). These narratives usually attempt to transform social differences and inequalities into national mythologies. Deconstruction allows the opportunity to recognize the conformation of national narratives. Since there are no "natural" or "essential" sources of identity, these are constructed through meanings and utterances.[16] What these constructionist perspectives rarely explore are the ways in which such narratives are read, contested, and fought over by empirical readers.

Rather than nations understood as discourses or narratives, what should be explored is the social construction of national meanings as utterances that are open ended and shaped over time. In this context, readership has generally been an unthinkable topic in literary criticism, most of the time concentrated in textual(ist) interpretation. This gap has impeded the exploration of how cultural forms, such as historical interpretations, essays, or novels, are embedded in institutional locations and cultural practices (Jauss 1982; CCCS 1980, 238). Similarly, debates on nationalism and national identities have emphasized the interpretation of the elite's discourses, and the ways in which those discourses are decoded has received scant attention (Johnson 1993a; 1993b). One of the multiple implications of these methodological decisions seems to be the depiction of national identities as uncontested representations. What is at stake is precisely how "empirical" readers such as peasants have interpreted images that consider them as crucial actors in the configuration of nationhood in Costa Rica. Despite claims made by historical accounts and philosophical speculation that the rural life and the peasant culture are the sources of the Costa Rican being, some autobiographies analyzed here show in various ways that the peasants perceive themselves through the stigmas constructed about them by hegemonic discourses (A. P. C., 24; H. A., 121). They feel excluded from a nation that, according to many commentators, has its origin precisely in the freeborn peasant. Some peasants consider themselves conchos, and they know the stigmatized meaning of the word, associated frequently with their lack of "proper manners" (H. A., 121, 133; H. S. Z., 93; L. E. S., 21). Narrating his childhood experiences, one of the authors told how he was an object of derision by urban children. They asked him, "'Concho, is it true that horses can fly in Santa María?' I did not reply, since speaking was shameful for me" (L. E. S., 20).

Peasants locate themselves as outsiders in the city, which is perceived as a place of threat and humiliation. The city is identified as a monster and as a prison from which one cannot be freed. Peasants don't know how to cross the streets; they feel that the ways in which they dress, talk, walk, or eat are not proper. These meanings are frequently related to the body, which is a primary bearer of distinction or exclusion (L. E. S., 20; F. V. Z., 248, 259, 262, 269; H. S. Z., 53). They perceive themselves the way that respectable "others" do. This social and cultural exclusion is translated into their own subjectivity in the form of shame, silence, and fear. It is hard to speak when one knows that one's Spanish is not the best or when unfashionable clothing makes it difficult to take part in certain "social" activities.[17] Interestingly, autobiographies written by Nicaraguans (see chapter 4) show that they have been interpellated in similar ways.

This internalized exclusion, however, does not always entail a passive assimilation of constraints. One of the authors notes, "While newspaper headlines highlight the best boxer, the best center forward, and the best artists who earn money dancing or singing, there are no news items about the best manual worker or the best coffee picker" (L. E. S., 18). This critical response illustrates an "oppositional reading" (Hall 1980b, 138) of national narratives but the respondent's autobiography also shows the way in which the author positions himself in order to speak (Hall 1991a, 51). In this case, the author wrote about his lived experience as a past event, locating himself as someone who is no longer a peasant. He recognizes his exclusion as a past experience and addresses the problem from a new location that is less marginal, confirming the extreme complexity of class and national identification processes.

While historical and fictional interpretations usually show coherent versions of national identity, the sense of national belonging present in the autobiographies is more ambiguous. It is not a permanent concern but is activated in particular circumstances. Rather than always considering themselves members of the nation, the authors sometimes locate themselves in local or regional areas of the country. There is also an ambiguous coexistence between the recognition of their own social exclusion as peasants and their loyalty toward idyllic representations of Costa Rica as a democratic nation. An autobiography written as a long poem provides a case in point.[18] Its author regrets that, as poor people, peasants live like rolling stones but at the same time, he does express his loyalty to the nation: "I never speak ill of my motherland; I always cover it with honor" (E. S. C., 65, 68, 80, 84).

This brief exploration of readership illustrates the complex circuits of cultural consumption of the elite's discourse on nationhood. National narratives intersect with other discourses in different sites and are read by different social agents. If one does not pay attention to the ways in which such narratives connect with empirical readers, there is a risk of reducing cultural processes to mere intellectual debates that sometimes have only slight repercussions beyond academic circles. Peasants, who are supposedly the "origin" of the Costa Rican nation, consider themselves among the people most excluded from nation-building projects. In other words, the analysis of circulation of the narratives highlights how difference and exclusion are present in the Costa Rican "imagined community."

Unimagined Communities

So far in this chapter I have attempted to show contested discourses on nationhood in Costa Rica. It is relevant to recognize sets of inclusions, but ways in which exclusions are embedded in nation-building projects are also important. A step forward demands that we explore ways in which this sense of nationhood has been closely related to the exclusion of those who, according to the liberal elite, did not fit into the desired nation. As Perceval (1995, 17) notes, history, as well as other social sciences, has been more concerned with the recognition of social ideals than with the inquiry into social fears and collective silences.

"Race" has historically been a structuring dimension in Latin America. During the nineteenth century the political elite aimed to identify themselves with European modernity. Richard Graham notes, "Latin Americans faced a difficult intellectual dilemma regarding race. On the one hand, racial heterogeneity characterized most of their societies. On the other, many Latin Americans aspired to an ever-closer connection to Europe and sought to follow its leadership in every realm" (1990a, 2).

Recent contributions have held that the liberal projects of nation building and nationhood in Central America during the nineteenth century also involved processes of exclusion (Bourgois 1994; Acuña Ortega 1995; Palmer 1993, 1995; Taracena 1995b). Striking a balance, Acuña Ortega states, "As a consequence of the exclusion of most peasant and indigenous populations, the liberal nation was rather a nation of 'ladinos,' citizens and people with some access to the written culture. The liberals created republics, but perhaps no nations" (1992–93, 48–49).

These institutional exclusions of black and indigenous communities have also been expressed as representations. Indigenous people have usually been absent in the national narratives. Generally, the freeborn peasant replaced the aborigine as the crucial character. Even now, being called Indian is a frequent form of derision. *Mamita Yunai* (Fallas 1986) illustrates how even radical and realist literature reinforces stigmatized images of indigenous peoples. The first section of the novel describes the narrator and principal character, Sibaja, going to the community of Talamanca, in Costa Rica's Atlantic region, in order to represent the Peasants and Workers' Front in a national general election. Sibaja discovers the fraud that had been devised by official party leaders that convinced most of the indigenous people to support them: alcohol was offered in exchange for their votes. He cannot understand why the indigenous people have accepted the offer, since they were ostensibly to be part of the Left. This disenchantment is translated into a series of aesthetic and moral judgments: "good-looking girls wearing men's clothes" (15–16); "that small and pallid Indian" (30); "a dirty and disheveled indigenous woman" (34); "some naked, skinny, long-haired Indian men coughed desperately, twisting like worms" (35); "every half hour children went out to 'make water'" (35); "some naked, others wrapped in rags" (39); "an old crooked mulatto" (46); "sleepless Indians went out to the big house and they were looking at me like idiots" (46); "the kitchen was filled with Indians that had caught cold, including some subdued and dirty Indian women" (49); "an Indian entertained himself by picking his nose" (60). The long-term and interfused connection between ethics and aesthetics is reestablished and Indians' political disloyalty is evaluated through aesthetic criteria. They do not appear as subjects of the plot; they are just drunks and liars. In the course of the novel, the reader cannot recognize Indian subjectivity. They have no names; they are just "Indians."[19]

The national condition of indigenous population has been a permanent challenge in Latin America. Liberal perspectives considered that the mixed ethnic background of most of the population, the mestizaje, had solved the dilemma. But it has remained unresolved, even from Marxist perspectives. Indigenous people are not peasants or proletarians, nor are they citizens. *Mamita Yunai* does not seem to challenge this tendency, though in its second part the novel presents a less negative description of indigenous people. The working-class characters—Herminio, Calero, and

Sibaja—reflect on their conditions of life, express their fears, and weep. Indeed, *Mamita Yunai* is one of the novels where masculine working-class characters cry most frequently. They remember by weeping (129); the death of Calero, flattened by a tree, is experienced again through weeping (169). The end of the novel is also defined by weeping (180). In this sense, the novel offers a reflexive perspective on working-class masculinities. Nonetheless, the characters do not seem to change; their views are not altered by the different issues they face. Sibaja knows almost everything; he and his readers experience few surprises (Ovares et al. 1993, 252).

The Constitutional Court of Costa Rica did not recognize the indigenous people as citizens until 1993 (SC 1993). Previously, indigenous people did not hold national identity cards. However, their newly gained citizenship has not improved their deprived living conditions. Public services such as health, education, housing, and community infrastructure are highly restricted in the areas where they live (PNUD 1999, 86). Overall, despite being an ethnically mixed population, national imagery has represented Costa Rica as a white nation. Being mestizo is generally interpreted as synonymous with whiteness. Again, the contrast with other nations of Central America where mestizaje was less intense could be the origin of this "white" representation (Palmer 1995).

As Peter Wade (1993) and Jeffrey Gould (1997) have argued, mestizaje has been a concept taken for granted in most debates on ethnicity and "race" in Latin America. Mestizaje designates the mixing of peoples from diverse ethnic backgrounds but also entails deep assumptions; it is a descriptive concept but above all a prescriptive one. Mestizaje seems to suggest that racialized differences do not exist but at the same time upholds the desired character of "whiteness." On the other hand, mestizaje has not only masked racialized representations but also gender issues, since the "mixing" of Spanish and indigenous peoples was frequently characterized by rape committed by landowners and public authorities, including priests (Acuña and Chavarría 1991, 130–32; Lobo 1997, 20, 53).

This exclusion of the indigenous population from national narratives and nation-building projects has been a common issue in Latin America. Such exclusion might be a consequence of the fact that, as Nancy Stepan notes, "The educated upper classes in Latin America wished to be white and feared they were not" (1991, 45). In this context, diverse projects were designed to attract European immigration, a common national policy in many Latin American countries by the end of the nineteenth century (ibid.; for Costa Rica's efforts in this direction, see Alvarenga 1999). The rule seemed to be "The whiter the better," as Thomas Skidmore (1990, 9) states in the case of Brazil. Toward the end of the nineteenth century, official discourses on immigration rested on an idealization of whiteness. Costa Rican governments attempted to settle "white" immigrants in the Central Valley, where the lack of labor force was a chronic problem especially on coffee farms. However, these attempts were not very successful (Alvarenga 1999, 12). Meanwhile there were also discourses on "undesired immigration," associated especially with Chinese, Arab, Turkish, Syrian, Armenian, and Romany citizens—whose entry into Costa Rica was forbidden by law in 1897 (Palmer 1995, 75, 80). Still, most "foreigners" were considered "necessary immigration." Black people, especially from Jamaica, arrived to work on the construction of the Atlantic railway and later in the establishment of banana plantations (Alvarenga 1999).

Since the "desired immigration" did not attract Europeans as the liberal elite had hoped, the government made claims for "self-immigration," a policy meant to improve health conditions and reduce child morbidity, a eugenic policy present in most Latin American countries. As in other nations, "To govern is to populate" seemed to be the rule (Stepan 1991, 43; Palmer 1996, 113). Self-immigration was proclaimed under the assumption that the population that was going to reproduce more quickly was the "white" one. Early in the twentieth century, the liberal politicians seemed to be convinced about the whiteness of the Costa Rican population, which was compared with a few other countries in Latin America such as Argentina, Chile, and Uruguay (Palmer 1995, 79).

Ideas of eugenics attracted the liberal politicians. As Stepan notes: "The new sciences were particularly attractive to the modern, secular, liberal intelligentsia, because they represented rational approaches to the natural and social world which were unencumbered by traditional religious considerations" (1991, 41). Costa Rica was no exception; Clorito Picado, a well-known scientist, wrote: "OUR BLOOD IS TURNING BLACK! And if it continues like that, from the crucible will emerge not a grain of gold but a piece of coal. There might still be time to rescue our patrimony of European blood, which is perhaps what has saved us until now from falling into decayed African systems" (in I. Molina 2002, 130–31; emphasis in original).

Oreamuno, who is known for her critical assessment of patriarchal values, is less attentive to "race." Her descriptions of blacks, probably written in the mid-1940s, are close to Picado's concerns: "The black has a rough thinking and a slow imagination, is as passionate as a zealous animal, but *he* orients himself according to his instincts. . . . The white imagination, more wide-awake and sophisticated, has created the myth of the sensual black. . . . A twenty-five-year-old black is a child whose legs have grown enormously, and with *his* mentality in early stages, is unreflective, obedient, submissive, and happy" (1961, 172–73; emphasis added).

The ideologies that supported modernization after the 1950s did not offer a different approach to black people either. Facio, writing in 1942, considered them "an uprooted and miserable population that extends through several regions of the country. . . . As a consequence of transferring its activities from one place to another according to its needs and interests, UFCO [United Fruit Company] created a black population, unadjusted to the national outlook, that floods the entire country, without benefit to the country or themselves" (1975, 60–61).

The media images representing immigrants as a wave emerge again here as a flood. Blacks were not recognized as national citizens until 1949. The first black candidate to the parliament was proposed in 1949 by Liberación Nacional (Solís 1992, 203, 324).

Perhaps one of the most naturalized representations of being black is present in a children's story, *Cocorí* (Gutiérrez 1977a), first published in 1949. The plot revolves around the arrival of a ship. The main character, Cocorí, a black child, wonders what it looks like before he sees it. One of the passengers is a little girl who has never met a black person. When she sees Cocorí, she exclaims, "Mum, look. What a strange child." She wonders why Cocorí is completely "sooty." She tries to scrub the soot off his black skin. The little girl remains nameless. Instead, she is identified by her whiteness. The narrator even states in italics that "in this country of blond men, the little girls and the flowers are the same" (20). She is surprised by the presence of monkeys around the beach, and Cocorí promises to catch her one. In return she kisses him and gives him a red rose. *Cocorí* is widely read in primary schools and children dramatize its plot. Unfortunately, its racialized representations do not seem to be a major focus of concern.[20]

The Historical Constitution of the Nicaraguan Other in Costa Rica

Disputes over the control of the San Juan River have had a key geopolitical relevance in the formation of both states and their national identities. In 1824, Nicoya, which historically had belonged to the colonial province of Nicaragua, decided to annex itself to Costa Rica (Obregón 1993; Kinloch 1998).[21] This decision was made in a context characterized by power disputes between Nicaraguan political elites located in Granada and León and as a result of the tensions between federalist and autonomous impulses in the constitution of the new Central American states (Taracena 1995a, 149; Casanova 1995, 278).[22]

The instability of Nicaragua and the isolation of Costa Rica began to constitute a pattern of comparison in the nineteenth century. While Nicaragua was not declared a republic until 1854, Costa Rica acquired that status in 1848, nine years after of the end of the Central American Federation (Taracena 1995b, 56). San José was proclaimed the Costa Rican capital early in 1824, which resulted in commercial agreements with Granada and Leon and the beginning of the state's control of national territory. Managua did not become the capital until 1846 (Casanova 1995, 287). The conflicts between Nicaraguan elites displaced people from their local communities and many of them went to Costa Rica (Kinloch 1998; Obregón 1993, 135, 155, 179). In 1846, as would be the case 150 years later, an official report stated, "A number of poor families, a multitude of peasants, are emigrating to the state of Costa Rica, where they are settling. They do not return to their desolate motherland. Their homesickness is at odds with their needs" (in Kinloch 1998).

The disagreements regarding the borders were not only focused on Nicoya. Expanding commercial activities, especially those related to coffee exports to England, demanded an efficient route. However, neither Nicaragua nor Costa Rica had routes or ports on the Atlantic. The exports started from the Costa Rican port of Puntarenas, traveled through the Pacific Ocean down to Cape Horn, where they turned into the Atlantic. Exportation meant long, expensive journeys.

After independence, the construction of a canal using the San Juan River, which forms much of the border between the two countries, was perceived in both countries as a path to modernity. The Nicaraguan elite felt a canal that could link both oceans would introduce Nicaragua to "cosmopolitan culture" and "the world economy." The Enlightenment and the Industrial Revolution in Europe, with their consequences for technology, production, and transport, had raised expectations that the canal would connect Nicaragua with these processes and bring the end of internal political struggles. A new Nicaragua would emerge with the canal, wrote the newspaper *El Correo* in 1849 (in Kinloch 1995, 266–67; Kinloch 1994, 50–52).

How to get such resources without losing the state's control of the national space, the center of the national project, became a serious dilemma (Kinloch 1996). The expansion coincided with the presence of the imperial powers in Central America and the Costa Rican and Nicaraguan governments signed agreements to build the canal with different companies. Nicaragua was close to the interests of the emergent United States in the region, while Costa Rica looked toward the possibility of attracting British investors. The British had left the Atlantic region of Nicaragua in 1787 but they returned in 1830, by which time the region had acquired geopolitical relevance in the context of imperial disputes with U.S. administrations over the construction and control of the canal. Although the proposed canal was finally built in what is now Panama, these geopolitical and commercial interests defined the border between both countries in a dispute between "local" and "global" powers.[23]

These conflicts were crucial in the beginning of nation-building projects and nationhood in both countries. One state contested the initiatives made by the other. Meanwhile, the relations between Nicaragua and Costa Rica with their other neighbor nations, Honduras and Panama respectively, have not represented a similar source of concern. Generally, historians from both countries have written their interpretations with a high sense of loyalty to their own nation. As I mentioned at the beginning of the chapter, the establishment of history as an academic discipline actually contributed to a sense of nationhood. In particular, disputes over borders were a crucial matter of inquiry among politicians and historians. The first historical interpretation of Costa Rica, written by Felipe Molina, was published in 1851 in the context of the conflicts with Nicaragua. In the course of these controversies, Molina maintained that Costa Rica was characterized by "perfect homogeneity among its inhabitants" (1851, 6). The basis for this description was comparison with other nations: "Despite the fact that the number of conflicts in Costa Rica, which might be called revolutions, seems to be considerable, they have not had fatal implications, as elsewhere" (Molina 1850, 5). Molina also described the dispute between Costa Rica and Nicaragua, and his comparison of citizens from the two republics is relevant in this context: "As everybody knows, the people of Costa Rica are industrious and peaceful. . . . The inhabitants of Nicaragua, despite having many good and brilliant attributes, unfortunately offer a contrast to this picture" (1850, 22).

These early examples illustrate a long-term configuration that is still present. The Costa Rican national identity has been historically defined through different versions of uniqueness with regard to other Central America nations. In particular, the construction of the Costa Rican national identity and the Nicaraguan other have long been closely related processes. It is not possible to approach the formation of a sense of nationhood in Costa Rica while ignoring how, simultaneously, the Nicaraguan began to be depicted as an indispensable "other."

Meanwhile, the internal conflicts between conservatives and liberals continued in Nicaragua. In 1854 the latter received support from a group of filibusters from the U.S. South, led by William Walker. They intended to annex Central America to the United States and establish slavery in the region (Obregón 1993; Kinloch 1998).[24] The war against the filibusters diminished the tension between the Nicaraguan and Costa Rican governments as well as among conservatives and liberals in Nicaragua, who were facing a major challenge. The threat posed by the filibusters, and the War of 1856 against them, began to be additionally interpreted as sources of nationhood in both countries. Steven Palmer (1993, 173–81) notes that the sense of national belonging in Costa Rica gained strength when the War of 1856 was considered *the* "national battle" in the context of the threat posed by the federalist attempts at the reunification of Central America in 1885. Similarly, the Battle of San Jacinto, when local troops defeated the filibusters, began to be celebrated in Nicaragua as the triumph of the nation against the invasion of Walker (Fumero 1995, 316–17).

In 1858 the Nicaraguan and Costa Rican governments signed an agreement regarding the borders: Nicaragua recognized that Nicoya belonged to Costa Rica, and both countries were to have access to commercial navigation along the San Juan River, although it was under Nicaraguan sovereignty. For most of their history, the border between Nicaragua and Costa

Rica has given rise to disputes associated with the high point of mercantilism. These disputes were employed by the emerging commercial and political elites in both countries as symbols in the construction of meanings about "national" space. In a long-term process, the interests of coffee exporters—most of them also active politicians—in the construction of the canal were going to be "nationalized" and thus fought over as "national interests." In the process of defending the national interest, a sense of nationhood would be created.

Toward the end of the nineteenth century Nicaraguans began to be considered an other associated with violence and criminality in the emerging Costa Rican imagination. Marc Edelman (1998) has explored how the devastation of the Guatuso-Maleku Indian community, as a consequence of the exploitation of rubber, was interpreted within the emerging discourses of nationhood in Costa Rica. Although during the transition between the nineteenth and twentieth centuries it was extremely difficult to distinguish between Costa Ricans and Nicaraguans, the rubber tappers were identified as Nicaraguans and were made responsible for such crimes, especially in narratives written by religious missionaries, who visited the region attempting to "Christianize their benighted brethren" (Bishop Thiel in Edelman 1998, 375).

The interpretation of the commodification of rubber in nationalistic terms is crucial. It is another link in the opposition between the "barbarian" Nicaraguan and the "civilized" Costa Rican. In 1919, Carlos Gagini published his *Diccionario de costarriqueñismos,* which attempted to define idiosyncratic Spanish words employed in Costa Rica. As Marc Edelman notes, his definition of "rubber tapper" is highly relevant in this context:[25] "Hulero: Person who extracts rubber. Those involved in this lucrative industry in the north of the country are nearly all Nicaraguans and for a long time they were the terror of the poor Guatuso Indians, whom they killed without piety or hunted to sell as slaves in the neighboring republic" (in Edelman 1998, 356).

This association between Nicaraguans and violence was also present in crime news items early in the twentieth century. In 1917 a local newspaper warned its readers about a dangerous criminal: "He is a cunning and dangerous fellow. Every citizen must do his best to capture him. He looks more or less like this: thirty years old, more black than brown, Nicaraguan type. He has a tattoo on his chest" (*EP* 4/24/17, in Soto 1998, 442).

The presence of the Nicaraguan other has not always been associated with criminality. During the transition between the nineteenth and twentieth centuries, Costa Rican intellectuals faced the challenge of conceiving a national literature. Some of them claimed that such a body of work had to depict the peculiarities of the peasant, the key subject of the emerging sense of nationhood. Others stressed that only a cosmopolitan perspective could allow writers to overcome a narrow focus on rural life (Montero 1995). Both groups illustrated their own thesis by quoting the most distinguished poet of that time in Central (and probably Latin) America, Nicaraguan Rubén Darío.[26] His international recognition became an example for writers who disputed the right to define *the* national literature. However, despite their differences, neither the "folklorists" nor the "cosmopolitans" envisaged local readers for their projects of a national literature. The inscribed reader of both projects was a "learned" European, whose gaze would make international recognition of Costa Rican literature possible. Even though Rubén Darío, the "learned" and "universal" Nicaraguan, was the most eminent writer in Central America, the Nicaraguan plebeian began to be associated with violence and criminality by the media. However these intellectual and aesthetic debates did not alter the constitution of the Nicaraguan as an "other." The split between the "universal" Darío and the "plebeian" Nicaraguan also questions the extent to which intellectual debates are the best location to grasp national identities, especially in societies like the Latin American, where there is a deep gulf between "learned" society and the "plebeian" classes.

The Inscription of the Nicaraguan Other in Realist Literature

While Darío became a literary reference, Nicaraguan workers became crucial characters in the social-realist literature published in the 1940s in Costa Rica, works that are today widely read in primary and secondary schools. Early in this chapter, some of these novels were shown to illustrate how fictional writing challenged the idyllic representation of a "rural democracy" and a "freeborn peasant" depicted by historical accounts. Now I will explore these novels critically, seeking to demonstrate how the plebeian Costa Rican agrarian classes were considered subjects of their own enunciation but also how new "others" have taken their place. The "foreigners," interestingly many of them Nicaraguans, emerge as the "others" within a more inclusive national narrative.

Bananos y hombres, the first novel about banana plantations in Costa Rica, was published in 1931 by Carmen Lyra (1988, 109). Estefanía, the main character, was seen for the last time in one of the trains "full of black men who were laughing loudly and black women who dressed in vivid colors and squawked, like Nicaraguan parrots, with low voices." Estefanía is constructed through the contrast with blacks and Nicaraguan parrots. Neither her ethnicity nor her nationality are named, but they can be inferred through difference with Costa Ricans. Blacks and Nicaraguans are used to emphasize the Costa Rican "white" character.

Nicaraguans are also present in *Mamita Yunai* (Fallas 1986). Pancho, a Nicaraguan contractor, is depicted as the best boss in the region, since he pays a little bit more and offers better meals (108). He is also, however, represented as a violent man when his wife is several minutes late with the workers' breakfast one morning. Suddenly, the workers hear her screaming because he has threatened to wound her with a knife (110). In another passage, however, Sibaja, the narrator, acknowledges that workers are exploited independently of their nationality: "Bones of nicas, bones of ticos [Costa Ricans], bones of blacks. Bones of brothers." Serious structural violence exists that does not make any distinction among nationalities. At the end of the novel, the death of Jérez, an old Nicaraguan worker bitten by a snake, is an opportunity to prove their solidarity (Fallas 1986, 156, 179).

Gentes y gentecillas (Fallas 1947) also expands the national characters, as mentioned above. Nevertheless, attributes associated with the "foreigners" do not change throughout the novel and they are most of the time associated with violence and immorality. Jerónimo, the main character, is informed that in his new job in the railway company, there are a lot of cruel people, including "Nicas" (228). Zacarías, who seems to be Colombian, is the most violent foreigner (52, 56, 58, 92). Panchón, a Salvadoran and the Black Devil, a Jamaican, are the best gamblers (241); they trick people and steal workers' money when they go to the casinos. Time and again, Costa Ricans are implicitly associated with positive attributes.

In *Juan Varela,* where the agrarian injustices are also the crucial issue, Juan is taken prisoner because the police caught him producing alcohol illegally, after his failures in agriculture. Meanwhile, his son died and his wife went to Parrita—a southern Costa Rican village, where UFCO also had banana plantations—with her new partner, a Nicaraguan. The reader does not know who he is nor why he is a Nicaraguan. He is an outsider within the plot who has not appeared before in the narrative.

Puerto Limón (Gutiérrez 1976 [1950]) is another novel written by a member of the 1940s generation. Its main plot revolves around a strike that paralyzes banana exports.[27] The strike is presented through the life of a landowner, Héctor Rojas, who finds his plantations threatened because the railway is not running and UFCO cannot receive his production. Rojas blames the movement's organizers, but in this context, Silvano, the landowner's nephew, lives his own transformation, becoming critical of structural injustices. Silvano listens to his uncle but he is also able to talk to the workers; he is a bridge between the principal family and the workers.

The main leader is Paragüitas, a Nicaraguan, and the second leader is Trino, a Costa Rican. Toward the novel's end, Paragüitas explains his nickname to Trino. When he was in Nicaragua, a child was playing soccer in the street and his ball muddied one of the U.S. troops that had occupied Nicaragua. In response, the soldier killed the child with the butt of his gun. Paragüitas sharpened the rib of an umbrella and took revenge for the child's murder. *Paragüitas* is the diminutive of *paraguas,* the Spanish word for umbrella. Trino remains fairly anonymous.

After the strike, nothing is the same. The other characters are just "workers," or more precisely "strikers"; it is not possible to travel through their private lives. The workers are perceived through the landowner and the reader hardly knows anything about them. They have no opportunities to directly express their own views, fears, and dreams. The novel is fiction and therefore it does not need to describe every detail, but certainly the strike is experienced only indirectly by "ordinary" workers, who seem to remain in the shadows.[28] How the workers survived during the long strike in the 1930s is unknown to the reader.

Bananos (Quintana 1962), a novel by a Nicaraguan, a former worker in banana plantations located in Costa Rica, offers additional images of the Nicaraguan "other." Manolo Cuadra argues in the novel's preface, "Many contemplatives and idealists are going be astonished to know that in the navel of the continent (in Costa Rica!) thousands of workers believed in a minimum of democracy but found only a maximum of exploitation" (1962, 6). Traveling by train in Nicaragua and Costa Rica, Emilio Quintana

(1962, 44–45) does not find fundamental differences between them. In both countries there is poverty; the latest fashion and the rags of the poor exist side by side. Nicaraguans are also represented in negative ways. They are suspected of having committed assaults and murders, and some Nicaraguan contractors do not pay fair salaries. In another case, a Nicaraguan worker—who represents the writer—is considered the person behind the workers' protests against the poor meals (Quintana 1962, 24, 26, 38). As in *Puerto Limón,* the leader of the protest is also Nicaraguan.

Quintana (1962, 13) perceives Costa Rican women as "white" and "pretty," and the Nicaraguan workers are going to spend their money with white prostitutes; they will be held tightly by feminine white arms, as they have never been in Nicaragua. Their desire seems to suggest that the celebrated Costa Rican whiteness, considered a key ethnic distinction by the hegemonic version of Costa Rican national identity, has been internalized in the ways in which people from other Central American countries perceive Costa Ricans. Nicaraguan workers were going to spend a night with a "white" woman for the first time.[29] Interestingly, the main character of *Bananos* harbors doubts about Costa Rican democracy, but the identification of Costa Rica as a white nation does not seem to be questioned.

From the above, it might be argued that these novels, examples of the radical and realist literature, offer new angles. However, this representation of "foreign" workers is frequently stigmatized. Their exclusion is not based on class but on nationality and "race."[30] In particular, Nicaraguans are frequently the "others" in the face of whom a more inclusive and critical conception of nation is constructed. Their depiction as criminals or "radical agitators" might be interpreted within the long selective tradition that considers Costa Rica a pacific country exempted from violence. The protagonists of conflicts are foreigners or the conflicts are located in other countries (Bourgois 1994, 272; A. Quesada 1998, 244, 276). Thus, the Nicaraguan other is associated with those antivalues excluded from the hegemonic Costa Rican national identity.

Private Correspondence: A Glimpse into Lived Experience

The U.S. interventions in Nicaragua and the civil war (1927–32) meant the death or displacement of thousands of Nicaraguans.[31] Augusto César

Sandino reported that one hundred twenty thousand people died between 1909 and 1931 (in Selser 1974, 247). This figure could represent about twenty percent of the Nicaraguan population at that time, and even if it is exaggerated, it indicates the significance of the war and the violence during this period, especially in a rural society with a low density of population. The war of intervention not only meant the loss of thousands of lives, but also the institutionalization of a culture of violence penetrated through the National Guard, which underpinned the Somoza dictatorship (Selser 1974, 233–35). Part of the displaced population sought opportunities in Costa Rica. Gregorio Selser (1974, 332) estimated that at least thirty thousand Nicaraguans arrived in Costa Rica during the 1940s, fleeing from repressive actions committed by the National Guard and the U.S. army. According to the census of 1927, 20,642 Nicaraguans lived in Costa Rica, nearly five percent of the total population (Alvarenga 1999, 28). In the 1960s the number was estimated at sixty thousand (P. Cuadra 1987, 62), though the Costa Rican census of 1963 reported only 18,722 Nicaraguans (Schmidt 1979, 47).

The privatization of indigenous lands and the low salaries paid on coffee farms in Nicaragua also prompted the arrival of Nicaraguans in Costa Rica and Panama (Gould 1997, 72). They usually went first to the Costa Rican province of Guanacaste and later arrived at the Atlantic coasts of Costa Rica and Panama, where most of them found jobs in construction of the railway, and later in the banana plantations (Bourgois 1994, 246). Similarly, Costa Rican workers displaced from their lands in the Central Valley went to the Atlantic looking for jobs.

In 1934 approximately twelve thousand workers went on strike because of the deplorable labor conditions on banana plantations. The government, UCFO, and the press claimed that the Communist Party and Nicaraguan workers instigated the movement. The latter suffered the worst police repression; many of them were arrested and later expelled from the country (Acuña Ortega 1984, 35, 45; Cerdas 1994, 95).[32] Similar images were constructed regarding the strikes that took place during the 1950s and the 1980s (Bourgois 1994, 279–81). The principal outcome of these representations has been the association of the Nicaraguan other with social protest. These images of "troublemakers" combine diverse repertoires. Sometimes "criminality" is the main issue, but after the strike of 1934 the association of Nicaraguans with communism began to gain salience.

During the second half of the twentieth century, the presence of the Nicaraguan other in Costa Rica was no less prominent. Many Nicaraguans joined forces with members of the former Communist Party and other defeated forces in the civil war of 1948 (Ibarra 1948; A. Cuadra 1977). This served to reinforce the association of Nicaraguans with communism and violence. Francisco Ibarra noted this tension in 1948:

> It is really painful and alarming, what is going on with the Nicaraguans in Costa Rica after the advent of the new revolutionary government that, in successive public manifestations, has claimed its desire to return peace and tranquility to the inhabitants, whether nationals or foreigners. . . . This sad belief among the average Costa Rican population that all Nicaraguans are pernicious criminals is related to the ignorance of many and the small effort made by the schools in dispelling these painful prejudices, perennial sources of discord between brother countries. (1948, 3, 11)

The winning forces in the civil war and the Somoza dictatorship in Nicaragua maintained mutual animosities. Anastasio Somoza García, the first member of the dynasty, supported an invasion organized after the civil war by the defeated Costa Rican forces. In 1954, José Figueres, the leader of the civil war in Costa Rica, aided an attempted coup d'état against Somoza. In turn, Somoza gave his support to another invasion to Costa Rica in 1956 (Solís 1992, 286, 350). Although the Nicaraguan population did not represent more than four percent of the total Costa Rican population at that time (P. Cuadra 1987, 62; Schmidt 1979, 47), they were criminalized. This means that the emergence of racialization is not a simple consequence of "immigration" but a result of long-term processes of constructing an imagined community through difference and inequalities.

The lived experience of the Nicaraguan community during this period has been little documented. I was very fortunate in having access to the private correspondence of doña Carmen Bustos and her children, a Nicaraguan family whose members arrived in Costa Rica in the 1930s. Most of the letters were written by her daughter, Rosa, and were addressed to doña Carmen. This collection also includes some letters sent in turn by doña Carmen, her son Pedro, and her daughter Regina. Rosa and Pedro spent most of their life in the southern Pacific region of Costa Rica, where after the mid 1930s the banana industry began activities and offered unskilled jobs. Communities such as Golfito, Puerto Cortés, and Quepos are often mentioned in the letters. Doña Carmen lived most of her life in Rivas, the closest Nicaraguan province to Costa Rica. About seventy letters written between 1930 and 1960 were preserved by Rosa and later by Juan Ramón, one of her sons.

Interestingly, sisters, not sons, used to write more often to their mother. In fact, the most common concern in Rosa's letters is the illness of her mother and Pedro's resistance to staying in touch with doña Carmen. While Pedro used to spend his money on drinking, as Rosa noted in one of her letters, she was especially worried about the vulnerability of her mother.[33] Rather than broad debates regarding their situation as immigrants, what really mattered for her was Pedro's refusal to travel to Nicaragua to visit doña Carmen. Rosa sent as much money as she could and was anxious to confirm that her mother had received her letters and the money she was able to save in Costa Rica. Rosa also sent to her mother medicine and in 1968 she even wrote her that a package of cookies was sent with a friend that traveled to Nicaragua. Meanwhile, doña Carmen asks frequent questions regarding Pedro's silence and she requests a photo in which all her children that lived in Costa Rica would appear together.

A significant number of letters refer to the possible trip of doña Carmen's children to Nicaragua, especially during the Easter holidays. The obstacle is to contact Pedro but Rosa always insisted that the next Easter it would be feasible. The motivation for these trips seems to be the possibility of family reunification, which is permanently postponed. At Christmas 1954, Rosa received a letter from which she learned her mother was seriously ill. Rosa attempted to sell a sewing machine, "my only treasure," but received an offer so low that she did not sell it. Doña Carmen did not wish to die before reuniting with her son Pedro and, in 1950, she wrote to him asking again when he was going to visit her, since seven years had passed since he left Nicaragua. Doña Carmen was anxious to see him, since she was losing her sight and she had been informed that Pedro was ill, too.

The letters also refer to other Nicaraguans who were living in Costa Rica at the time, which seems to confirm that many Nicaraguans left their country, seeking opportunity, especially in banana plantations, in Costa

Rica. But issues of nationhood were not a topic in the correspondence. This relative absence might be interpreted as a relative autonomy of family life and more personal surroundings from the political events at that time. A letter sent in 1949 mentioned a strike that had taken place recently, and there were also references to unemployment in Quepos in the same period, but these are rather incidental references. This lack of political references is particularly relevant because this correspondence coincided with the civil war of 1948 and, as mentioned above, Somoza supported military coups against the new government and many Nicaraguans supported the defeated forces.

Nationhood and "immigration" do not seem to have been of particular interest, especially among inhabitants of remote regions of the country, such as Golfito or Quepos. It might indicate that conflicts among political elites do not always arouse the same interest and involvement among plebeian classes. Equally important to consider is the extent to which nationalist discourses made by political elites are able to convince "ordinary" people about their "belonging" to particular nations in the first decades of the twentieth century in Central America. Sometimes it is supposed that wide-ranging groups easily internalized nationalist ideologies without major analysis of readership and processes of appropriation and contestation of such discourses. From this correspondence it might be suggested that the family's principal form of belonging was tied to kinship relations, with doña Carmen as the center of an extended family. This correspondence also points out that immigration has been a long-term process through which many Nicaraguan and Costa Rican families have joined each other. These letters make clear that the Costa Rican nation—as probably also many others—constitutes itself through multiple and diverse relationships.

Chapter 4

Belonging and Racialization as Lived Experience

Up to now this project has analyzed extended narratives about national identities, such as news items, literature, and historical accounts. These cultural forms are usually located in the public sphere and are professionally produced for defined circuits of distribution and cultural consumption. A different and complementary location is to recognize the interplay between such extended representations and everyday life, exploring ways in which different social actors have contested such narratives. This chapter is based on fieldwork undertaken between January and June 1999 in Costa Rica.

Despite growing interest in "immigration" issues—which have become synonymous with "nicas"—neither the media nor academic accounts have paid much attention to the relationships between how Costa Ricans represent themselves and their images of the Nicaraguan community. Accordingly, the methodology of fieldwork was to triangulate sites and methodological strategies. Since the overall objective is to explore ways in which national identity has frequently been constructed on the basis of difference and exclusion, I concentrated most of my efforts on the analysis of representations and practices performed by Costa Rican citizens. This has meant focusing on the "perpetrators" of exclusion and related processes rather than on the "victims" (Gabriel 1998, 12), though I have also explored how these processes interpenetrate the Nicaraguan community in Costa Rica.

An important stage of this fieldwork was carried out with primary and secondary school students.[1] Thirteen state and private institutions were selected. Primary school children in the sixth grade (average age: twelve) and secondary school students in the eleventh grade (average age: seventeen) were chosen. Table 4.1 shows a brief description of the selected institutions, whose students come from different economic and social backgrounds and geographical locations. Lincoln High School, for example, is one of the most expensive educational institutions in Costa Rica; it is a liberal-oriented center with close ties to the U.S. educational system. In contrast, La Carpio is situated in one of the most deprived communities of San José, and about fifty percent of its total population, approximately twenty-five thousand inhabitants, are Nicaraguans. The group from La Carpio comprised thirteen Nicaraguans and seventeen Costa Ricans. Poás, Siquirres, San Carlos, and Sarapiquí are counties in which coffee and citrus farms as well as banana plantations offer jobs to Nicaraguan workers. These employment patterns shape the narratives written by students in different ways.

Table 4.1

Schools Selected for the Study

School	Economic Background*	Type	Location
PRIMARY SCHOOLS			
La Carpio	shantytown	state	urban
Rincón Grande	working class	state	urban
Los Sitios	working class	state	urban
D. Alighieri	lower middle class	state	urban
Conbi College	middle class	private	urban
SECONDARY SCHOOLS			
Sarapiquí	rural working class	state	rural
Siquirres	lower/middle class	state	rural
Pavas	lower middle/working class	state	urban
San Carlos	middle/working class	state	rural
Poás	middle class	state	rural
Vargas Calvo	lower middle/middle class	state	urban
Saint Clare	upper middle class	private	urban
Lincoln	upper class	private	urban

*These are rough distinctions since I have no precise figures for family incomes.

Since there were no statistical criteria in the selection of these groups, I followed the concept of saturation suggested by, among others, Daniel Bertaux (1988), which suggests that when new cases (e.g., institutions) repeat previous patterns, the selection of institutions can be considered sufficient. The students were asked to write two stories. The first one was to describe "Costa Rica as a nation"; the topic of the second was "Nicaraguans in Costa Rica." The activity was introduced as a research project undertaken at the University of Costa Rica about the opinions of the younger generation about their country. The students did not know the second topic until they had written the first story. In a second session, we discussed their pieces. In total 300 written pieces were gathered about Costa Rica and 263 on Nicaraguans in Costa Rica.

Students were asked to write their stories using metaphors. As rhetorical device, the metaphor offers the possibility of recognizing symbolic and emotive representations associated with their own nation and the "other." Sander Gilman asserts that "we learn to perceive in terms of historically determined sets of root-metaphors, and they serve as the categories through which we label and classify the Other." Metaphors are mutable and constantly shifting. "They reflect," Gilman continues, "certain perceptual categories, which are in turn projections of internalized, often repressed models of the self and the Other" (1985, 22–23). Furthermore, another important concern during this stage of the research was to explore the importance of media discourse in the shaping of these metaphors. Overall, the responses offer a wide range of ways of representation, which will be discussed in the course of the following pages.

The work with students was complemented by an analysis of three collections of history textbooks employed in primary schools. This textual analysis endeavored to discover possible links between the stories written by the students about Costa Rica, which are highly homogeneous, and the representations of the nation in these textbooks. Indeed, most of the metaphors on Costa Rica are constructed about ecodemocracy as the nation's key identification. The analysis of textbooks also provides an important mediation between the historical formation of nation and nationhood in Costa Rica and the interpretation of historical issues by primary and secondary school students. Those possible links do not suggest a simple reproduction of contents by students; rather the aim was to explore the interplay between representations in textbooks and subjective images of belonging in their metaphors. In fact, the analysis of the textbooks came after the workshops.

Another kind of inquiry was undertaken through autobiographies. Nicaraguan citizens in different provinces of Costa Rica—including San José, Alajuela, Heredia, and Limón—were invited to write about their lived experience as immigrants. Furthermore, several radio and television programs allowed me to publicize this initiative, which was launched in January 1999 and ended April 30, 1999. By the end, twenty-six autobiographies were gathered. Twelve pieces were written by women and fourteen by men from many different regions of Nicaragua. Some were teachers, students, public servants, and technicians who left Nicaragua looking for jobs in Costa Rica. At the time of writing, all the women worked as domestic workers in Costa Rica. Men had jobs in construction and agriculture, and a few got opportunities in the service sector. We met in a workshop and discussed the experience of writing about oneself. Over coffee and tortillas, copies of the received autobiographies were distributed. Two awards ($75 each) were given to the pieces considered the most reflective accounts of being an immigrant in Costa Rica.

This activity had a threefold aim. First, it attempted to document how the experience of exclusion and racialization is lived by Nicaraguans. Second, the autobiographies offer a crucial method of exploring ways in which members of the Nicaraguan community contest racialized discourses, since they usually do not have the opportunity of taking part in public debates. Besides their material deprivation as low-paid workers, Nicaraguans experience what Mikhail Bakhtin (1981, 346) has described as an intense struggle within themselves for hegemony among various available verbal and ideological points of view, approaches, directions, and values. They consider themselves good workers but they know they are racialized on the basis of ethnic and cultural criteria. The autobiographies attempt to explore these tensions. Third, writing about oneself reconciles meaning and agency; the authors described their own experience and were able to contest critically diverse racialized discourses that circulate in Costa Rica. As Carolyn Steedman argues, "Writing does indeed bring new forms of selfhood into being" (1997, 123). The autobiographies were also an attempt at dialogue. The goal was to consider Nicaraguans, not as "objects of inquiry," but as subjects of their own knowledge, a distinction not always made by commentators on the "Nicaraguan problem."

The stories average two paragraphs each, most written during a Spanish lesson. The twenty-six autobiographies—varying in length from fifteen hundred to eight thousand words—were completed within twenty weeks. While the students' stories explored different responses regarding nationhood, the autobiographies attempted to know ways in which members of the Nicaraguan community address their own racialization (Sandoval 2000).

Ecodemocracy and Its Discontents

The metaphors about Costa Rica are characterized by their homogeneity. Most are highly positive and based on two key references: natural landscapes and political values such as democracy, freedom, and peace. About two-thirds of the pieces give positive images of Costa Rica as a nation. Both positive images of nature and those related to political values constituted 51 percent of the total (see table 4.2 and appendix 5). A free white bird is a common metaphor of the nation, as are images of paradise and treasure. A student from Lincoln High stated that in national celebrations "schoolchildren replace the army, reflecting that in our country innocence rules over guns."

While political values have been the core representation of Costa Rica in the last fifty years, ecological images are emergent icons. They probably arose in the context of the tourist promotion of Costa Rica as an ecological paradise. Indeed, tourism has become the second most lucrative economic activity in Costa Rica, after coffee exports. The number of tourists visiting Costa Rica rose from 278,000 in 1987 to 811,000 in 1997. In 1999 the number reached 1 million for the first time (PNUD 1999).

Representations of Costa Rica either as a rural democracy or as a middle-class nation have dominated much of the official imagery during the second half of the twentieth century. Now nature rather than society seems to be the key source of belonging. Ecodemocracy can also be considered as a reelaboration of old versions that identified nature and nation (see chapter 3). However, this "naturalized" belonging is now located in a global arena where the tourist's gaze plays a crucial role. It does not renounce previous versions of identity but enlarges them with images in which tradition and modernity coexist and complement each other. The local makes sense through the so-called global since, as Jonathan Rutherford points out, "cultural difference sells" (1990, 16).

Table 4.2

Students' Representations of Costa Rica and the Nicaraguan Community

School	Nicaraguans in Costa Rica						Costa Rica as Nation					
	FEMALES			MALES			FEMALES			MALES		
	+	+/-	-	+	+/-	-	+	+/-	-	+	+/-	-
Lincoln	15	-	-	13	-	2	17	-	1	15	-	-
Saint Clare	16	2	2	10	-	3	16	-	4	10	1	2
Conbi	2	2	3	7	3	2	2	3	2	7	1	4
Poás	13	3	3	4	1	1	16	1	2	5	-	1
Vargas Calvo	5	2	4	5	1	2	2	-	8	4	-	4
Dante Alighieri	5	2	5	6	3	8	7	-	5	9	2	7
Pavas	1	4	6	5	1	1	4	-	7	5	-	2
San Carlos*	-	-	-	-	-	-	6	7	5	4	3	8
Siquirres	1	3	2	5	1	1	2	-	4	7	-	-
Sarapiquí	6	-	1	-	1	5	7	-	-	7	1	-
Los Sitios	7	4	3	4	2	-	11	2	2	5	-	2
Rincón Grande	6	-	1	4	-	-	8	-	1	4	-	-
La Carpio	10	-	2	13	2	4	10	1	1	15	-	3
Total	87	22	32	76	15	29	108	14	42	97	8	33

This table is a synthesis of information included in appendixes 5 and 6.

The signs +, +/-, and - indicate the students' opinions regarding both topics: + indicates positive comments, +/- indicates a combination of positive and negative views, and – indicates negative images.

*The pieces written by students from the San Carlos secondary school were discarded because the teacher asked them to write about Nicaragua and not about Nicaraguans in Costa Rica.

Among the students the tourist's view is an important reference when they emphasize the ecological representation of the nation. Interestingly, the students of the Dante Alighieri primary school, who showed the strongest hostility toward Nicaraguans, were also most likely to mention tourists (28 percent) as conferrers of legitimacy for their sense of nationhood. Tourism is also perceived as a confirmation of positive national attributes among students of Conbi College (a primary school) (21 percent) and the Poás secondary school (16 percent). The students made a distinction between "foreigners," some of which are "tourists" and others "nicas." This split confirms that the "other" is always situated, relational, and historical. A piece by a primary school student illustrates the distinction: "I think the Nicaraguans must leave the country because they cause much violence—[and] because half the Costa Rican population is Nicaraguan and because they take land and bring drugs, and the tourists don't like to live close to the nicas." Another student made a similar comment: "It is fine that Cubans, Chileans, Americans, Chinese come to Costa Rica but no longer the Nicaraguans. I don't understand why they come here if they have their own country."

These representations of tourists also rework an old icon: at the end of the nineteenth century the image of Costa Rica as the Switzerland of Central America was supported by travelers' testimonies, appropriated in turn by historians, and later presented in advertisements (see chapter 3). Nowadays the tourist has replaced the traveler; but the gaze of the modern other remains. Both narratives register similar portrayals; sadly, the new ones hardly show any novelty. While holidays in Latin America and elsewhere might aim to experience "the primitive," "the effect of which is to confirm westerners' sense of their own 'advancement'" (Gabriel 1994, 146), for the "natives" their presence is a way of making sense of their own belonging to a "unique paradise" now involved in a global world. However, tourism is sometimes associated with a loss of identity. It is a relevant concern among students of San Carlos secondary school, in Costa Rica's northern region, where tourism has increased considerably during the last years, introducing new kinds of jobs and activities in a region that has been traditionally devoted to agriculture.

On the other hand, some stories linked the exaltation of nature with great hostility toward Nicaraguans. The risks posed by deforestation and pollution to natural attributes such as flora and fauna are explained by the presence of immigrants. Dirtiness associated with them seems to be interpreted as a risk to the environment—reminiscent of recent debates over pollution in the United States. As Gabriel (1998, 122) points out, the environment provides an array of metaphors (pollution, overheating, toxicity, and contamination) to use in connection with "recent" immigrant populations. Some stories written by students of Conbi show this tendency. A male student, for example, wrote: "Costa Rica has plenty of forests everywhere. Costa Rica is very nice because it has many animals, nature, volcanoes, and beaches. Despite being a small country, Costa Rica has many nice things. But people don't care, Costa Rica doesn't have enough trees; garbage is everywhere; the sea is also full of garbage."

In his piece about Nicaraguans in Costa Rica, the same student explicitly links Nicaraguans with "disorder": "Some of the Nicaraguans not only steal but also burn forests and defile Costa Rica." It might be suggested that when these ecorepresentations seem to be under threat by deforestation and other sources of risk, some of the anxieties are projected onto outsiders, especially Nicaraguans. As Ghassan Hage (1998, 168–69) found in the case of Australia, nationalist ecology often links the nation with fantasies of the natural, and polluted others seem to disrupt the sustainability of national ecology (L. Young 1994).

Metaphors associated with political values were the second group of representations, with 18 percent of the total. The principal references were to democracy, freedom, and peace. An interesting feature of these attributes is their comparative framing; Costa Rica is often represented through comparison with other nations, as in a piece by a female student from Poás secondary school: "Costa Rica, Center of Peace. Costa Rica is one of the few countries that has no military protection; it is defended by means of words." A male student from the same school wrote, "Costa Rica is the democracy of the Americas; since it has no army, it is the free motherland of the continent."

This positive description of Costa Rica is not affected by gender or age differences, which shows that processes of political socialization take place in primary school, where children learn a consolidated official history, including peace, democracy, and the abolition of the army. These attributes have a close connection with the interpretations offered in secondary education as we will explore below.

Meanwhile, intense discontent with idyllic representations appears in urban state-supported secondary schools. There seems to be an important link between social class and age; at the end of secondary school students have to make crucial decisions, either continuing higher education or finding a job. Opportunities diminish drastically for new generations from lower-middle-class or working-class backgrounds. Indeed, only one out of ten students who begin primary school gets a place in a public university. New generations find well-paying jobs hard to get, and young people with incomplete secondary schooling show the highest rate of unemployment (PNUD 1999, 48).

A small group of students (about 5 percent) wrote that a concentration of power and wealth is taking place and there is an increase in social injustices. During the workshop in the Vargas Calvo school, the students considered it a contradiction to emphasize that Costa Rica has the best living standards in Central America when there is a deficit of about five thousand classrooms. They knew the figures and, most important, they interpreted this decline in standards of public education in terms of a devaluation of their own academic diplomas. A student at Vargas Calvo provided an interesting image: "Costa Rica seems, I don't know, perhaps it is like a train looking for things everywhere and after a short time the only ones who get onto the train are always those who have money. From time to time we notice that only the wealthy people rule."

The nation is a train that does not have room for all citizens. That this injustice is noticed only "from time to time" seems to indicate that it is not an obvious conclusion. The example quoted above shows also that images of decline and threats of exclusion appear together with a lack of confidence in politics and politicians. In a national survey of young people, 67 percent reported a lack of confidence in politicians (PNUD 1998, 10).

Overall, class seems to be a crucial factor in the students' stories; those written by upper-class students, for instance, are characterized by positive images about Costa Rica. In particular, ecodemocracy is the most frequent representation of nationhood. Conversely, students from public urban secondary schools more frequently challenged consolidated images of Costa Rica as an egalitarian nation. An aspect that requires further research is the extent to which age makes a difference among students from similar social and economic backgrounds. A case in point is the contrast between the stories written by students from the Vargas Calvo secondary school and the Dante Alighieri primary school, institutions that attract students from similar backgrounds and are located in the same area. Whereas Vargas Calvo's students were critical of Costa Rican nationhood, Dante Alighieri children showed more conventional views on Costa Rica and a considerable hostility toward Nicaraguans. Developmental psychologists have suggested that adolescence is a crucial period for identity formation and during which concern for ideals and social issues acquire more salience (Rosenthal 1987, 157).

School Textbooks: Forging the Nation

The presence of recurrent versions of an ecodemocracy among the students led me to explore possible sources of such images. The textbooks employed in primary schools constitute an important reference, since they are recommended by the Ministry of Education and constitute the "official" bibliography. During the past fifty years there have been several textbook collections written by different teams and published by various printing houses. I chose three collections that show a diversity of representations of the nation, though they do share some similarities.

The first collection of textbooks was written by Adela Ferreto, Carlos Luis Sáenz, Carmen Lyra, and Carlos Meléndez, a group of very well known intellectuals. These books were not published simultaneously; the first ones might have been written early in the 1940s, with many editions in the following decades, even in the 1980s. (Unfortunately, the later editions do not indicate original publication dates.) The initiative was the first to provide textbooks for primary and secondary teachers. Students did not read this first collection themselves. Previously, teachers frequently used the books written by Ricardo Fernández Guardia and Carlos Monge-Alfaro (see chapter 3).[2] The second collection, one of the major private initiatives, was published in 1995 by Santillana. The third collection was the result of an agreement between the Ministry of Education and the University of Costa Rica, by which the latter was contracted to produce a new collection, "Toward the Twenty-first Century" (1996). On average a new collection of textbooks has been printed about every fifteen years. The students who wrote the metaphors might have studied especially the last two series, the Santillana and "Twenty-first Century." I have explored some keywords such as *nation, "race," democracy,* and *peace,* which are introduced in the textbooks throughout the explanation of certain historical issues. Rather than being a systematic discourse analysis, this section highlights certain relationships between these keywords and the metaphors written by students. In this sense, the reading of textbooks has been guided by the students' writings and not vice versa.

The definition of the Costa Rican nation offered to second- and fourth-grade primary school students by the Santillana editions elaborates essentialist arguments about nation. The second-grade book maintains, "A nation is a group of people with the same ethnic origin who speak the same language and have a common tradition" (Morales et al. 1995a, 69). Meanwhile, the fourth-grade version states, "Costa Ricans share a history, a past that justifies the Costa Rican way of life; a territory, an ensemble of places, landscapes, and regions that belong to us; a culture, customs, knowledge, and way of life that characterize us in every way" (Morales et al. 1995b, 78).

This "ethnic" definition of nation is paradoxical given the diversity of the Costa Rican population. If one followed such a definition, Costa Rica would not be considered a nation, since its inhabitants do not share the same ethnic origin. This ethnic homogeneity does not take into account either indigenous or black peoples who still speak other languages. In the second definition, the homogeneity is not ethnic but cultural: history and space—key sources of belonging—are shared by the citizens.

Thus, the nation is represented in terms that are simultaneously ethnic and cultural. That is hardly surprising, since diverse ideas of exceptionalism have associated Costa Rica with whiteness and cultural difference. What makes these textbooks unusual is their cultural circulation: they are not intellectual debates, like those discussed in the last chapter, which usually involve a very selective readership; on the contrary, these are manuals that are consulted by many students as their key references.

Moreover, there is a remarkable homology between the ethnic and cultural representation of Costa Rica as a nation and the processes of ethnic and cultural racialization of Nicaraguans. Both the self-definition of nation, as well as the images of the racialized Nicaraguan other, are worked out through ethnicity and culture. I am not suggesting that the processes of racialization of Nicaraguans are a consequence of these definitions, but they do constitute an intellectual framework in which ethnic absolutism and uniqueness are mixed in such a way that they might engender hostility and authoritarian attitudes. Meanwhile, the third-grade textbook published within the collection "Toward the Twenty-first Century" brings another perspective: "The Costa Rican population is like a family tree. It has indigenous, European, African, Asian, and Latin American roots. . . . We can appreciate and appraise our differences without forgetting that all of us are equal as people" (Pérez et al. 1996, 35). Instead of homogeneity, this version is constructed around the tension between diversity and equality.[3]

Democracy and *peace,* other keywords in the national vocabulary, are also present in the textbooks. Ferreto and Sáenz, for instance, recreated a deep-rooted image—"Costa Rica has more teachers than soldiers"—inaugurated by the Liberal president Ricardo Jiménez in the 1930s. They also wrote, probably late in the 1950s, in a second-grade textbook that by 1981 had been reprinted twenty-three times, "My father says that in Costa

Rica there are no military parades because our country is peaceful without an army, that our army is made up of school children, the young people that study in order to know more and more; aiming to make Costa Rica into a more and more cultured country in which all of us can live with dignity and respect" (1981, 24).

Even periods characterized by social protest are summarized in optimistic terms. In August 1934, for instance, workers on banana plantations went on one of the most important strikes during the twentieth century in Costa Rica (see chapter 3). Many Nicaraguan workers who took part in the protest were expelled from the country. Also, a decree forbade the transit of "colored" people from the Atlantic to the southern Pacific coast (Meléndez 1981, 92; Casey 1979, 130; Bourgois 1994, 141). However, the balance of this period presented in history textbooks for primary school children is highly apologetic. Ferreto and Meléndez described the personality of Ricardo Jiménez, the president of Costa Rica at the time this legislation was approved: "When he was president he endeavored to maintain respect for human rights and people's freedom in every corner of the nation. He was against racial and religious discrimination, against any limitation of free speech and a free press" (1981, 232).

Although during this period black and Nicaraguan workers were strongly discriminated against, these schoolchildren's ideas coincided with the idyllic representation of the liberal period. Three decades later a similar image seems to remain. The Santillana edition for sixth grade offers an interpretation of nation building in which diverse issues followed a certain "historical democratic will." The War of 1856, for example, is considered a crucial issue:

> When the national campaign of 1856 ended, the Costa Rican compromise with freedom and peace began. Accordingly, the past generations were organizing the republic from a democratic perspective, with social justice and equality, in which other ways of life were never accepted. (Morales et al. 1995c, 47)

A similar depiction is constructed of the twentieth century:

> In 1948 the Constituent Assembly decided to abolish the army through the elimination of an article of the constitution of 1817. . . . Our coun-

> try has given a lot of importance to the human being, since Tomás Guardia made the decision to abolish the death penalty. Don Pepe [José Figueres], as he was known, emphasized the importance of consolidating the civil democracy. . . . This decision turned the world's attention toward us, since a small country located in a conflictive region like Central America made a transcendental decision [to abolish the army]. (Morales et al. 1995c, 87)

Interestingly, a similar balance is present in the sixth-grade version of "Toward the Twenty-first Century": "Elections without conflicts and electoral purity have become part of the national tradition and the country's international image. The incorporation of women in political life is not questioned" (Fonseca et al. 1996, 119). Time and again, the gaze of the other—called world attention or international image—becomes crucial. It is another important similarity between the students' writings and these textbooks, since Costa Rican democracy is legitimated through the opinion of "significant others." Little attention is paid to the fact that women, for instance, are scarcely elected, a fact that has been a central preoccupation of feminist campaigners in recent years. The omission is crucial precisely because the readers are the generation who might change this tendency.[4]

Overall, historical analysis seems sometimes to be overlapped by a sort of epic narrative in which loyalty to the nation—not exceptional among historians—is more important than historical debates. Through certain teleological patterns, different processes follow a national will which is usually identified with democracy. Politicians and events not precisely characterized by democracy are portrayed in such a way that, sooner or later, they fit into a sort of epic narration. This teleological pursuit is generally worked out through the sequence equilibrium-breakdown-restoration. The equilibrium is generally identified with the colonial period, a sort of paradise in which poverty made possible equality, and later democracy. The breakdown emerges in the context of events such as the dictatorship of Tomás Guardia (1870–1882) or the civil war of 1948. However, even these issues are remembered by their peaceful outcomes: the former abolished the death penalty and the latter got rid of the army. Restoration is undertaken by certain politicians, who work as "primary definers" of situations. Although there is a certain "historical will" that endures through the changes, the equilibrium that is restored is not identical to the one that existed, as Tzevetan Todorov (1991b, 88) has found in other texts.[5] Controversial periods become a source of progress.

This plotting of equilibrium-breakdown-restoration enacts "preferred readings" that are inscribed in the texts (Hall 1980a, 134). Students do not face alternative explanations of controversial issues. They are not invited to consider that the representation of history is itself a contested historical event (McClintock 1995, 10). Nonetheless, certain developments escape this teleological narrative. The dictatorship of General Federico Tinocos Granados (1917–19) remains, for example, generally unmentioned (Solís 1995, 9). Another loaded issue is the decision to ban the Communist Party (PC) after the war of 1948. Both the Santillana and Twenty-first Century sixth-grade textbooks blame the PC itself for that decision, rather than considering the authoritarian context. The Santillana text maintains, "The Popular Vanguard [Communist] Party constitutes a special case. It was banned between 1949 and 1974 on account of extremist ideas, alien to democracy" (Morales et al. 1995c, 120). The Twenty-first Century text offers a similar explanation: "Given its leftist ideology, the Communist Party, founded in 1931, was excluded from the electoral processes after the civil war" (Fonseca et al. 1996, 118).[6]

The principal difficulty of these narratives is that they present themselves as *the* past rather than merely an interpretation of it. Nevertheless, democracy has been also the subject of dispute. As Sue Wright argues, "No ideology, however hegemonic and entrenched in institutions and everyday life, is beyond contest" (1998, 10). Indeed, a female student at San Carlos secondary school wittily addressed this contestation: "Costa Rica is a country whose inhabitants almost literally enjoy peace, freedom of speech, respect for human rights, and social and individual guarantees. I say 'literally' because all this seems to be written only in history textbooks or in tourist brochures."

Meanwhile, references to tourism are nearly absent from the textbooks, which might indicate that the formation of the image of ecodemocracy seems to result from the peculiar mix of contents offered in formal education, especially those related to political values and media advertising. Ecodemocracy might be interpreted as a "structure of feeling" (R. Williams 1977), reworking previous versions of national identity under new economic and cultural conditions. It provides an example of how the local—a small country with no major consequence beyond Central America—fits into the "new era" of global capitalism. Conversely, it is worth noting that national representations constructed around the images of the freeborn peasant have become residual among new generations, even for those who still live in semirural areas.

Images of Nicaraguans: Good Workers and Threatening Others

The stories about Nicaraguans show different kinds of representation. A common image considers them "seekers of opportunity" in Costa Rica, as emphasized by 20 percent of the written pieces (see appendix 6). Those who consider the Nicaraguans to be seekers of opportunity usually hold a very positive representation of Costa Rica too. This correlation is especially present among students from private institutions such as the Lincoln and Saint Clare schools. It might be suggested that these images contain a certain dose of philanthropic condescension. Roberto DaMatta has argued that "the dominant, triumphant sectors of any society always read its history and social structure as a narrative of solidarity" (1991, 139).

Several pieces are constructed around the metaphor of a wounded bird looking for a place of refuge. Interestingly, the bird metaphor is used both for Costa Rica—"a free white bird"— and for Nicaraguans. Another important group of stories depicts the Nicaraguans as good workers (15 percent). A frequent representation identifies them with ants, insects that usually work hard despite the fact that anything can destroy their work. Students from different class backgrounds, age, gender, and location used this image. A male student from the Saint Clare school summarized these images: "The Nicaraguan is the one who cleans, watches over, and builds Costa Rica."

Sometimes, metaphors associated with hard work seem to be constructed for an instrumental reason. Nicaraguans are required inasmuch as they undertake undesirable jobs; otherwise, there is no reason to admit them. In fact, certain metaphors that considered Nicaraguans good workers also compared them with "pests," "plagues," or "drugs." These metaphors were written especially by male students. A student from Saint Clare school wrote: "They are a great but necessary pest. They are a social pest when they bring their diseases and poverty into the country, creating a worse Costa Rica for all of us, but some of them are good people because they undertake jobs that Costa Ricans don't like to do." A student from Lincoln school provided a more articulate justification of "plague": "Nicaraguans are a plague. What I mean is that they are eliminating a modus vivendi [present among certain Costa Ricans] that is not necessarily good, characterized by vagrancy and laziness. Nature [Nicaraguans] is controlling a way of life that was suffocating us."

Nicaraguans are "regulating" the labor force in Costa Rica, eliminating those who are inefficient, and in this struggle for survival, a sort of social Darwinism will generate progress. In this case, the plague metaphor is not explicitly related to pollution but is associated with the survival of the fittest. This instrumental utility of Nicaraguans is diminished by the threats associated with them. They are required for undesirable jobs but they are also, for instance, considered carriers of diseases. Profitability and threat of pollution cross each other. A Saint Clare student, condensing this ambivalence, compared Nicaraguans with drugs: "They are necessary but they can kill you." The students' representations do not result from a sense of being swamped—an image discussed below—by Nicaraguans; instead it seems to be an association with loathing. *Plague* is usually used to describe a large number of organisms that threaten personal and social health. Topographically, plague is located in low places and, as Stallybrass and White argue, "in the slum, the bourgeois spectator surveyed and classified his own antithesis" (1986, 128). But these images are not beyond contestation; a primary school student from the Dante Alighieri school, for example, addressed these metaphors of pest and plague written by secondary school students: "For many people, the Nicaraguans are a pest, but they come here painstakingly seeking better economic conditions. Last year, I met a Nicaraguan classmate who had to come to Costa Rica with her family, searching for a better situation. She told me that working as a 'housekeeper' there [in Nicaragua], one earns five thousand colones [about $20 in 1999] monthly."

It might be suggested that there is an emergent discourse on human rights and equality among students. Pieces written regarding equality, sadness, and discrimination constituted 21 percent of the total. A Costa Rican female student from La Carpio, where Nicaraguans were nearly half the group, wrote, "Nicaraguans are people like us; they have the same rights as we do. . . . Many Nicaraguan children face problems in their studies because their families have faced economic problems; the parents can't work." This image of "human beings like us" is also present in the Los Sitios school: "I perceive the Nicaraguans as any other people. I see them just like the Canadians that come to Costa Rica. Well, I wrote that because they are people like us. They are not strange beings [*bichos raros*] or anything like that. They have feelings like any other person, and they come to Costa Rica looking for jobs because there are no opportunities in their country."

A female student from the Vargas Calvo school interpreted such discrimination in terms of class: "I suppose that we perceive them [Nicaraguans] as the bourgeoisie of our country perceive the lower class here." Another female student from Saint Clare school even questioned why one has to belong to a certain nation: "I believe nobody belongs to a single place; anyone can experience new and different things." Most of these representations about discrimination, human rights, and equality were written in state schools where images about criminalization against Nicaraguans were also strongly present. In contrast with the homogeneity among private secondary schools, the state-run ones—which accept especially working-class and lower middle-class students—show more contradictory representations. Thus there is a tension between the recognition of rights and images of threat.

Another important set of images does indeed portray Nicaraguans as "threatening others." This menace is represented by the metaphor of being swamped. Nicaraguans are also considered to be "too many" and as people who are "taking Costa Ricans' jobs." Some pieces even strongly suggest that they must leave or be expelled from Costa Rica. Such images made up 13 percent of the total. This racialized politics seems to be stronger among those who belong to the lower middle class. The decline of public investment in social services such as education, health, and housing has not only meant material changes, such as those discussed in the next chapter, but also subjective shifts, especially among the less prosperous members of the nation.

Furthermore, this social decline has coincided with the growth of consumption as a way of social distinction. It has meant a society in which high expectations are promoted within a range of limited possibilities of access to income and spending. Such opposite tendencies engender "unintended consequences" (Giddens 1986, 9–14) that can be diminished but not extinguished. Thus, students who feel profound hostility and xenophobia can be considered members of the lower middle class. The schoolchildren at Dante Alighieri, for example, argued that Nicaraguans are taking jobs that were formerly occupied by Costa Rican workers. This hostility might indicate that social actors threatened by the fear of their own social exclusion tend to project their menace onto racialized others.

Stallybrass and White called this process displaced abjection, "the process whereby 'low' social groups turn their figurative and actual power, not against those in authority, but against those even lower [than themselves]" (1986, 53). Although the latter are located in a "lower" position, they are perceived as all-powerful and such an exaggerated threat justifies and makes rational diverse forms of hostility. The geographic location of schools is important in this context. Students from schools such as Dante Alighieri, Pavas, and Vargas Calvo—who wrote the most hostile images—generally live in the eastern and western sectors of San José, where prosperous neighborhoods have attracted many commercial facilities and therefore the contrast between the upper middle class, integrated by young professionals, and the working class is more pronounced. This proximity might increase anxieties related to fears of social exclusion since there is daily exposure to prosperous lifestyles which are more or less inaccessible to the lower middle class and working class. In this context, as Norbert Lechner (1998, 182–83) argues, the fear that the "we" has of the other exhibits not the potential hostility of the other, but the vulnerability of the "we."

This hypothesis also seems to be confirmed by quantitative indicators. According to the balance provided by the United Nations Development Program for Costa Rica, while the percentage of families below the poverty line from 1994 to 1999 represented about 20 percent of the total, the "index of vulnerability to poverty," which estimates the number of families facing the possibility of descending below the poverty line, reached 31.1 percent, in 1999, the highest level during the nineties (PNUD 1999, 103–4). In nations such as Costa Rica where all want to be winners, it is not easy to reveal one's own vulnerability.

This hostility toward the Nicaraguan community is not as strong among students who live in the most deprived shantytowns, where material facilities are extremely restricted and whose inhabitants earn low incomes. In particular, the Costa Rican children of La Carpio primary school, in which about 50 percent of the students are Nicaraguan, manifested less disagreement with their Nicaraguan classmates and neighbors than those schoolchildren that scarcely come across Nicaraguans in their everyday life. A Nicaraguan girl from La Carpio primary school made a remarkable comment: "Well, Costa Rica is nice but there are Nicaraguans who also love Costa Rica. Well, I think that Costa Ricans and Nicaraguans are equal. The difference is their accent. They come from different countries but all of us are equal. Like there are no differences between women and men. So why should we fight each other?"

Among students from the upper middle class there is a similar image of Nicaraguans. When I asked, for example, students from Saint Clare high school why they thought Nicaraguans were good workers, one-third of them declared that in their houses the domestic worker was a Nicaraguan woman. In other words, proximity seems to be a source of positive representations, or at least it seems to neutralize hostile images. Indeed, most of the students who show the highest hostility against Nicaraguans do not share a common space with them.[7]

A case study carried out in another shantytown, La Carpio 2, reported similar outcomes. Despite the deprivation present in the neighborhood, there was no strong division between nationalities. Nicaraguans associated xenophobia with employers but not with Costa Rican neighbors, churches, or schools (Gómez et al. 1999). This is an important conclusion in a community without many institutional facilities or public services. A similar conclusion arose from a countrywide survey of young people. Those who live in shantytowns expressed less hostility toward Nicaraguans than did the average respondents in the national sample. Both groups were asked about their threshold of tolerance toward the Nicaraguan community and other stigmatized groups. While 29 percent of the national sample disagreed with the presence of Nicaraguan population, only 15 percent of young people who live in these very deprived communities expressed similar feelings (PNUD 1998, 13; Garita 1999, 11). Again, those who have more frequent contact with Nicaraguans show less hostility than those who do not interact with them.

On the other hand, it might be suggested that the media provide most of the framing through which Nicaraguans are represented. A student from Sarapiquí wrote that the immigration of Nicaraguans "is like an invasion from another planet with different inhabitants. . . . The reason for this is that there are frequently bad incidents in the media, most of them committed by Nicaraguans." Similarly, a student from Los Sitios school stated, "I have seen on TV that Nicaraguans take school grants away from Costa Rican children." During the workshops I asked the students how many Nicaraguans were in prison. Most estimated that Nicaraguans made up 50 percent of the prison population. When I inquired into the sources of their estimates, most had based their answers on the media. In fact, Nicaraguans make up only 5 percent of the total population in prisons (see chapter 5).

Generally, people are becoming increasingly dependent on the media for both knowledge about and evaluation of current issues, given their limited and segregated sphere of experience, as research on media dependency has shown in recent years (Wolf 1994; Morley 1999). This dependency on media representations is highly relevant in Costa Rica, since most of the media institutions have been historically close to right-wing and conservative political perspectives. Despite the processes of modernization experienced in diverse fields, there are no examples of consolidated liberal or leftist media institutions. The explosion of new TV channels, for example, has not meant more alternatives (Sandoval 1994). The principal repercussion of this structural constitution of the public sphere is that the right has positioned itself at the center of political debates (Hall 1988). This tendency has been reinforced in the last decades by neoconservative and neoliberal ideologies in politics and economics, respectively. Meanwhile, most of the radical media do not have an important political presence beyond intellectual and militant groups. In this context, racialized representations have been incorporated into everyday life without major public criticism.

Being an Author/ity: Contestation over Racialized Identities

Being an author was a new experience for almost all the participants in this research.[8] Although some had entertained the possibility of writing about their lives as immigrants, only a few had already started. An important constraint was lack of time, but perhaps their principal impediment was not considering themselves writers. As Said notes, *author* has the same etymological roots as *authority* and both engender potent notions of mastery and property. Writing can also be considered, as McClintock (1995, 300) points out, an entry to the political authority of self-representation. What was at stake in this study was not only the matter of writing itself, which used to be reserved for a select group, but also the location of the host institution: the university was perceived as very exclusive and far from their everyday lives. Elmer, a teenager who left secondary school in Nicaragua to look for a job in Costa Rica, wrote: "Respectfully, I apologize if my writing has caused any offense or displeasure, but since you gave me the opportunity to express my opinion I have done it very cheerfully, and I thank you sincerely for it."

The students' distance from "learned society" is evident in the first or last lines of their pieces, where they apologized for their unfamiliarity with the "proper" written skills in Spanish and repeatedly expressed their thanks for being invited by the university to write about themselves. Vicente, an agricultural worker in his fifties who used to be a primary school teacher, appreciated the "opportunity": "Thanks for considering us. You know well about the racism against us; we are not perfect but we are good workers." Aleyda—a single mother of three, formerly a secretary and now a domestic worker—wrote, "Thanks for your attention and [my] apologies for some spelling mistakes. I don't know how I managed to find time for writing."

An invitation to write down a selective account of their lives might be interpreted as a way of revictimization, since most of their memories are painful remembrances. However, as mentioned above, their writing attempted to reconcile deconstruction of racialized representations and agency. As Walter Westerman argues in the context of testimonies brought by Salvadoran refugees in the United States in the 1980s: "Testimony is about people rising from a condition of being victims, objects of history, and taking charge of their history, becoming subjects of it" (1994, 177). The writing also endeavored to overcome the boundary between the private—humiliation, shame, silence, tears—and the public. Overcoming that divide is even more important when the authors are immigrant women and men, most from rural or working-class backgrounds, who are usually "ignored" in debates about subjectivity (Steedman 1986, 11–13). The invitation to write about their lives also meant conceiving this research not only as an intellectual exercise aimed at getting academic recognition but also as a modest political intervention in the current debates on the "immigration problem." This experience sought to demonstrate that the boundary between "academic" and "participatory action research" can be overcome by situated research questions (Hajdukowski-Ahmed 1998).

Autobiography as a genre has been the subject of several debates. There have been warnings about the risk of considering autobiographical accounts as synonymous with "authentic" lived experience. But as Penny Summerfield notes, "The story that is actually told is always the one preferred amongst other possible versions. . . . Since discourses tend to be multiple, contradictory and fractured, the narrator must also find words for what discourses marginalize or omit" (1998, 17). One of the authors, July, a teenager, did warn me that she was aware of the shortness of her piece and excused herself by saying she had lived in the Nicaraguan countryside and felt ashamed of writing about her rural background. She did not know, being a teenager in San José, how to write about those rural experiences. Her situation makes evident the selectivity of any autobiographical writing, which is always located in and responds to a particular moment in time.

In turn, my reading is also located and selective. I have chosen certain topics and omitted others. Certain aspects have been highlighted and others remain undiscussed. My situated reading is part of the ongoing debate on identities and immigration in Costa Rica. In fact, autobiographical writing produces a particular account of the self but also of a selective and potential addressee that is inscribed in the texts. Morson and Emerson state that "what speaks in us most often is not direct experience or memory but a narrator with an imagined other's values and intonations" (1990, 217). These writings, for instance, contest racialized discourses present in media discourse and everyday interactions. The addressees are frequently described as Costa Rican university students, but there are also inscribed possible Nicaraguan readers. Overall, as Joan Scott maintains, "experience is at once always already an interpretation and is in need of interpretation" (1992, 37).

Guadalupe, a clerical worker and single mother of six who later got a job as a domestic worker in Costa Rica, wrote in the introduction to her autobiography: "I thank you for giving me this opportunity to draw on all this from inside. Since I wrote this, I have not been in pain or grief anymore. I feel that somebody else, after reading this, will sympathize not only with me, but also with all the people who are going to write." Being a writer is a way to overcome grief and loneliness. This overcoming is made possible through writing but also through dialogue with potential addressees. Guadalupe suggests that her piece has an addressee who is not a specific reader but, as Bakhtin (1982, 318–19) points out, a "super addressee," an ideally responsive listener, who can be considered as a third party or space.[9] Personal stories are shared by other people: "Now other people know what we are going through," said some of the workshop participants. Alba, a single mother and primary school teacher who is currently a domestic worker, wrote, "Sorry, I might be going off the topic but let me relieve my pain. I would like to write a book telling the long list of experiences I have lived in this beautiful country. I would like my memories to be published in the newspapers of my country and here too." In other words, the stories make sense not because they are considered symbols of authenticity but because they can circulate within communities. What is at stake is the possibility of constructing a sense of community under severe material and ideological constraints. Writing can be a part of broad processes of collective recognition and empowerment. Autobiographies can be considered a third space of contestation, in which neither authenticity nor racialization can be sustained.

An interesting difference among the authors is illustrated by the ways in which they positioned themselves in order to speak (Hall 1991a, 51). Generally, men seem to locate themselves in a more public arena, addressing their chosen topics in terms of political conflicts rather than by speaking about personal experiences. They usually externalize public concerns to broad audiences. Pánfilo, a driver who traveled from the northern region to attend the workshop at the university—which is in San José, in the center of the country—wrote, "I am going to talk in a simple manner, in the popular language of my people. I am going to describe my experiences here. In order to do so, I need to make an outline of what is going on in Nicaragua. I claim the right to speak about my people because I am one among many." Octavio starts his piece in a similar way: "Although we are in an alien land facing many disadvantages as a consequence of those brothers that have committed undesirable acts, I say to the Nicaraguan brothers that they should not be ashamed of being Nicaraguans."

Women seem to position themselves in a less public and external discourse and cross the public/private divide more frequently. Michelle, a single mother of three who arrived in Costa Rica after crossing the mountains when she was two months' pregnant, considered herself part of a history of suffering people. "We are not perfect but we are good and honorable workers. . . . we can stop eating and bring shelter and clothing to others. Do you know why? Because we suffered war, hunger." Partners and children are often absent from male testimonies, whereas the separation between mothers and children is a painful theme of women's narratives. They usually leave their children in Nicaragua and the grandmothers take care of them. Aleyda remembered that she decided to go back to Nicaragua because she could not bear being separated from her children. Aracely, a single mother, also wrote that she was in tears when she left Nicaragua, since her child had been left "without any milk or shoes." Verónica, who had experienced domestic violence for several years, also wrote about her relation to her children: "I always got paying jobs but I couldn't make ends meet because I earned only fifty dollars [per month] in Nicaragua. . . . They kept saying: 'Mom, I want this, I want that'; and I couldn't give them anything. I was renting a house and sometimes I didn't have money to pay for it. I used to go to bed with my two children in tears, because I had nothing to feed them."

Although feeling guilty about the children is frequent among women, they have become more autonomous since they do not depend on their partners. The sense and composition of the family is also changing. The absent father is a common issue and now the biological mothers are not permanently present, though most telephone their children on weekends. Grandmothers usually take care of the children, as in an extended family. This also illustrates that, for thousands of Nicaraguans, immigration has implied leaving not only a nation but also kinship relations and networks of solidarity. Indeed, many have come to live in a city for the first time. In turn, domestic work and the construction industry have become the main points of entry to the urban world for women and men respectively. Further research might explore the long-term implications of these changes in family patterns.

Ethnic Markers as Sources of Identity

Accent constitutes a marker of cultural difference between Costa Ricans and Nicaraguans. The Costa Rican way of speaking is implicitly considered to be standard Spanish. The Nicaraguan accent is a source of racialization, especially in jokes, and thus has become a source of shame among Nicaraguans. Nereyda, a domestic worker and single mother of three, wrote, "The scorn for our accent, clothing, color, or gestures hurts us deep in our hearts." Leoncia points out a similar concern: "The worst thing is the treatment that [Costa Ricans] give us. It is not fair that they even make fun of our words, our clothing." Elmer also emphasized how accent has became an ethnic marker: "We Nicaraguans that come to Costa Rica for the first time speak with our own accent, as any other foreigner would do, but when we express with emotion what we want to say, Costa Ricans make fun of us. Many times we are rejected for being nicas." Similarly, young Nicaraguans interviewed by Patricia Alvarenga (1997, 19) said they disguised their accent in order to avoid being ashamed.

A lack of "proper" Spanish is interpreted as ignorance. It marks the Nicaraguans as outsiders, as those who do not share the same culture (Gilman 1985, 178). This emphasis on language and accent seems to suggest an identification between race and nation, in such a way that those who do not achieve the standard language do not belong to the nation. Accent as a distinctive ethnic marker might be interpreted through the distinction, suggested by Bakhtin (1981, 270–75), between centripetal and centrifugal forces present in language. While the former call for boundaries, order, and control, the latter produce heteroglossia. Centripetal forces play a key role in the configuration of national belonging since they "serve to unify and centralize the verbal-ideological world." However, Bakhtin notes, "alongside verbal-ideological centralization and unification, the uninterrupted processes of decentralization and disunification go forward" (272). Language, Bakhtin stresses, is languages. "Every concrete utterance of a speaking subject serves as a point where centrifugal as well as centripetal forces are brought to bear" (ibid.). The more "alien" people are to "standard" Spanish—which, implicitly, is the Spanish spoken in the Costa Rican Central Valley—the less they belong to the nation. Interestingly, accent is also deployed to make distinctions among Costa Ricans. Peasants are considered bad Spanish speakers, as are the people who live, for example, on the Pacific and Atlantic coasts (see chapter 3). Hence, centrifugal and centripetal forces make distinctions about language that are used to establish geographic boundaries. Centrifugal forces draw concentric rings around the nation's center in such a way that these disputes do not take place outside the material world. As Morson and Emerson note, "Language is not an autonomous or semiautonomous whole that comes to interact with extralinguistic forces. Rather extralinguistic forces are constitutive of language and its history" (1990, 170).

But Nereyda and Leoncia did not only mention accent; they noted clothing, gestures, and color as other distinctive ethnic markers. Verbal and nonverbal languages come into play together. Taste, Bourdieu argues, is a unitary set of distinctive preferences present in clothing, language, or body habitus. Such preferences avoid being selected and instead appear as "logical" and "natural" (Bourdieu 1986; 1993, 64, 79). Aracely interpreted these associations in terms of class exclusion: "Here in Costa Rica, if one doesn't have references, one is lost. There are people who discriminate a lot on the basis of class. They divide people into three groups: lower, middle, and upper classes. According to them, the lower classes are considered uneducated and brutish people—polos—which means they dress badly and don't know how to speak, but it isn't true."

These ethnic markers highlighted by Aracely are present in everyday practices. For example, the Costa Rican police have checkpoints along routes located close to the Nicaraguan border. Buses are stopped in order to verify the passengers' passports or other official documentation; however, policemen do not inspect all of them. Instead, they choose those passengers whose dark skin and dress are associated with Nicaraguans, illustrating the extent to which implicit assumptions of who is Nicaraguan have been internalized and how these signifiers are institutionalized in police work.

In this context, the emphasis in Bourdieu's writings on the epistemological rupture between common sense and scientific knowledge—an insight of Gaston Bachelard's, also present in Louis Althusser's books—demands some caution: Nereyda, Leoncia, and Aracely show us that common sense is "ordinary" but by no means always a simplified understanding of everyday life. They were able to recognize the close internal relations among diverse ethnic markers. Aracely in particular links their racialization with class divisions. She suggests that certain stigmas are applied both to Nicaraguans and to Costa Ricans, not as a consequence of their nationality but because "they dress badly and don't know how to speak." They are considered polos, a social category discussed in chapter 3. Thus representations like nicas or polos articulate class and race divisions, confirming that what makes national identities powerful is precisely that other identities are inscribed (or suppressed) in a sense of nationhood without overt recognition.

From Maids to Prostitutes

Racialized discourses have also represented Nicaraguan women as prostitutes. Leoncia recalled that "some time ago, it was said in a newspaper that 60 percent or 80 percent of the prostitutes in this country [Costa Rica] were nicas, but it is not true." She continued: "The only thing that they [Costa Ricans] don't make fun of and view with hypocrisy is our labor force, because we are efficient and do any job except prostitution or theft." The association of Nicaraguan women with prostitution is widespread. In a conference regarding the situation of the Nicaraguan community in Costa Rica, the then vice minister of state, Carlos Castro, argued that a large number of Nicaraguan female children were involved in child prostitution. Other Nicaraguan women were single parents without an established family, the vice minister claimed (Castro, comm. to Foro de Población Migrante, 1999). Interestingly, no data supporting such statements were provided.

This articulation of sexualized and racialized images is present in everyday life, often through jokes such as the following:

> There are three men in a brothel in San José: one Chinese, one Costa Rican, and the third Nicaraguan.
>
> What are they doing there?
>
> The Chinese owns the business, the Costa Rican is a client, and the Nicaraguan is waiting for his wife.

This link between Nicaraguan women and prostitution is worked out through class and national identifications. Nicaraguan women are situated and historical others; they are poor and outsiders. "The sexuality attributed to the proletarian is the sexuality and libertinage of the Other," as Gilman has noted (1985, 48, 53). Conversely, those who tell the joke do not belong to the same social class as the Nicaraguan women portrayed as prostitutes. Nor do they share the same nationality.

This transcoding of Nicaraguan women into sexualized representations might be related to their jobs as domestic workers. Maids, argue Stallybrass and White (1986, 152), represent a boundary between "respectable" society and the "nether" slum. However, they commonly perform "intimate functions" among bourgeois families, not only in Europe, but also in Latin America. Thus, male desires for "low" women emerge in the context of relationships with maids as, for example, the writings of Sigmund Freud and Walter Benjamin seem to suggest. Maids represent a boundary between the high and the low, the public and the private, but at the same time they personify the possibility of transgressing such boundaries. The socially proscribed returns in the form of psychic desire, White and Stallybrass insist (167). It also shows, as McClintock notes, that "gender is not a separate dimension of identity to which one adds, accumulatively, the dimension of class. Rather, gender is an articulated category, constructed through and by class" (1995, 94). This representation about prostitutes also highlights ways in which images of the nation, frequently related to the public sphere, connect with the private and the "cult of domesticity" (5).[10]

Domestic work has been historically one of the most excluded jobs. Interestingly, the Constitutional Court refused an appeal that asked for its inclusion in the current labor legislation. The court argued that domestic work has an "exceptional character" and, in consequence, is still regulated by a special legislation. During 1999 and 2000, domestic workers campaigned in the parliament for change. However, they have received little support. A member of the parliament (1998–2002), Rina Contreras, claimed that in exchange for long workdays, domestic workers receive salaries in kind, such as meals (*LN* 2/1/00). This justifies, according to her, the fact that domestic work is regulated by a specific rule and not according to the labor law.

"Why Are We a Burden? Help Me Find an Answer, Please"

Workshop participants asked why they are represented as a burden if they make a substantial contribution to the Costa Rican economy. Vicente notes: "If there were a law expelling all the foreigners from the country, I assure you that the Costa Rican economy would collapse." Elmer argues, "Many Costa Ricans say that we are a burden, but the things we are doing for the benefit of this country are not recognized." The paradox of being badly paid but at the same time considered a burden engenders anger and undermines self-esteem. There is an internalization of social exclusion that has been scarcely recognized. Leoncia points out:

> Another outrage is that [Costa Rican] President Rodríguez, with the respect that he deserves, is asking for help from the U.S. government because, he says, it is impossible to sustain us.[11] It is, dear friend, shameful. These politicians are corrupt. If the tragedy of Hurricane Mitch hadn't taken place, there wouldn't have been any amnesty [see chapter 5]. It is all business and those who get the worst part of it are the poor, because if there were no dead and wounded people, tears, and pain, there would be no amnesty. My poor people, we have suffered earthquakes, heavy seas, wars, hurricanes, drought, and the worst, bad governments, and here [we find] outrage and violence. But nobody cares nor listens. Nobody is condemned; there are just people who are exploited. You can't imagine how sad it is being far from your children and husband, as in my case.

Being Nicaraguan has become an offense in and of itself, and the autobiographies provide evidence of how such racialized discourses have addressed the Nicaraguan community. Lissette notes, "When we say something or it is simply recognized that we are Nicaraguans, immediately they humiliate us; they tell us that we are thieves, that because of our nationality we are bad people." It is not only that they are badly paid—the most common concern among liberal critics—one might say that there is also an economy of subjectivity that has not even been discussed, since being repeatedly considered a burden and garbage does leave scars. Aleyda, for instance, writes that she was falling into depression. However, working-class subjectivity has been generally absent from psychoanalysis and other perspectives interested in subject formation, as Carolyn Steedman (1986) has stressed. The concept of the self, for instance, has not been explicitly related to particular social groups but seems to refer to middle and upper classes. With respect to the anxieties caused by modern society, the institutional support offered by various sorts of secular counseling such as psychotherapy or psychoanalysis has been separated, at least in Latin America, from the "ordinary people." Indeed, members of the working class do not normally employ words such as *depression* in their everyday conversations. Nonetheless this devaluation of their economic contribution has been contested by their own recognition of their everyday efforts. Vicente pointed out a similar concern: "For Costa Ricans we are like strange animals without any access to the privileges of this country; they discriminate against us, they humiliate us, we are treated very badly because they don't recognize that the economy of this country has improved enormously with the nica labor force."

Elí, who left Nicaragua in the 1980s as a consequence of compulsory military service, remembered that some time ago, one of his children had asked him, "Daddy, do I have Nicaraguan blood?" "Yes," answered Elí. "So how can I get rid of it?" replied his son. His question, which arose in the context of arguments with other children, suggests a mode of address organized around an extreme version of biological racism: Nicaraguan blood is a bearer of a nationality that he does not want to claim. This case also indicates that for children the negotiation of their identity presents different challenges since they are growing up in Costa Rica but sometimes face hostile relations with their peers. Meanwhile, their attachment to Nicaragua is not so strong, since they have spent most of their life in Costa Rica.

Graffiti has become a common cultural form through which racialized discourses are expressed. For example, Nicas Are Garbage (*nicas basura*)—sometimes accompanied by a Nazi swastika—has been written in several public spaces on the east side of San José. This association of Nicaraguans with garbage has two implications. First, it identifies Nicaraguans with filth, as opposed to the purity that would characterize Costa Ricans; second, it locates Nicaraguans spatially as the lowest. Both meanings contribute to configuring control and limits. Nicaraguans belong to the nation neither hygienically nor spatially. Garbage, as several scholars have noted, transgresses social boundaries and lies beyond cleanliness (Douglas 1966, 36; Stallybrass and White 1986, 127; McClintock 1995, 152–53). Being repeatedly considered a burden, garbage, and strange animals has resulted in an accumulating anger and impatience for an opportunity to protest. Aracely highlighted this point:

> Our life is not easy in Costa Rica. Sometimes, when we travel by bus, we hear people criticizing us, calling us: bastards, sons of bitches, people dying of starvation [*muertos de hambre*], and rascals. They express themselves in a vulgar and hostile way. Some of us get angry and face up to them. It affects us because, although we come here with no visa, we are helping to build up this country, doing those jobs that Costa Ricans don't like to do.

Aleyda and Lissette recalled their nonstop jobs as domestic workers. Lissette stated:

> I have experienced very shameful and painful experiences as a domestic worker. They [Costa Ricans] consider the domestic worker a slave, without values and feelings. For them we are less than a human being: without opportunities, with schedules from 5:30 A.M. to 9 or 10 P.M. Our bosses never value our work, which I think is very important because it allows them to be successful in their jobs since their children are well cared-for.

Many domestic workers live in the house in which they work, thus sharing a very private space but at the same time feeling like outsiders (Chaney and García 1993, 14). "I used to feel lonely," Aracely wrote, "among people who saw me as a thing without value; the lady didn't like me sitting in the armchairs in her hall. I suppose that for some in the Costa Rican upper class, we, the nicas, are the garbage in their right eye. It is sad for us." Living in another person's house reminds her that she does not have one of her own. Meanwhile, La Merced, a park in downtown San José, has become a common place for Nicaraguans to meet. Especially on weekends, small groups, integrated most of the time by newcomers, talk and exchange information. The park gives them a sense of collective identity and seems to overcome the loneliness that Aracely mentions. The park they have chosen is significant since it was formerly known as the drunks' park, a space in which marginalized people used to stay during the daytime. The "drunks" left it when the park was refurbished in the early 1990s. Among Costa Ricans it is now sarcastically called Managua, and there have been periods in which it has been intensively policed. However, Nicaraguans have remained there. It is one of the few public spaces in which they feel like citizens. Some of them like being photographed in the park, and through these photos La Merced is perceived in Nicaragua as an icon of all those complex displacements that have taken place in Central America during recent decades. La Merced might be interpreted as a form of reterritorialization of their identities after having left Nicaragua. Furthermore, their presence in the park would not be understandable without taking into consideration that downtown San José is not the ideal site for shopping or leisure for the middle classes. With the boom of malls, exclusive consumption is now located in suburban areas, and in a certain way the center has become periphery; abandoned spaces are now occupied by less prosperous consumers.

Contestation Is Not a Matter of Discourse Alone

Contestation under situations of extreme social inequality is especially difficult. When jobs are at stake and there are not many alternatives, protest goes beyond the simplistic dichotomy of reproduction/resistance. Contestation does not take place in a discursively sealed vacuum; it is located in contexts in which the possibility of response is minimal, such as workplaces or while one is listening to a radio program. Nicaraguans in Costa Rica sometimes seek to move beyond the reproduction-resistance dichotomy circle, but after hours and hours working at a construction site, in a factory, or as a domestic, it is a major challenge (Sandoval 1997).

The undermining of trade unions—on banana plantations and in other activities within the private sector in Costa Rica—is an important reason for the absence of collective action. The defeat of strikes on banana plantations in 1985 and 1994, for example, left the workers without major possibilities of institutional representation (Sandoval 1985a; SITAGAH/CODEHU 1994). Hence, multiple injustices take place without major notice. Vicente wrote that he and his coworkers were discharged from their jobs because the contractor did not want to pay their Christmas bonus, which in Costa Rica is equivalent to a month's salary. The boss argued that the immigration authorities were looking for "illegal immigrants," and since the workers did not have official visas they would be expelled from the country. They left their jobs and received nothing.

Sweet bananas are frequently nurtured with bitter tears. Tobías described one of the most painful injustices. There were nearly two hundred workers, most of them Nicaraguans, on a banana plantation in the Atlantic region of Costa Rica. Although in agriculture salaries are normally paid weekly or twice a month, the contractor told them that they would be paid at the end of the month. After the first month, he did not pay but assured them that the following month he would pay the accumulated salaries. They received no pay for six months. They protested, but he escaped to Honduras, where banana plantations are also an important economic activity. The workers decided to remain in the *baches,* small rooms that banana companies offer to single male workers. They went on strike and the Immigration Police were sent in to remove them, yet they resisted. Then the plantation owners decided to surround the baches with mounds of putrefying bananas; the unbearable smell forced the workers to abandon the plantations. Finally the local Catholic church offered them shelter for a few weeks.

Nicaraguan women in domestic work have experienced similar hard times. Guadalupe narrated a conflict with her employer, a "learned" and "feminist" woman: "I told her that although she was my employer and the mistress of the house, she had no right to humiliate me. Before I was a maid, I told her, I was a human being with the same feelings and rights [as she had]." This and other cases illustrate how class divisions preempted possible gender alliances and how even feminist and "learned" women became hard-line employers. Leoncia wrote that she had spent an entire day washing tennis shoes and denim trousers in a middle-class house. In the afternoon, she felt really hungry since she had not had any breakfast or lunch. The final straw came when the lady of the house asked Leoncia to clean the toilet but would not allow her to use gloves:

> I couldn't take it anymore. . . . I locked myself in the bathroom. I took the bleach and the soap and spread them all over the place. Then I sat on the toilet, waiting for time to pass. Later I came out, closed the door, and told the lady that I had finished. . . . Carlos,[12] I can't stop myself from crying as I write all this because I don't understand why there is so much indifference, when in God's eyes we all are equal. My heart burns with pain when I think of the millions of people who will starve to death today, tomorrow, and always.

Aracely made a similar comment:

> If Jesus always told the truth and always defended himself, why shouldn't I do the same? Why shouldn't I defend my rights here and anywhere? . . . I wonder why they [Costa Ricans] humiliate us if before God's eyes we are all brothers and sisters. We are one family. I believe that racism and social divisions should not exist, but unfortunately they exist here. There are also a few nice people though, like those from the house in which I am working now.

As Guadalupe, Leoncia, and Aracely made explicit, their contestation is based on religious notions of justice and human rights. These critiques might be grounded in experiences and practices within the popular church in Nicaragua. Beyond differences attributed to nationalities, there must be common human rights, they insist. As Stephanie Linkogle (1996, 229–30) notes, values like solidarity and equality became critical common sense through discourses and practices underpinned by the popular church. Religion does not mean waiting for recognition until after death.[13]

The testimonials and debates held during the workshop also addressed the racialized discourses published by the media. Interestingly, the media were not suggested as a possible topic when the participants were invited to send their testimonials. However, some participants offered criticisms that give an idea of the weight of media discourses among the Nicaraguan community. Vicente, for example, wrote: "Here in Costa Rica there are nice people as well as unscrupulous monsters. In any part of the world there are bad and good people. It is inevitable. But here, if a nica makes a mistake, there is not enough space for the scandal in the newspapers' pages. But if a Costa Rican gang robs a bank or murders or rapes (or both), it is not that serious in the eyes of the news."

Similar comments were made about radio programs in which Nicaraguans are depicted as a burden to Costa Rican society. Some of the participants in the workshop did not understand why some commentators are so hostile toward Nicaraguans. Gary, a father employed in commercial activities, noted in the workshop: "I do listen to such programs—not because I like them but because I want to know what they say. One would like to contest such comments but it is difficult." Gary knows that such images about Nicaraguans are not fair but he cannot make his disagreements public, highlighting the complexity of "resistance" and "contestation." Racialized discourses are read and interpreted in an "oppositional way" (Hall 1980a, 138); however, there is a complex institutional and political gap between an oppositional reading of received messages and the real possibilities of contestation. The former does not guarantee the latter.

Michelle made this point explicit: "What we do here is not for leisure but out of necessity, not because we like being humiliated and being considered strange and ignorant animals. . . . we keep quiet, avoid saying what we feel, but it is only out of necessity." The absence of collective ways of resistance and contestation is a crucial element. That absence makes contestation highly unequal because it must be addressed to corporate media, to which they have no access. When Nicaraguans appear in the media, generally they are represented as a crowd, as objects of debate, but not as subjects of their own enunciation. Pánfilo argued during the workshop that Nicaraguans have to get organized: "What's going to happen after this meeting?" Diverse critiques have noted that an "active response" to media discourses has sometimes been considered "resistance" (Gray 1997, 96; Morley 1997, 121). However, there has been less attention regarding the links between oppositional readings and the possibilities of collective contestation. These missing links reveal the complexities of challenging racialized representations beyond academic circles.

Instead, Nicaraguans locate their resistance more in communal sites, where they share, as Gilroy (1987, 234) noted in British black communities, particular sets of values and norms in everyday life such as mutuality, cooperation, and identification. They have forged networks of solidarity beyond national boundaries. Racialization comes out in the context of class relations and not just as a nationalist antagonism—for example, when those who perpetrate racism are employers. Costa Rican and Nicaraguan families offer their humble houses to newcomers, even where there are no kinship relations. Alba reported that a Costa Rican family warmly received her and her little daughter in a small house that is shared by seventeen people. In contrast, she was teaching the daughter of the former Nicaraguan ambassador in Costa Rica and he did not show any interest in her case.

At the institutional level, important efforts have been undertaken by the Asociación de Trabajadoras Domésticas (ASTRADOMES; Domestic workers association), a grassroots organization that offers support and advice to domestic workers. ASTRADOMES established a hostel that provides shelter to domestic workers who have been discharged from their jobs. The Catholic Church and other ecumenical groups are carrying out other important efforts. Relating these communal experiences to media projects might be a crucial step. In this sense, new radio programs addressing the Nicaraguan community began transmission in 1999. They might constitute very important forums for debates about immigration and identities. Other media projects are also being considered. How greatly commercial pressures will allow critical and creative broadcasting to flourish is another unexplored question. Meanwhile, Aracely dreams of establishing a *comedor infantil* (children's canteen) in which children of her neighborhood in Nicaragua can have their meals, and Leoncia would like her children to inherit a better future, free from injustice, in which they realize their dreams.

Learning to Listen?

In recent years, some nongovernmental organizations (NGOs) have emphasized the economic contribution of the Nicaraguan community in Costa Rica as a way of changing public opinion about immigration issues. However, racialized politics have not been transformed drastically. These important efforts seem to have two weak sides. First, the emphasis on the economic contribution made by the Nicaraguan community is at risk of becoming part of an instrumental rationality based on utilitarian criteria: since they undertake undesirable jobs, they must be appreciated. Interestingly, this instrumental account is also present among students, as discussed above.

Second, there is no lineal relationship between being exposed to "positive" images of immigrants and any change in attitude toward them. Racism does not work exclusively on a rational basis. It is, rather, a projection of internal fears and desires onto outsiders (see chapter 1). Hence any attempt at change has to address the historical sources of such feelings. Rather than an attempt to give voice to the voiceless—a common promise in Latin America—these testimonials endeavor to enact ways of listening. Nicaraguans—as well as women, blacks, and peasants—have always had a voice. Listening, perhaps the most complex dimension of communication, is what is often missing. For instance, Michelle says that when someone humiliates her, she looks firmly at the person's face in such a way that she or he is the one who is ashamed.

However, the current situation is not always the most promising one, as can be illustrated by the responses of some NGOs toward these testimonials. The Foro Emaús (Emaús forum), constituted by diverse NGOs and ecumenical organizations, showed an initial interest in the possibility of publishing these. The NGO El Productor, a member of the Foro that was going to offer financial support for the initiative, examined the material concluding that some testimonials provided "exaggerated" accounts of discrimination and were in turn an example of Nicaraguan xenophobia toward Costa Ricans. The assessment made by El Productor meant that the Foro lost interest in any publishing initiative. This decision was resisted by ASTRADOMES, which considered that despite disagreements with some testimonials, the whole document had to be published because "the autobiographies cannot be ignored," as Rosita Acuña, leader of ASTRADOMES, pointed out (interview, 12/12/99). This illustrates how social control works in Costa Rican political culture: since there were disagreements regarding the testimonials, the decision was to prevent the publication of the document. Rather than inviting public debate about the representation of nationhood, the decision was to prevent any dialogue. In short, differences of opinion regarding key issues seem to be unspeakable, even among NGOs, which are supposed to represent liberal and critical views.

Top-down analyses, commonly employed in research on national identities, usually focus on a single cultural form, especially literature or media representations, but it is necessary to look at how different cultural forms are appropriated in everyday life, where "everyday genres" play an important role in the representation of nationhood. Throughout this project, the analysis of autobiographies has provided important methodological insights. While they were used in the last chapter as a way of exploring contestation of historical representations of nationhood, in this chapter they have illustrated how hegemonic views on current issues are also an object of dispute. In both cases they were an important resource for the understanding of both public and more personal versions of nationhood.

Liberal commentators and NGOs have raised concerns about discrimination against Nicaraguans. A further step might be to consider discriminatory practices as part of broader processes of national identity formation that have historically excluded indigenous people, peasants, blacks, and other undesired "immigrants." This step forward would also challenge recent "immigration studies," whose focus is either on the "integration" of Nicaraguans into Costa Rican society or on employment patterns. Although *integration* is not defined, it seems to indicate that Costa Rica is an already constituted nation where "immigrants" have to find their own place. In other words, the situation of Nicaraguans in Costa Rica could be an exceptional opportunity to address the sense, commonly taken for granted, of Costa Ricanness.

Chapter 5

Material Decline, Dislocation, and Racialization

Racialization is not only a discursive phenomenon; it is, rather, linked to material factors, though such relations cannot be formulated in deterministic terms. Although the constitution of the Nicaraguan other has been a long-term process, the last two decades of the twentieth century have witnessed an increase in the ways in which nationhood in Costa Rica has been represented by reference to the Nicaraguan community. Two main factors seem to be at work in the stigmatization of Nicaraguans in Costa Rica. First, there has been a political transition from cold war ideologies, in which the main opposition was the former Sandinista government, to a racialized politics through which the Nicaraguan community as a whole is usually stigmatized. This regional political change occurred after the defeat of the FSLN in the 1990 general elections and coincided with the bankruptcy of the political regimes in Eastern Europe. The second factor is the decline in public investment, especially in health, housing, and education. The public investment in 1997, for instance, did not reach the amount provided in 1980, in a context characterized by chronic tax evasion. It has meant a decline in public services such as housing, health, and education.

Being middle-class—a key way of belonging to the Central American "electoral democracy"—is becoming harder and harder. The most prosperous groups manage to avoid this decline by means of a continuous privatization of their everyday life: selective neighborhoods policed by Nicaraguan guards, private education, exclusive consumption, and exotic vacations far away from the "masses." Overall, being a citizen both in terms of living conditions and political participation is becoming highly restricted, and it is difficult for a broad segment of the population to come to terms with these structural transformations of the nation. Thus the material basis of a nation, which considers itself to be unique, is being undermined and this decline gives rise to anxieties, especially among the less prosperous social groups, which in turn are projected onto the Nicaraguan community.

This undermining of institutional and material infrastructure has been accompanied by processes of secularization and modernization that have altered the patriarchal foundations of a traditional society. The public recognition of domestic violence, among other factors, has also aroused uncertainties and anxieties. Nations are usually judged by their public domains, but in this context what undermines the motherland seems to be the subversion of private matters. "Costa Rica is not the same anymore" is perhaps one of the most common expressions that sum up this sense of distrust. There is a crisis that can be solved only by returning to tradition and family values.

How Did the Communist Nicaraguans become Nicas?

The war of liberation against the Somozas' dictatorship won significant support in Costa Rica. Former president Rodrigo Carazo (1978–82) publicly recognized his government's backing of the insurrectionist struggle, and according to a survey about 55 percent of the population supported his decision (Umaña 1989, 57–58). However, the economic crisis experienced by Costa Rica, as well as the escalation of U.S. intervention in Nicaragua, transformed relations between the two countries. During the 1980s the Sandinista government was represented as a communist threat by both the media and the political elite in Costa Rica.

The decline of coffee prices in the international markets and the increase in oil values toward the end of the 1970s created a critical economic situation in Costa Rica. At the beginning of the 1980s the GDP decreased by about 5 percent and the national currency was devalued approximately

450 percent (Umaña 1989, 119). Agreements with the U.S. Agency for International Development (USAID) played a key role in the processes of economic stabilization and further initiatives toward privatization. Between 1983 and 1989, USAID transferred $592 million to the Costa Rican government, the equivalent of 10 percent of the GDP (Edelman and Monge, in Raventós 1997, 117). The former U.S. ambassador stated that between 1983 and 1986 the U.S. government's transfers to Costa Rica totaled about $813 million (in Sojo 1991, 240). Meanwhile, the Reagan administration restricted U.S. sugar imports from Nicaragua by 90 percent as part of a major attempt at economic strangulation (Sojo 1991, 208) and supported military counterrevolutionary groups (the so-called Contras) that organized their attacks from Honduras and Costa Rica.

The administration of President Luis Alberto Monge (1982–86) declared the neutrality of Costa Rica in the regional conflicts in 1980. However, the economic compromises reached with USAID meant that these claims were hardly feasible. Indeed, hostility became a permanent feature of relations with the Nicaraguan government. Costa Rican authorities maintained that the Sandinista army was fighting the Contras within Costa Rican territory. Although the Costa Rican foreign minister did accept that the Contras were launching their attacks from Costa Rica, he argued that it was impossible to control them (*LPL* 2/29/84, in Umaña 1989). The media played a crucial role in the framing of these hostilities. In 1981, *La Nación* introduced a Central American edition that addressed current issues from a confrontational perspective. Additionally, *Nicaragua hoy* (Nicaragua today), a weekly supplement published by the Contras, was included in the regular editions of *La Nación* (Umaña 1989, 81, 93).[1]

The communism-democracy opposition became part of everyday life through the demonization of the popular church in Nicaragua. Certain priests who held posts in the Sandinista government were made icons of a threat to the Catholic Church, the hierarchy of which, in Costa Rica and Nicaragua, has been traditionally aligned with conservative politics. The effectiveness of these images also remained fixed in the ways in which nation and gender were meshed. The Sandinista government was depicted as a rapist of the nation's territory. Key signifiers such as *penetration, violation,* and *military harassment* became crucial tools in the war of words. Politics was transcoded into subjectivity through metaphors associated with the body and sexuality.

This period saw the emergence of a number of important right-wing groups. Among those that achieved high public visibility were the Asociación Democrática Huetar Norte (North Huetar democratic association), located in the border region between Costa Rica and Nicaragua, and Alerta (Alert), which was among the most active groups and—significantly—made up of women, most of them descendants of prominent politicians. Also worth mentioning are the Comité Cívico Pro-Defensa de la Dignidad Nacional (Civic committee for the defense of national dignity), Asociación Democrática Costarricense (Costa Rican democratic association), Juventud Democrática Costarricense (Costa Rican democratic youth), Instituto Costarricense del Sector Empresarial (Costa Rican institute of the private sector), and the Unión Solidarista (Solidarity union). What these groups had in common was an all-out anticommunism that recalled similar views held by El Movimiento Costa Rica Libre (MCRL), the most consolidated far-right-wing group in Costa Rica since the 1960s.[2] The group's slogan was, I Love Costa Rica: Fight Communism. But while the MCRL maintained high public visibility through the media (publishing a weekly page in *La Nación* for many years) and included two paramilitary groups, these new right-wing organizations were less permanent and had the advantage of not being considered a part of the far right; they defined themselves as patriotic.

The presence of these groups meant an increasing political polarization characterized by a sharp hostility toward the Nicaraguan government, which became a daily war of words. The MCRL even envisaged the possibility of a military offensive against the Nicaraguan government. In 1983, remembering the War of 1856 (see chapter 3), they argued, "This country has to demonstrate to those who do not believe in freedom that, as in 1856, we are ready to offer our blood for the defense of peace and democracy and against the aggression of a gang of mercenaries that is today usurping power in Nicaragua" (in León and Ovares 1983, 62).

They believed that the Costa Rican government held a weak position in relation to what they regarded as the "Sandinista threat." Some of these voices were even represented within the Monge administration. In regard to the proposal for neutrality the former vice-minister of state, Enrique Chacón, argued, "I do not believe that each person in Costa Rica has to be neutral. . . . It is cowardice. You are either a democrat or a communist" (*LN* 5/13/84).[3] Liberal and leftist groups contested this far-right politics.

In 1984 trade unions, universities, and other progressive groups organized an important demonstration by calling for peace and negotiation. This was a clear expression of disapproval of the government's support for the Contras and U.S. foreign policy in Central America.

An important arena of confrontation took place in the northern region of Costa Rica, close to the border with Nicaragua. In 1983, for example, a radio station, known as Radio Costa Rica, was installed in the region on the initiative of President Monge, who asked President Reagan for support in order to "rescue the broadcasting [Costa Rica's] sovereignty" in the region. Officially, the radio was an initiative of the Asociación Costarricense de Información y Cultura (Costa Rican association for communication and culture), since Costa Rican legislation does not allow foreigners to own broadcasting media—although 60 percent of the programming of Radio Costa Rica was provided by the Voice of America (Sandoval 1985c, 14–15). Despite the diverse social organizations that considered the installation of Radio Costa Rica an intervention of the Costa Rican government in the conflict between the Reagan administration and the Nicaraguan state, the station continued broadcasting until the end of the Sandinista period. The station's transmission facilities were patrolled by members of the Asociación Democrática Huetar Norte, one of the most active right-wing organizations in the border region between Costa Rica and Nicaragua. It began activities in 1982, claiming to stop the violation of territory by the Sandinistas and supporting the Contra groups that were fighting the Costa Rican government, often from within Costa Rica itself (Sandoval 1985b, 10).

These political and military activities in Costa Rica's northern region achieved international prominence when journalists and members of a Contra group known as the Alianza Revolucionaria Democrática (ARDE; Democratic revolutionary alliance), headed by Edén Pastora, were attacked during a press conference held in May 1984 in the community of Pocosol. Three media staff were killed and eighteen were wounded. What was supposed to have been an unnoticed event received extraordinary coverage since the victims were journalists of diverse political persuasions. The initial version claimed that the attack was planned by the Sandinistas against Pastora, but later it was revealed that the attack had been organized by the CIA with the object of killing Pastora, since he refused to join the Frente Democrático Nicaragüense, the most far right faction of the Contra groups, based in Honduras (Avirgan and Honey 1985, 1989). Further investigation made clear that this event was connected with the Iran-Contra scandal, in which the U.S. government sold weapons to Iran and used the profits to support the Contras' activities in Nicaragua. One of the "local" connections between the CIA's "global" operations in Central America at that period was John Hull, who began to be mentioned in the early 1980s as the key link between groups such as the Asociación Huetar Norte and the Contra organizations (Sandoval 1985b, 9; Avirgan and Honey 1989).

Other right-wing groups were focused on political work, emphasizing the threats posed by the Sandinista government, which was labeled a satellite of the Cuban and Soviet regimes. Foreign policy and media discourse were the principal objects of inquiry about this period by academic research (Umaña 1989; Sojo 1991). No attention has been paid to those "civic groups" that insisted that a stronger stance should be taken by the Costa Rican government against the "Nicaraguan threat" (Sandoval 1985b). It is particularly important in this context to look at the formation of Alerta. At that time, most of its members were over sixty years old, and although they had belonged to different political parties, anticommunism played a powerful role in mobilizing them into political action. They used to meet in different social activities and collected a small budget that allowed them to publish frequent propaganda in the newspapers. Their slogan, Where Are the Costa Rican Trousers? addressed men's lack of interest in the defense of the nation.

Alerta organized mobilizations at the Ministry of Foreign Affairs that protested the "weak" political response of the Costa Rican government to the Sandinista "invasions." They also organized a rally in the center of San José, calling for the sacking of the former security minister, who had maintained a moderate attitude in conflicts with the Nicaraguan government. The interviews, almost two decades later, with three former members of the group showed how they had thought of the memories of their political participation within new contexts.[4] Although such interviews took place individually, each participant interpreted his or her participation as part of a patriotic legacy from distinguished ancestors. Being descendants of politicians enabled participants to defend the nation even beyond ideological differences. Their fathers and other relatives played important roles in key political processes, such as the War of 1856 against the filibusters, the Tinoco dictatorship (1917–19), and the civil war of

1948. Through these genealogies of patriotism, they made links between origins, national belonging, and destiny in a critical period. One insisted, "Forging the nation is my obsession" and "I am a fanatic of the motherland." The connection between family and nation is so close that the latter is naturalized. Another maintained that "the motherland is acquired by means of breeding; it becomes part of your blood." These women became responsible for the nation's future.

They learned how to respect the nation at the dinner table, connecting manners and political attitudes. "Love of the nation is learned in the family. . . . whoever respects his or her own home, respects the constitution and the law," stated one. Respectability was also associated with tradition and authority. Another remembered that her grandfather used to read a manual of good manners at the dinner table. In other words, the internalization of authority arose not only in public institutions but also in forms of private socialization where the most crucial links between representations and subjectivities are produced. As Elias (1982) has shown, the history of manners has an enormous importance in the ways in which the body is socialized. Social hierarchies and topographical rules are internalized through manners (Stallybrass and White 1986, 93). Respect for family values is translated into respect for the motherland. Under these forms of sociability, defending the nation was interpreted as defending a patriarchal order internalized at home. The nation was seen as an enlarged family, showing that the sense of belonging is constructed by reference to the authority of the father.

Meanwhile, the defeat of the Sandinistas in the general election of 1990 as well as political changes in Eastern Europe left undermined the communism-democracy opposition as a key political identification. Cold war hostility has been generally replaced by a racialized politics in Central America and elsewhere (Gabriel 1994, 181). In 1989 graffiti in a men's restroom at the University of Costa Rica read, "Sandinistas, Get Out"; "Communists, Get Out"; "Russians, Get Out" (in Araujo 1991, 171), ten years later the targets have shifted: "Nicas, Get Out" is frequently written in some areas of San José. With nicas no political adjectives are required or, to put it another way, *nica,* a racialized representation, has been politicized and become part of everyday life.

While Nicaraguans call themselves nicas, as a collective identity, Costa Rican newspapers and the Costa Rican people use the term every day in such a way that the Nicaraguans' national identity itself becomes a stigma. The word *nica* works through different ethnic markers, denoting dark-skinned, poor, violent people who do not speak "standard" Spanish, just to mention a few characteristics. Ethnic markers associated with the other are also used to characterize Costa Ricans as "white," middle-class, peaceful people. *Nica* is an arena of social struggle over the power of representing the "other." It illustrates how a word is inhabited by past and present voices under asymmetrical power relations. An important dimension of any utterance is intonation, which according to Michael Holquist is "a kind of portrait in sound of the addressee to whom the speaker imagines he or she is speaking" (1990, 61). In this particular context, the intonation imparted by the speaker in *nica* bespeaks a hierarchical relationship in which the addressee is at the bottom. Bakhtin observes,

> When we seek to understand a word what matters is not the direct meaning the word gives to objects and emotions—this is the false front of the word; what matters is rather the actual and always self interested *use* to which this meaning is put and the way it is expressed by the speaker, a use determined by the speaker's position (profession, social class, etc.) and the concrete situation. Who speaks and under what conditions he speaks: this is what determines the word's actual meaning. (1990, 20; emphasis in original)

Still, it is necessary to specify that not all Nicaraguans are nicas. Despite a generalized stigma against Nicaraguans, a more careful analysis reveals that both men and women have a clear class inscription; they are poor and dark-skinned people. Nicaraguan businessmen (businesswomen are not frequent) or members of the middle class do not seem to have been racialized by the media. Similarly, Sergio Ramírez, a well-known Nicaraguan writer, was depicted as a "universal Nicaraguan." While he is frequently interviewed in the cultural sections of newspapers, the poor are generally to be found in crime news. The former, one could say, is a Nicaraguan; the latter are nicas. An investor or an intellectual is presented as an individual, whereas the nicas appear as an anomic collective, a wave; they are undifferentiated, they have neither name nor personality.[5] This opposition between the "learned Nicaraguan" and the plebeian nica is not a new one. Almost one hundred years ago the same distinction was made between Rubén Darío and the Nicaraguan other (see chapter 3). In a similar way, Europeans or North Americans who visit Costa Rica are not considered foreigners or outsiders; on the contrary, they are called tourists. In other words, a foreigner is not always an impoverished outsider. This point has theoretical implications: subject positions are not chosen freely; Nicaraguans in Costa Rica are not free to choose their identity. Any configuration is historical and these processes of racialization and exclusion are grounded in long-term class inequalities (Bradley 1996, 212). The so-called death of the social and the subject do not obliterate class inequalities, either as materiality or as representation.

Conversely, Costa Ricans suspected of having committed irregular acts are not defined overtly by their nationality. Ethnic distinctions seem frequently to be linked to outsiders, as several researchers have demonstrated in different cultural contexts. As Gill Seidel (1988, 9) notes, "we," the established, have "culture"; the others, the outsiders, have "ethnicity." Following Stuart Hall (1991b, 21), one might argue that Costa Ricans always manage to hide behind their negative constructions of otherness. But at the same time the other is historical and socially located. The Nicaraguan other is crucial precisely because it articulates racialized and class-based meanings of difference and material inequalities.

Nonetheless, the boundaries between cold war politics and racialized discourses have been blurred in specific circumstances. An important continuity between anticommunism and racialization took place in 1994 in the banana plantations owned by the company Geest Caribbean. About six hundred Nicaraguan workers were discharged in response to a strike that they had organized some months earlier (*B* 5/12–14/94). The strike had been provoked by the constant fluctuation in salaries paid by the company and by the flight of some subcontractors without paying the salaries they owed (*LN* 5/15/94; *LT* 5/14/94).[6] The company reactivated old mechanisms of political persecution, such as the firing of those workers who were affiliated with the trade union (historically considered communist), and the regional immigration office refused to extend visas to those Nicaraguan workers who went on strike (SITAGAH/CODEHU 1994).

Racialization was accompanied by renewed waves of anti–trade union propaganda. The company produced a video in which the abandonment of banana plantations in Costa Rica's southern Pacific coast was used as an example of what could happen if the trade unions organized strikes in the Geest Caribbean plantations, located in the Atlantic region. The workers were asked, for example, "Did you think of your family when you decided to join the trade union?" (SITAGAH/CODEHU 1994). The video elicited many concerns among the workers; indeed they mentioned it several times in the declarations to the Human Rights Commission that brought about the strike of 1994. Ironically, similar action was taken in the strike of 1934 (see chapter 3) (Acuña Ortega 1984, 33). Sixty years later, a new chapter of an old story was written; again class and racist exclusion were intrinsically meshed.

How Many Nicaraguans Live in Costa Rica?

The progressive erosion of patriarchal values, the decline of public services, and the rise of criminality are some of the symptoms identified by the media as belonging to a disease that threatens Costa Rican uniqueness, a self-representation that gained strength after the 1950s. Frequently, internal problems are explained as the result of external factors. Nicaraguans have become central actors in the elaboration and condensation of these dislocations. Four key representations of Nicaraguans are often repeated: there are too many of them, they threaten the Costa Rican national identity, they have exhausted the welfare state, and they commit most of the crimes.

News reports, editorials, newspaper columns, and letters to the editor provide examples of ways in which such dislocations are represented. My reading is not an exhaustive inquiry, but it can provide us with some links between internal factors and the representations of Nicaraguans as a threat from within. *La República* provided a summary of dislocations and presumed causes:

> A population that is more than 10 percent foreign can change a nation's identity. . . . These foreigners consume a significant amount of the national budget, which includes public services, but they scarcely pay taxes. . . . The three hundred thousand "illegal" Nicaraguans demand services, which means a constant and increasing load for Costa Ricans. . . . Costa Rican authorities believe that the massive immigration increases the crime rate because 40 percent of the prison population is

> Nicaraguan. . . . The government of José María Figueres [1994–98] believes that the arrival of thousands of Nicaraguans in Costa Rica causes instability in the economy and generates an environment of insecurity in the streets. (3/5/95)[7]

The number of Nicaraguans in Costa Rica has become a matter of debate and, above all, speculation. According to the Costa Rican Office of Immigration, there were 99,940 permanent Nicaraguan residents in 1997 (Castro and Morales 1998, 12). Most of them acquired their documents after two immigration amnesties, implemented in 1992 and 1994, that were designed to provide official documents to "illegal" foreigners, most of them Nicaraguans. About eighty-seven thousand people were documented in the two periods (Samandú and Pereira 1996, 14; Alvarenga 1997, 15). After Hurricane Mitch, various organizations put pressure on the Costa Rican government to establish a new immigration amnesty for Central Americans either holding temporary residency or lacking any "legal" documents. This third amnesty ran from February to July 1999; those who entered Costa Rica before November 9, 1998, were able to apply (*LG* 2/29/99). Most of the 155,886 applications (over 97 percent) were from Nicaraguan citizens (*LN* 7/27/99). According to the 2000 census Nicaraguans represent about 6 percent of the total population (see introduction) (INEC 2001, 5). This figure is somewhat higher (perhaps 8 percent) during harvest seasons, when temporary agricultural workers arrive from Nicaragua.

Representations of Nicaraguan "immigration" have been characterized by speculation as to its numbers, similar to reactions in England and the United States since the 1960s (Hall 1990, 20; Gilroy 1987, 84; Chaves 2000, 12). Most commentators have tended to exaggerate their estimates. A liberal intellectual, once critical of national stereotypes, has claimed, for example, that the Nicaraguan "demographic invasion" has reached one million people (Cersósimo, interview, 4/9/99).[8] Exaggerating the number of immigrants justifies stronger measures against them. Rooted in a positivist epistemology, numbering is a way of validation and gives "true nationals" the possibility of maintaining control of the "national space." The threat can be quantified (e.g., "10 percent is too much"), and that gives a sort of objectivity to the above arguments. However, any quantification is extremely relative: the Jews formed about one percent of the German population and most of them were murdered (Elias 1996, 304). In turn, attempts to challenge the numbers game have to accept the ways in which the media frame the immigration issue. As Stuart Hall argues in the case of England,

> If you establish the topic as "the numbers of blacks are too high" or "*they* are breeding too fast," the opposition is obliged or constrained to argue "the numbers are not as high as they are represented to be." This view is opposed to the first two: but it is also imprisoned by the same logic—the logic of the "numbers game." . . . However, changing the terms of the argument, questioning the assumptions and starting points, breaking the logic—this is a quite different, longer, more difficult task. (1990, 20; emphasis in original)

The argument about the number of immigrants works through an interesting link between quantification and space. As Hage argues in the case of Australia, "The classification as 'undesirable' always assumes a space where the undesirable is defined as such." Nations constitute an imaginary space where too many "represents the possibility of becoming out of control and losing the status of being an object of the will of the nationalistic manager" (1998, 92; see also 37, 43).

A more elaborate threat resides not only in numbers but in the danger posed to "national identity." A letter to the editor argues, "The described phenomenon [the presence of Nicaraguans] alters the culture, displaces workers, and produces a demographic explosion that increases poverty" (*LR* 4/10/96). There are no specifications about what is to be understood by *culture* and *identity* and what changes could take place. Identity seems to mean a perennial homogeneous formation, shared by all the inhabitants, without relationships with other cultures. Thus, Costa Rican identity seems to be perceived as a fixed and naturalized system. Furthermore, while positive aspects define the identity of "true nationals," the identity of the outsider is assumed to be negative.

Nicaraguans are represented, following Paul Gilroy (1987, 48), as "a problem or threat against which a homogeneous, white, national 'we' could be unified." They are economically excluded but politically required as the historical others, with reference to which various discourses on identity and nation in Costa Rica are articulated. During the 1990s, *immigrant* and *illegal* became synonymous with *nica.*

Recently, news reports (*LN* 12/5/99) have acknowledged that the number of Nicaraguans in Costa Rica does not exceed four hundred thousand. Such recognition has meant a more reflexive media representation, avoiding xenophobic and jingoistic stigmas. What such news reports do not explain is why the number of Nicaraguans in Costa Rica was exaggerated in the first place. It is not a technical problem regarding statistics but a ritual of portraying the immigrants as a major threat. Nor is it suggested anywhere that the media are precisely the institutions that have represented the Nicaraguan community as a wave that swamps national boundaries.

Amnesty 1999: New Scenarios, New and Old Racisms

Racialized discourses that have emerged in the context of the amnesty circulate on the Internet as well as in graffiti and jokes and do not seem to be the expression of institutionalized groups, but they do manifest very aggressive views that might be articulated politically. The arguments in this contestation combine elements of both "new" cultural racism and also recycled biological racism. Nicaraguans are represented as a threat since they "invade" the national space, and undermine the national identity, but also because they are "genetically different" and reproduce themselves faster than the "true nationals." These representations show that the distinctions between "new" cultural and biological racism cannot be generalized. Both types of racialization are articulated and activated in particular contexts. For example, I asked some "cybercitizens" about their opinions regarding the amnesty. One replied, "For me this is SHIT. It was bad having a massive inflow of Nicaraguans, but now it is even worse because they won't stop coming. I'm so angry with the authorities of this country. They've been fucked up the ass [*meter el bollo*]" (emphasis in original).

Here the amnesty has been interpreted as a lie and emphatically identified with excrement, the lowest signifier through which is possible to express detestation of Nicaraguans. The body, as Stallybrass and White (1986, 10) note, time and again transcodes the social and the subjective. Body images, in their view, "speak" social relations and values with particular force. The lowest in the social scale is signified through the lowest part of the body. Excrement is a signifier of a detested otherness. Furthermore, a rooted metaphor of homosexual rape is used for the threat posed by their presence in Costa Rica. Interestingly, the nation as rape victim is identified with the male body, not the female. The invasion of the social is interpreted as an invasion of the male body. What is challenged in this case seems to be male respectability. And, as in the news items published in the 1980s and discussed earlier in this chapter, invasion is identified with penetration, which confirms the overlapping of images of nation and sexuality.

While in the former example the keyword is *space,* another example from cyberspace is constructed around *time:* "Sometimes I would like them [nicas] to leave us alone, like in colonial times. Thank God, Costa Rica is a beautiful country protected by the Virgin of the Angels. But where there is Good, there is Evil. If there is day, there is night. Historically, Costa Rica has been genetically privileged—it is recognized worldwide—so why do we want to ruin this heritage?"

The present is threatened since the peaceful colonial heritage is menaced. The clue to the future resides in the past; the past is the future. The nation, a secular institution par excellence, is interpreted as a consequence of a holy wish: God and the Virgin of the Angels have provided Costa Ricans with a beautiful country. This religious insight is complemented by essentialist oppositions, for instance day versus night, in which Nicaraguan immigrants are associated with darkness. Although nationalism is considered a modern and secular development (Gellner 1983), these sacred oppositions reveal that the distinction between modern and traditional and secular and sacred are blurred frequently. God is quoted as a justification of secular enterprises, as Billig (1995, 77) states. In a similar perspective, McClintock argues, "Despite the commitment of European nationalism to the idea of the nation-state as the embodiment of rational progress, nationalism has been experienced and transmitted primarily through fetishism—precisely the cultural form that the Enlightenment denigrated as the antithesis of Reason" (1995, 374).

National belonging is constructed by means of rituals, myths, loyalties, fears. The nation, a secular and contingent form of social organization, becomes sacred. However, these sacred and naturalized attributes do not guarantee the nation's security, since genetic uniqueness and cultural racism are rejoined by a biological source of belonging: Costa Rican identity is genetically determined. New scenarios are perceived through both "new" and "old" racisms. National representations regarding golden ages are frequent, but biological arguments are not usually explicit. Interestingly, there were no critical responses to such arguments in the online edition of *La Nación.* These views are frequent on the Internet. An argument in a chat room provides further examples:[9]

> There are many communities in Costa Rica where the ticos ARE ALREADY A MINORITY. The peaceful and quiet Costa Rica is gone. Girls can no longer walk without being harassed by drunken Nicaraguan troublemakers at ANY HOUR OF THE DAY. Crime is constant. Your unpatriotic [*vende patria*] attitude will mean that some day we will lose this country. Their [Nicaraguans'] birthrate is higher than the national rate, and soon this country of peace, democracy, and freedom will be a country of war, anarchy, and totalitarianism. . . . They threaten Costa Rica; we don't threaten them, we repudiate their attempt to take possession of our country simply using the "tico" style (with jokes, for instance). The xenophobic ones are the Germans, who attack and discriminate by skin color. We respect our cultural variety. All of us are Costa Ricans: Indians, blacks, whites, browns. Ticos pay less attention to our poor dear Indians than to those drunken, ungrateful Nicaraguans. (emphasis in original)

These representations are similar to those depicted by the media and analyzed in chapter 2: the motherland means peace, democracy, and freedom; Nicaraguans, on the other hand, imply war, anarchy, and totalitarianism. Those women who feel insecure in the streets represent the threatened motherland; they are both the embodiment and the bearers of the nation's honor (Yuval-Davis 1997, 45). The implicit narrator is a man, one who considers himself in charge of the nation's security. The "other" is constructed as a rapist, a common feature within racialized contexts (see above). The threat posed by the Nicaraguans is also biological, since these "drunken, ungrateful" people reproduce themselves with greater frequency than do Costa Ricans; therefore, the latter could lose their country. The national destiny depends on the biological capabilities of reproduction in such a way that gender and race are tied to the politics of national identity (26–27).

On the Internet, the frequency and radicalism of exchanges are usually influenced by media attention on certain issues. In 1998 and 1999, for instance, disagreements between the Nicaraguan and Costa Rican governments elicited many letters to the editor in the online edition of *La Nación*. Eight out of ten letters addressed immigration as a problem. Interestingly, most of the messages did not receive critical responses. These messages seem to constitute the voice of a considerable group. As Elisabeth Noelle (1993) states, the media tend to produce a "spiral of silence" through which certain points of view are portrayed as being supported by a strong majority and other perspectives are silenced and appear as expressions of minorities or dissidents. Perhaps the most important consequence of this spiral of silence is that extremist representations enter into the mainstream public sphere without major resistance. They are not perceived as extremist but as just another point of view. Racialized politics seem to silence competitive interpretations and, in the process, become stronger.

Opinion polls constitute an important tool in the formation of public opinion. Gallup polls, for example, explore periodically what they consider the principal problems of the country. The questionnaires provide a preselected list of problems and, in turn, the results are released as public opinion, avoiding any comment on the ways in which such results were gathered. Thus, according to public opinion, Nicaraguan immigration has become a key problem in Costa Rica. Certain informal polls organized as part of TV news programs illustrate how the spiral of silence works in everyday life media reception. For example, in February 1999, the public was asked in a telephone poll, "Do you support the amnesty?" (TV4, 2/3/99). Ninety-three percent of the 580 callers did not support it. Another TV program asked a similar question in November: "Can *we* continue accepting Nicaraguans?" (TV7, 11/23/99; emphasis added). After one hour, they reported 3,340 calls, and 96 percent of the callers said no. In both cases, the way in which the question was asked suggested the desired answer, the one consistent with the editorial perspective of the program. The first poll was carried out in the context of the amnesty. The news items regarding this issue emphasized the rubbish dropped around the Costa Rican Office of Immigration by the long queue of applicants who had arrived the day before in order to get a place. Considering such framing, the results are not surprising.

A third case shows an interesting contrast. Again in the context of the amnesty, I was invited to a TV forum to discuss a variety of topics regarding the Nicaraguan community in Costa Rica (TV42, 2/2/99). The live program combines the guest's comments with live participation from the viewing audience. Ten viewers called in. At the beginning, most comments were negative, especially those made by men. But later, positive comments predominated, although many calls could not be answered, given the lack of time and technical resources. By the end, half the responses disagreed with "immigration" and half showed their solidarity with the Nicaraguans. The difference between this case and the first two highlights the effects of the media on viewers' responses. As Pierre Bourdieu argues, "Putting the same question to everyone assumes that there is a consensus on what the problems are" (1993, 149). The effect of such an imposition is predictable: "It creates the idea that there is such a thing as a unanimous public opinion, and so legitimizes a policy and strengthens the power relations that underlie it or make it possible" (150).

Jokes are another important cultural form that translates racialized imagery into common sense and everyday life (Barker 1989, 265). Depending on the context in which a particular joke is told, the person telling the joke may not be considered racist. Most jokes about Nicaraguans seem to be perceived as benign and funny with no major implications. They can be considered as key narratives of *inferential racism,* which can be defined, according to Stuart Hall, as those unquestioned assumptions that "enable racist statements to be formulated without ever bringing into awareness the racist predicates on which the statements are grounded" (1990, 13). Jokes are relevant not only in their content but also in the act of telling them (Fiske 1996, 78), which can create a hilarious environment and a sense of collective consensus, increasing "the threshold of the public acceptability of racism" (Hall 1990, 13). Indeed, it is difficult to have public disagreements about jokes in the context of informal meetings. Of fourteen jokes gathered by Sergio Morales (1997), four depend on symbolic violence and hatred, as in following two examples: "Why did God create nicas? So blacks would have someone to laugh at" and "If Hitler had known about Nicaraguans, he wouldn't have killed so many Jews." Both jokes associate hatred with racism in such a way that Nicaraguans, Jews, and blacks are related. Following Sander Gilman (1985, 35), one might argue that these groups were associated not merely because they were outsiders but because they expressed different images of difference.

On the other hand, racialization is not merely a representation; it also has a mobilizing power. One cybercitizen advocated expulsion of the Nicaraguans in view of their lack of education, "standard" Spanish, and "proper" behavior. The writer said they could stay as refugees, but in an isolated territory; this was an alternative to the amnesty:

> Costa Rica can't afford social spending for too many nicas, and this is a very small country, and you will see, if this thing continues like this, some day the number of nicas in CR will be half of the total population. And it makes me sad. Although, as I told you before, the nicas come here looking for better living conditions, and arrive with no education, morals, or health. And they are used to violence and horrible crimes; then when they arrive here they do the same, and criminality and mugging rise. And the worst is their accent. Poor people. I feel pity but enough is enough. The amnesty does not make sense to me. Instead of allowing them to live here, it would be better to find somewhere else and put them all together living as refugees.[10]

Significantly, these examples present a similar pattern: to exert control over immigrants is a crucial act. Control seems to represent a fantasy of domination generally displayed by men around certain boundaries and territories. The relevance of the Internet as a site of communication lies not only in the content but also in the anonymous form of most of the exchanges. It offers possibilities for making claims that in the course of an informal face-to-face conversation might be considered overt racism. In a similar way, graffiti demands repatriation as the solution to the "immigrant problem": Get Out, Nicas (*Fuera nicas*); Enough Is Enough! Death or Get Out, Nicas (*Basta ya! Muerte o fuera nicas*); and Nicas Are Garbage (*nicas basura*) have become part of the visual landscape. Interestingly, both the Internet and graffiti are anonymous forms of public communication.

How Violent Are Nicaraguans?

The violence and criminality attributed to Nicaraguans is a major topic of debate in Costa Rica. There is a representation that criminal offenses are rising, and Nicaraguans are seen as responsible for the increase. However, a broad perspective on violence and criminality might offer a different perspective. For example, it might be surprising, especially if one follows crime news, that the number of suicides in Costa Rica is slightly higher than that of homicides (see table 5.1).

Table 5.1

Suicides and Homicides Registered by the Judicial Police in Costa Rica, 1986–97

Year	Suicides	Homicides
1986	94	—
1987	122	114
1988	133	117
1989	158	116
1990	165	139
1991	133	132
1992	153	160
1993	163	160
1994	179	182
1995	224	184
1996	210	189
1997	—	210
TOTAL	1,734	1,703

Source: OIJ 1997, 1998.

During the 1990s 2,172 homicides were reported and suicides reached 2,367. The percentage of homicides committed by men increased from 88 percent in 1990 to 96 percent in 1999. Men were the victims of 81 percent of all homicides in 1990 and of 86 percent in 1999 (OIJ 2000a, 5). Meanwhile, men accounted for 88 percent of the suicides in 1999, which seems to confirm, among other factors, their low tolerance for frustration. Furthermore, 52 percent of male suicides in 1999 were by men between twenty and forty years old. It is also worrying that the number of Nicaraguans who committed suicide doubled between 1997 and 1999, rising from eleven (5 percent of all suicides) to twenty-two (9 percent) (OIJ 2000b, 8). Suicides, however, are not considered by the public to be a threat. This might be the result of a different quality and level of attention by the media; whereas homicides are crucial raw material for crime news, suicides are seldom mentioned. In a more general perspective, this silence reveals the difficulties a society faces in discussing those factors that might generate suicides, such as the gap between social expectations associated with consumerism, and the material and institutional means to satisfy them.

Nicaraguans accounted for 5 percent of the total prison population in 1998, a figure well below their proportion of the Costa Rican population as a whole (7–8 percent). Nicaraguans perpetrated almost 20 percent of homicides registered in Costa Rica during 1999 (2 percent more than in 1998) (OIJ 2001, 25). Meanwhile, the number of Nicaraguans who were victims of homicide also increased a bit between 1999 and 2000, from 12.8 to 15.3 percent (OIJ 2001, 20). The relationship between the nationality of the perpetrator and the nationality of the victims is not provided by the official statistics, but some cases reported by the media seem to indicate that an important number of homicides took place among Nicaraguans (Nicaraguan perpetrator, Nicaraguan victim). Most of the perpetrators of these homicides were men who lived in extreme poverty in rural areas. They intended either to rape or to steal; frequently the perpetrators and the victims were neighbors or relatives (*LN* 8/14/94, 3/24/95, 1/27/96, 6/22/96, 7/23/03; *LR* 3/24/95). These data suggest that crimes committed by Nicaraguans did not follow any nationalistic or ethnic patterns, but that they did take place in the context of deprived material conditions. Indeed, similar crimes have been committed by Costa Ricans against each other (*LR* 8/13/96). However, their nationality does not seem to be a matter of concern among the media. Rather than confirming higher criminality among Nicaraguans, the figures could be interpreted as part of a wider pattern of stigmatization. In this sense, Peter Wade notes, "The discourse of ethnicity is often based on remarks that derive from unspoken, taken for granted knowledge of 'typical' ethnic behavior and which allude to isolated characteristics in a practical context that illustrates that aptness of the allusion and implicitly discards as irrelevant all contrary instances" (1993, 166).

The Costa Rican prison population has increased, regardless of nationality, due to changes in legislation since 1994 (see table 5.2). The new legislation has meant longer imprisonment and lower benefits for people in prisons, noted by the Ministry of Justice (INC 1999, 5; Nagel 1999, 1).

Table 5.2

Costa Rican Prison Population by Nationality, 1994–98

Nationality	1994	%	1995	%	1996	%	1997	%	1998	%
Costa Rican	3,367	91.0	2,918	88.4	—	—	4,705	89.1	5,222	89.7
Foreign	331	9.0	384	11.6	—	—	574	10.9	599	10.3
Nicaraguan*	141	3.8	173	5.2	—	—	255	4.8	289	5.0
Total	3,698	100.0	3,302	100.0	4,705	—	5,279	100.0	5,821	100.0

*Data on Nicaraguans are given as a subset of all foreign data. They are not included in the totals for each column.

Source: INC *Población Penitenciaria Extranjen al 31-2-98.* San José: Mínisterio de Justicia, 1999, 6, 30.

These processes of criminalization illustrate a broad pattern of representation: "The established group tends to attribute to its outsider group as a whole the 'bad' characteristics of that group's 'worst' section. In contrast, the self-image of the established group tends to be modeled on its exemplary, most 'nomic' or norm setting section, on the minority of its 'best' section" (Elias 1994, xix). The "others" are responsible for public insecurity, and the exaggeration of their criminality justifies taking strong measures against them. In this sense, the outsiders constitute an ambivalent image; they are considered anomic but are, at the same time, necessary to make sense of social dislocations. This ambivalence of the Nicaraguan other becomes clear if one imagines what Costa Ricans' self-representation would be without this image of otherness. Despite being racialized and criminalized (or perhaps because of it), Nicaraguans are indispensable in terms of national representation. Indeed, the image of Costa Rica as unique, either regarding political attributes or ethnic markers, is fundamentally constructed through difference with the Nicaraguan other. However, current research on the Nicaraguan community in Costa Rica usually emphasizes their economic impact—either highlighting their contribution or alleging that they are a burden to the national budget. Their role in the configuration of national subjectivities has not been a major subject of concern.

Racialization might also be related to the emergence of authoritarian tendencies. In Costa Rica, for example, the death penalty was abolished in 1870, but a survey published in 1996 revealed that 58 percent of people consulted would support its return, 22 percent more than in 1994, and 78 percent considered it necessary to have a strong and energetic "man" in the presidency (*LT* 2/1/96; *LR* 11/8/96).[11] Some letters to the editor confirm this tendency. One letter, from the former governor of Puntarenas Province, bore the headline "License to Kill." It was about the murder of a mechanic by an elderly citizen, who argued that the victim was making too much noise. The letter can be summarized in two assertions: one, minors and elderly people effectively have a license to kill since they are not prosecuted, and two, Costa Ricans' high life expectancy means many elderly citizens and thus many licenses to kill. The letter concludes: "Deputies: Don't allow two kinds of citizens, those who have a license to kill and those who don't. Reform the laws; draw them up in such a way that potential murderers think twice before acting" (*LN* 1/9/96).

Theodor Adorno and his colleagues (1950) propose that "stereopathy" and personalization are crucial devices for the formation of authoritarianism.[12] While stereopathy avoids particular examples, personalization prevents any abstract analysis. Both are driven by rigid ways of thinking in which any chaotic situation is fixed under certain criteria. As described above, "license to kill" can be understood as personalization: a very particular case is generalized in such a way that elderly and young people threaten the nation. Stereopathy might also explain cases in which Nicaraguans are stigmatized as responsible for criminality, even when the figures do not support such claims. Different kinds of phenomena are construed as a web, without recognition of their specific differences. One example is unforgettable: "The arithmetical operation is very easy: arms + unidentified immigrants + poverty + insufficient police vigilance + guerrillas + drug dealing = VIOLENCE" (*LN* 1/8/96; emphasis in original). On the one hand there is law and order, and on the other, immigration, strikes, kidnappings.[13]

Being threatened by crime coincides with other experiences of dislocation, especially those related to moral values and ways of living (Hall et al. 1978, 146). Indeed, letters to the editor frequently call public attention to the fact that the nation has lost its traditional values: "It is a pity to realize how ethical, moral, and religious principles have been lost among our public servants in politics, those who were thought of as exemplars of our society. The result is that now, whatever the law does not punish is allowed" (*LN* 8/22/94).

An editorial summarizes research done in relation to this problem: "The four fundamental values of any society—truth, honesty, work, and solidarity—are in crisis in our country" (*LN* 4/7/96). Since most examples occur in the public sector, it has meant a strong relationship between neoconservative ideologies and neoliberal economic perspectives. In other words, if the size of the state were reduced, corruption would decrease. This formula might have derived some inspiration from Thatcherite populism in Britain (Hall 1988, 48). Another editorial claims, "After a brief inventory, what is surprising is the number and diversity of denounced or investigated cases of corruption in the public sector. These cases seem to show lack of transparency and nonobservance of the legal administration of public resources, but above all they exhibit the absence of essential ethical principles" (*LN* 11/5/96).

The moral crisis is present not only in the state but also within traditional forms of the family. Divorces and unmarried parents have been considered as undermining the roots of society. The divorce rate increased from 9 percent in 1976 to 40 percent in 2000, and the percentage of unmarried couples who live together rose from 18 percent in 1976 to 28 percent in 1999—staggering numbers for a predominantly Catholic country (in I. Molina 2002). The number of reported cases of domestic violence also skyrocketed, from 5,023 in 1996 to 20,996 in 1998 and to 32,643 in 2000 (PNUD 2001, 278). These figures have produced a sense of "family breakdown," which is thought to undermine the nation as well; both private and public sites of belonging have been diminished.

In this context, the past emerges as an ideal time. If the past were imitated, these permissive customs might be overcome. This line of argument is activated, for instance, during national celebrations such as Independence Day. An editorial summarizes possible alternatives in the face of these challenges:

> The egoism, the indifference, the conformism, the dislike of our best values, and the lack of patriotism have become obstacles that impede us from appreciating our country and what we have. . . . The Day of the Motherland [Independence Day] is the day for recovering many of the lost values that characterized our grandfathers, when to defend the motherland was to defend honor. . . . A return to our roots is important, a retrospective journey in order to analyze what has been lost and what should be rescued. (*LR* 9/7/96)

However, this nostalgia does not seem to effectively cope with contemporary social anxieties. What is at stake are the ways in which the achievement of consent has been legitimized in Costa Rica. Nicaraguans have been "made symbols for, and symptoms of, a succession of dislocations" (Hall et al. 1978, 160). While they are excluded economically—as will be discussed below—they have become politically central. Frustration and disenchantment are projected onto these undesirable historical neighbors that are frequently represented as the enemy within. In a society like that of Costa Rica, where differences between diverse social actors are usually unspoken in public, alleged threats to the nation play a prominent role.

Are Nicaraguans Taking Costa Ricans' Jobs?

The political and social injustices suffered by the other Central American nations have been crucial for the representation of Costa Rica as a singular democracy, but at the same time these nations are perceived as a threat to the uniqueness that characterizes Costa Rica's national identity. Immigration is perhaps the most explicit example of how being part of Central America is a source of both uniqueness and threat. As mentioned in chapter 3, historically Nicaraguans represent some of the most rooted antinational values in Costa Rica: dark skin in a country obsessed by whiteness, an idiosyncratic Spanish as opposed to the "standard" Costa Rican way of speaking, a violent character in a peaceful democracy. Above all, however, they are poor. Being poor is particularly threatening, given the decline in public investment since the 1980s, which has put an important sector of the Costa Rican population at risk of social exclusion. Although unemployment has not increased recently—5.7 percent in 1997, 5.6 percent in 1998 (PNUD 1999, 130)—the presumed displacement of Costa Ricans by Nicaraguan workers in the labor market as well as the cost of public services provided for them—especially housing, education, and health—has been a permanent arena of dispute.

Costa Rica has experienced a transition from an economy based on agriculture to an economy in which the service sector became considerably more important in the second half of the twentieth century. Young Costa Ricans, whose parents worked traditionally in agriculture or construction, have found jobs in the service sector. The proportion of people employed in the primary sector (mainly agriculture) declined from 55 percent to 20 percent between 1950 and 1997 (PNUD 1998). Conversely, the number of jobs in the service sector rose from 48 percent in 1987 to 56 percent in 1997. Meanwhile, the incorporation of women into paying work increased from 20 percent in 1973 to 34 percent in 1997 (I. Molina 2002, 117). Nicaraguans played a key role in this transition, since they replaced former workers in some parts of the primary sector and in construction and domestic work (Samandú and Pereira 1996, 10; A. Morales 1997, 118–19). In other words, there has been an expansion of the service economy without a decline of the primary sector, which has been based on an intensive employment of labor rather than on technological innovation.

Banana exports, for instance, increased from $149 million in 1985 to $649.3 million in 1995; meanwhile, the number of workers rose from 13,690 to 34,951 in the same period (Castro and Morales 1998, 49). In Sarapiquí County, a region in which banana plantations are the most important economic activity, the number of Nicaraguan workers was an estimated 40 percent of the total, according to Ramón Barrantes, a trade union leader (interview, 1/27/99). Construction is another field that employs a significant number of Nicaraguan workers, especially in unskilled work. The instability of the sector, characterized by recurrent expansions and contractions, requires workers for short periods. Nicaraguans usually fulfill this kind of demand and are then expelled from the labor market in times of recession (Sandoval 1997). Various reports agree that about 20 percent of domestic workers are Nicaraguan women (ASTRADOMES 1997; Castro and Morales 1998, 42). A survey carried out among Nicaraguan domestic workers found that while about 50 percent of the respondents work more than twelve hours a day—the maximum under the current law—they believe that their employers comply with the law. It might be argued that, given the high unemployment rate in Nicaragua, they are reluctant to complain about unfair labor conditions in Costa Rica. Indeed, nearly 90 percent of them did not previously do this type of work in Nicaragua (Barboza 1997, 21–22, 36).

Under previous legislation, the number of foreign workers was not permitted to reach more than 10 percent in any economic activity. However, in January 1999 the Constitutional Court allowed an appeal by certain companies that were seeking to abolish such restrictions. Generally, this quota was not observed and employers ran the risk of being prosecuted. These constitutional changes reveal the complexities of the dynamics of inclusion and exclusion. On the one hand, Nicaraguans are excluded as an undesired people; on the other, they are included so that they might be exploited for their cheap labor. Their exclusion is intended not to drive them out of the labor market but to keep them in low-paying jobs.

Debates about the labor market have focused on how the Nicaraguan labor force has contributed to the decline in salaries. Some interpretations suggest that the tendency has been for the minimum wages to become the maximum ones in economic sectors such as agriculture, construction, and domestic work (Ruiz 1998). Compared with salaries paid in 1987, real salaries in construction, for example, decreased by 11 percent in 1997. In the case of domestic work, the income patterns are hardly predictable; while in 1990, 1992, 1993, 1994, and 1996 salaries increased at a higher rate than the average woman's income, in the rest of the decade they declined (Castro and Morales 1998, 38).

Although it is indisputable that newcomers put pressure on salaries, little attention has been paid to the relationship between the presence of the Nicaraguan labor force and other economic variables in the income patterns in Costa Rica. A case in point is the second Program of Structural Adjustment in Costa Rica, supported by the World Bank, which aimed to promote nontraditional exports to new markets (Raventós 1995, 205). Citrus fruits, melons, and flowers were among these nontraditional exports. Costa Rica has been competing for such "thin" markets with many other countries. Being successful depends on the possibility of reducing costs. Generally, the real decrease of salaries is the most common measure taken in order to guarantee competitiveness. The arrival of Nicaraguan workers has allowed some investors to maintain regional advantages—better-qualified workers and infrastructure, political stability—but now with cheap salaries paid in unskilled jobs. This has been especially relevant in agriculture and certain industrial activities. In other words, income patterns have to be interpreted in this broader context of export economies and not only as a consequence of the arrival of new workers. With or without immigration, export economies have to decrease costs of production in order to be successful in the so-called global economy (López 1989).[14]

The location of these nontraditional economic activities in the northern region of Costa Rica is another important element, since it has brought the two sides of the border into sharp contrast. While the Nicaraguan side of the border has suffered historical isolation from the rest of the country, the Costa Rican north experienced strong support in the 1980s as part of its geopolitical importance to the conflicts in Central America. Meanwhile, other Costa Rican regions, such as the province of Limón, with the nation's highest rate of unemployment, have not received the same attention. In this context, immigration is not only the result of the critical situation of the Nicaraguan economy but is also a consequence of the investment in Costa Rica's strategic regions (Samandú and Pereira 1996, 22; A. Morales 1997, 23, 52, 88, 93).

Overall, the immigration debate has centered on costs; the accumulated wealth is unthinkable. Indeed, no information is available about the implications of such low salaries in the processes of expansion and capitalist accumulation. Ironing, cleaning, and cooking rest in Nicaraguan hands, but the surplus value produced by such "degraded" work is unknown. The same can be said of those "dirty" jobs in construction or agriculture. Nicaraguans cross the private/public divide without major notice.

Do Immigrants Collapse Public Services?

Another arena of dispute has been the social cost of Nicaraguan "immigration" into Costa Rica. As I mentioned earlier, education, housing, and health have been the most controversial topics. The number of Nicaraguan children in formal education in Costa Rica is about twenty thousand, approximately 3 percent of the total number of students. Each year the Costa Rican government distributes awards (93,500 in 1999, about $28 each) to the poorest students. In 1999 some authorities refused to give such awards to Nicaraguan children, arguing that they were foreigners. However, a Costa Rican principal appealed to the Constitutional Court, claiming that the decision was discriminatory, and the appeal was upheld (*LN* 2/20/99). The "awards affair" caused a public debate about the social costs of Nicaraguan immigration. The possibility of excluding Nicaraguan children from these awards elicited a strong critique by a Liberal politician, who considered that such attitudes provoke "loathing" (*LN* 4/3/99). In turn, an editorial in a monthly regional newspaper called the decision of the Constitutional Court "a slap in the face of national sovereignty" (*ND* ?/2/99).

Housing has also aroused public concern. According to Costa Rica's Ministry of Housing, the deficit of houses with basic facilities rose from 96,165 in 1994 to 152,494 in 1999, an increase of 63 percent in five years. Of those, 33,095 cases were classified as *tugurios* (shanties), which do not have "minimum" infrastructure or access to public services such as electricity or water. It has been estimated that Nicaraguan families inhabit between 40 and 42 percent of tugurios in San José (Román 1998, 3; *LN* 8/30/99).

A third area of dispute has been the health services provided for the Nicaraguan community. The national health authorities stated that in 1998 spending in health services for Nicaraguans rose to about $16 million, approximately 3.5 percent of the total annual investment in health (*LN* 2/6/99).[15] Clinics and hospitals that are located close to Nicaraguan communities have faced an increase in the demand for their services, especially treatment of emergencies and maternity cases. The Hospital of San Carlos, one of the closest hospitals to the Nicaragua–Costa Rica border, is a case in point. The maternity service reported 275 Nicaraguan patients from October 1997 to September 1998 (14 percent of all patients). Fifty-five percent of the Nicaraguan women had paid their fees, just like any other patient. The rest were not registered with the public health service. A study of this case highlighted the implications of spending on those women who did not contribute to the public health fund and the further implications for services provided for the national population (A. Carvajal 1997, 42, 62).

A survey undertaken in the province of Limón, where most of the banana plantations are located, provided data of a different sort. Nearly two-thirds (64 percent) of the Nicaraguan workers had health service certificates, and most of their health problems (64 percent) were related to their handling of pesticides used on the plantations (Foro Emaús 1996, 13). Another investigation, carried out in Matina County in Limón Province, explored health and labor conditions on banana plantations. Most of the workers (92 percent) belonged to the National Health Service (Caja Costarricense de Seguro Social) but they did not use it often, since they could lose their jobs as a result of frequent absences (García and Guzmán 1998, 113, 115).

Overall, the deterioration of public services in education, housing, and health facilities has been portrayed as a consequence of immigration. "Foreigners," many of them "illegal" people, are taking advantage of those facilities that should be the exclusive right of "true nationals," as right-wing commentators have argued (*LN* 3/21/97). However, little attention has been paid to the relationship between services provided to those Nicaraguans who do not pay taxes—basically as a result of their own social exclusion—and the decline of public investment since the beginning of the 1980s, when programs of structural adjustment took effect in most Latin American countries.

While social investment in Costa Rica represented 23 percent of GDP in 1980, it fell to 14 percent in 1992 (PNUD 1997, 118). The internal composition of social investment also changed: health and nutrition was reduced from 45 to 32 percent. Meanwhile, social benefits rose from 15 to 26 percent during the same period (Samandú and Pereira 1996, 9). This alteration has meant an undermining of long-term investment in social provision and an emphasis on piecemeal solutions, which are more politically profitable in electoral periods. Health investment, another disputed field, experienced a decrease of about 50 percent between 1980 and 1992. Although the number of public clinics for external consultation increased, no hospitals have been built since 1980 (PNUD 1997, 80). Consequently, there has been a reduction in the availability of hospital beds per inhabitant. Between 1984 and 1996, the number of beds per thousand inhabitants decreased from 2.9 to 1.9. A similar tendency can be observed in investment in medical technology. In turn, private medicine, as might be suspected, has expanded its services during this period.

In the housing sector the overall situation is scarcely discussed. Every year the deficit rises by twenty-five thousand new houses and the only solutions offered by the state do not satisfy the annual deficit. In other words, the lack of housing cannot be explained by the presence of Nicaraguans.[16] Despite the immigration debate, what really matters are the difficulties thousands of working-class families of any nationality have in finding a house. For a working family with two children and a monthly income of about $400, getting a mortgage is almost impossible. This is the case for men who work in construction and women who work in sweatshop factories, for example (Sandoval 1997, 135–36).[17] In 1984, for instance, it was reported that about thirty-six thousand houses were considered tugurios (in G. Carvajal 1994, 46), even when the number of Nicaraguans in Costa Rica was fewer than in the 1990s. In other words, this evidence suggests that the housing shortage is not simply a consequence of the immigration problem. However, among certain politicians and academics, there is a current identification of the tugurio as a Nicaraguan problem (Román 1998, 5).

In other words, what seems to be hard to recognize is the presence of poverty in a country where one of the most powerful contemporary national representations is of being a prosperous middle-class nation, an exception not only in Central America but also in Latin America. Public investment in education, for instance, decreased from 6.9 percent of the GDP in 1980 to 5.8 percent in 1997 (PNUD 1997, 97). In 1999 the deficit of state classrooms was over forty-five hundred (Fonseca 1999, 24). Conversely, private education expanded. The number of private primary schools rose from just over 1 percent to nearly 6 percent of all schools between 1980 and 1997, and private secondary institutions increased from 12 percent to 31 percent in the same period (I. Molina 2002). Low achievement and school truancy have turned public education into a matter of national concern. While the number of students who receive low marks in public secondary schools is 53 percent, it is just 26 percent in private institutions. Truancy from state primary schools is currently nearly 5 percent; from secondary schools it is approximately 15 percent. The institutions with the lowest performance are those that operate at night and those located in deprived rural areas. Meanwhile, few students are truant from private institutions—only 2 percent from primary schools and 1.6 percent from secondary schools (PNUD 1999, 83, 86). Overall, only one out of ten students who begin primary education in Costa Rica finds a place in higher education eleven years later (83).

The deficit of classrooms allows us to make practical sense of the impact of Nicaraguan students on the lack of appropriate educational facilities. Generally, each class has about thirty students and each classroom is used by two different classes on a daily basis: one class works during the morning and the other in the afternoon. If the number of Nicaraguan students were about twenty thousand as the authorities have said, they would require 333 classrooms (about 7 percent of the nation's deficit). The remaining 93 percent can be explained only as a consequence of the chronic lack of investment in education.

If a new classroom costs about $8,500, the construction of these 333 classrooms could cost over $2.8 million. Another important challenge arises in relation to the teachers required—approximately seven hundred. Since a primary teacher in Costa Rica earns about $6,000 annually, salaries for these teachers could exceed $4 million per year. The required investment in infrastructure for Nicaraguan children, including classrooms and housing, might rise to about $19 million. Meanwhile, the investment in education and health could reach approximately $14 million annually. This level of investment is impossible to attain, according to mainstream media and politicians. A comparative perspective may be necessary to make sense of these figures. The financial performance of banana corporations, which have expanded their activities on the basis of low salaries paid to Nicaraguan and Costa Rican workers, is a case in point. At the end of 1995 their debt with the public banks rose to about $84 million, which represented 7 percent of the public credit budget (Castro and Morales

1998, 52). Although that debt is considerably higher than the "costs" of immigration, it is scarcely considered a threat to the nation's finances.

Another situation that goes generally uncommented upon relates to those companies that have not paid for social security for their employees. Official and media discourses do not take into consideration that most of the time the contractors are the ones who avoid paying for social security. If the contractor does not register the worker, she does not have access to the service. In the worst case, the contractor reduces the worker's contribution to the health system but retains the money and does not register the worker. An official estimate revealed that the accumulated private debt with the National Health Service reached about $108 million in 1997. In 1998 fifty companies held 43 percent of the private-sector debt with the National Health Service (*LN* 7/20/98). The agricultural companies alone (most of them banana enterprises) located in the country's Atlantic region had an accumulated debt of approximately $37 million (PNUD 1998, 119; CCSS 1999). Interestingly, it has been impossible to make public the names of these enterprises. The health authorities maintain that they are inhibited by law from publishing such a list; however, they have made the services provided to the Nicaraguan community into a central media event.

The accumulated debt of private companies with the National Health Service makes it evident that the lack of an efficient fiscal policy has been another structural source of injustice. Even the World Bank has insisted on the necessity of improving it. Nevertheless, local politicians seem not to pay attention to this facet of neoliberal recommendations. What has been implemented with vigor is the reduction of public investment in health facilities. In 1984 the difference between income and spending in the National Health Service was estimated at $10.8 million and increased to $15.9 million in 1985 (Sandoval 1987, 4). Seventeen years later, the surplus was estimated at approximately $103 million. Meanwhile, the National Health Service has been contracting out to the private sector those services it is unable to provide, given the chronic underinvestment during the last two decades. This policy has institutionalized the financing of private health facilities with public money. In November 2001, *La Nación* revealed that between 1991 and 2001 the private services contracted by the National Health Service increased by 404 percent and the payments of such services grew 109 percent. The National Health Service paid about $12 million for such services, 50 percent more than the money required for the new equipment needed to provide the services in public hospitals and clinics (*LN* 11/23, 11/25/01). What goes unmentioned is that such policy has been strongly supported by neoliberal media and politicians, including *La Nación*.

Another way of conceptualizing the social spending needed by the Nicaraguan community might be by looking at economic incentives that successive governments gave to those who exported nontraditional products to nontraditional markets between 1973 and 1999. This policy was aimed at diversifying the Costa Rican economy, thereby lessening dependence on coffee and banana exports, which always face unstable international markets. These tax-credit certificates, known in Spanish as Certificados de Abono Tributario (CATS), consist of a bonus paid by the government to the entrepreneurs according to the value of their exports. CATS have indeed modified the composition of exports: while in 1980 nontraditional exports represented 67 percent of the total, they rose to 78 percent in 1991 (PNUD 1999, 319). In return, the government paid about $1 billion to exporters between 1984 and 1999. Although neoliberals have strongly criticized economic protectionism, this economic policy has not been the object of public debate. Despite the large amount of money involved, CATS have not received the same attention as the so-called economic burden associated with the Nicaraguan community, even though some of the recipients have been prosecuted for submitting false documents in order to claim their incentives (*LN* 9/27/99).

I am not suggesting that immigration to Costa Rica is a solution to the structural problems of Central America, nor do I underestimate the economic impact of the services provided to the Nicaraguan community. However, the decline of public services and the "threat" faced by the lower middle classes in Costa Rica cannot be explained as a consequence of immigration. Moreover, the emphasis on the decline in public investment and lack of fiscal policies cannot hide the internal processes of economic exclusion and corruption in Nicaragua. The so-called pact between Arnoldo Alemán and members of the Sandinista elite reinforced the loss of credibility of politicians among the population. "In order to compensate for their mutual weakness, they seem to need each other," says the annual report of the Nicaraguan Center for Human Rights, ironically (CENIDH 1998, 10). Interestingly, Alemán made the precarious situation of Nicaraguans in Costa Rica the raw material for a nationalist rhetoric "on behalf of" his fellow citizens. However, as has been stated by certain Nicaraguan NGOs, the Alemán government did not pay any attention to the structural sources of immigration (CODEHUCA 1998).

The privatization of 351 state enterprises favored high-ranking members of the former Chamorro government and some members of the Sandinista elite. Although these enterprises produced about 30 percent of GDP, the state sold them at less than 20 percent of their real value (CENIDH 1998, 32; Dijkstra 1999, 305). Rural properties distributed by agrarian reform programs have not been legalized, and therefore the owners have no access to credit, provoking a severe recession in agriculture at a time when the "informal urban sector" has proved unable to absorb people who are looking for a job. Although the Nicaraguan economy was expected to grow by 6 percent during 1999, the highest rate in Central America, private consumption did not follow the same trend. Indeed, the distribution of income became more unequal in the 1990s, and poverty increased to the point that remittances have become a crucial resource for survival (Dijkstra 1999, 306; *LN* 9/24/99). In 1995 the remittances sent by Nicaraguans who live in Costa Rica and the United States to relatives in Nicaragua amounted to $50 million. Seven years later, in 2002, official and unofficial figures put remittances at between $600 and $800 million. Meanwhile, in 2001 exports from Nicaragua reached $620 million, and international aid to Nicaragua is currently estimated at $500 million (Grigsby 2002, 18, 22). In other words, remittances have become a key resource for thousands of Nicaraguan families.

Most of the foreign investment has been allocated in the service sector. In turn, the weight of consumer goods within the imports has increased from 17 percent in the period between 1986 and 1989 to 29 percent between 1991 and 1995 (Dijkstra 1999, 304). The gap between exports and imports has grown from $555.2 million in 1997 to $866.5 million in 1998 (UCA 1999, 11). Investment has been activated by the return of prosperous Nicaraguans from Miami, who brought with them ways of life associated with so-called global consumption. Downtown Managua now contains new shopping areas, fast-food outlets, and gas stations. Thus the contrasts between expectations and actual consumption have become even sharper. On average, salaries declined 30 percent in the past ten years (Rocha 2002, 20). At a time when being a citizen usually means being consumer, most Nicaraguans are neither.

Alemán's government (1997–2002) subscribed to hard-line market fundamentalism. "Don't solve anything; leave it to the market. After all, we control it" has become the prevailing conventional wisdom (UCA 1999, 5). But the extent of corruption has been compared with the Somozas' dictatorship, when the state and the family business were indivisible, and a kind of neo-Somocista kleptocracy has been developing.[18] Alemán's personal worth rose 980 percent from 1990, when he started his tenure as mayor at the Managua city council, to 2002, when he finished his presidential term. Meanwhile, the inequalities are astonishing. The director of the Nicaraguan Central Bank during Alemán's administration received a monthly salary of $12,000, which is 240 times greater than that of a primary school teacher. This only serves to accentuate the paucity of Nicaragua's investment in education, the lowest rate in Central America. A similar tendency affects health: in 1986 health investment was equivalent to $65.39 per citizen; a decade later, in 1997, that amount had diminished to $16 (CODEHUCA 1998, 26; CENIDH 1998, 12). The recently elected president, Enrique Bolaños, has promised to stop this tendency and began by reducing the megasalaries of high-ranking bureaucrats by 35 percent (UCA 2002, 12). In January 2002 a denunciation signed by more than sixty thousand citizens demanded an investigation into the enrichment of Alemán's family (UCA 2002, 6). On December 12 the Nicaraguan National Assembly voted to strip his parliamentary immunity from prosecution. He has been charged with money laundering and the theft of state funds.

In any case, immigrants are not responsible for the ways in which economic and social policies have been conceptualized and implemented in Nicaragua and Costa Rica. In the latter country, for example, public investment has grown since 1993, but it has not reached the level reported in 1980. Despite an increase of 22 percent in 1997, it is still 1.3 percent below 1980 figures (PNUD 1997, 118). This recovery, rather than being unique to Costa Rica, coincides with the obsolescence of market fundamentalism within the context of increasing processes of (and new ways of) social exclusion in many Latin American countries. Regional development in Central America is another unexplored alternative. Although immigration has become a structural problem regionwide, there are no broad projects for sustainable development. The arrival of Nicaraguans in Costa Rica is a particular example of this tendency, which has displaced more than 3 million people from their countries. Policing immigrants has replaced the debate and design of long-term strategies.

I have emphasized material determinations and the ways in which policymakers have represented them. A key tenet of this research is that representations and subjectivities cannot be narrowly conceived as autonomous domains, as exclusively discursive dimensions. As Pieterse states, "Probably the single most important feature of representations of otherness is the role they play in stabilizing and maintaining social inequality" and the fear that social hierarchies might diminish demands the permanent reassertion of boundaries (1992, 234, 223). Racialized representations are intrinsically related to (and are an expression of) material antagonisms. Any attempt to challenge racialization needs to tackle social injustices. Rather than blaming Nicaraguans for the deterioration of public services and other institutions, what is necessary in Costa Rica is the discussion and debate of alternatives to neoliberal policies that, after twenty years of hegemony, have increased the privileges of few and the anxieties of many.

Conclusion

This project has attempted to show that nations are formations of difference and inequality. The Nicaraguan other, for instance, has seen a long-term construction intrinsically related to the formation of nationhood in Costa Rica. This analysis of belonging and difference has been located throughout this research within two crucial tensions present in cultural studies as well as in debates on national identities.

The first is related to the multiple links between historical and literary narratives, media discourse, and everyday life. Each of these sites is situated in different temporal and spatial locations but there are multiple and diverse links within and between them. Nonetheless, they seem to be considered autonomous dimensions. Media discourse, for instance, is often assumed as a source in historical analysis, without major discussion of the political location of the media institutions themselves. Conversely, historical analysis is often missing in media discourse analyses and ethnographic perspectives. More generally, the distinction between social sciences and history has been a damaging one to both sides. A last, but by no means least important, boundary distances media discourse analysis from ethnographic perspectives. The deconstruction of texts frequently evades the empirical analysis of circulation and appropriation of these texts within specific institutional sites. Meanwhile, ethnographic research sometimes interprets the active role of audiences as an example of resistance against dominant ideologies.

The second set of tensions arises from the multiple links between representations, subjectivities, and wider institutional and material conditions. An exclusive analysis of representations, for instance, might produce an unchallenged sense of nationhood, characterized by hegemonic images and institutionalized ceremonies. In this sense, this project has also attempted to explore empirically some of the ways in which such representations addressed subjects and are contested by them under particular institutional constraints. These links illustrate that nation-building projects and the constitution of a sense of nationhood have been closely related developments. Nationhood not only lies in representations but is part of material developments.

These tensions between historical interpretations, media analysis, and ethnography, on the one hand, and representations, subjectivities, and material factors, on the other, illustrate the complexities of a nonessentialist perspective that renounces both primordialist perspectives and merely discursive versions of national identity. If meanings of nationhood are neither natural nor encapsulated in discourses, it is necessary to explore some of the diverse relations between cultural forms, practices, and institutions. A major difficulty of mapping these diverse sites of national identity formation is precisely how to avoid deterministic views, emphasizing either hegemonic or more inclusive representations. Perhaps an important methodological outcome of this project has been to combine an antiessentialist perspective on national identities with a multilocated empirical analysis of diverse spatial and temporal sites—chronotopes—where nationhood is represented and contested. This multilocated perspective has shown that there is no single hegemonic version of national identity, but several disputing the power of representing nationhood. Hegemonic versions are under contestation and their possibility of success depends on the possibility of being translated into common sense and everyday life.

Weaving Some Threads

The formation of the Nicaraguan other in Costa Rica can be interpreted in the context of (post)colonial conflicts in Central America since the nineteenth century. Border conflicts between the two governments, initiated by the possible construction of a canal along the San Juan River, have created mutual animosities. As recently as March 2000 a new disagreement regarding the interpretation of the border treaty became once again a media event in newspapers along both sides of the frontier (*LN* 3/6/00). Furthermore, the expulsion of Nicaraguan peasants from their lands as a consequence of coffee expansion led thousands of them to Costa Rica, where the construction of the railway to the Atlantic region required workers. Overall, the Costa Rican nation has been constituted, over a long period, out of syncretic relations among diverse peoples—in particular indigenous populations, Europeans, mestizos, blacks, Asians, and Nicaraguans. Despite this diversity, the sense of nationhood in Costa Rica has been characterized by its ethnic and political uniqueness, which includes a strong sense of difference with regard to other Central American nations. The first historical interpretations, for instance, used comparisons with Nicaragua as a way of highlighting Costa Rica's unique character.

This constitution of the Nicaraguan as an other seems to articulate racialized and class-based representations. Indeed, if Nicaraguans were not such a dark-skinned and poor people, they would not be others. A Nicaraguan investor, for example, is recognized first of all as a businessman and secondly as a Nicaraguan. The term *nica* is reserved for the *poor* Nicaraguan. These racialized and class-based representations have been closely related to criminalization and social protest. For instance, the genocide of the Guatuso-Maleku community, located on the border between the two countries, has been interpreted within a nationalistic frame. The perpetrators were identified by their nationality and not by their economic interests in the exploitation of rubber. Similarly, banana plantations have been represented over the years as beyond the boundaries of the national territory, without morality and law. After the active participation in the strike of 1934 and the civil war of 1948, Nicaraguans became not only criminalized but also labeled in more explicit political terms as communists. This latter identification is especially relevant in Costa Rica, where the distinction of being an exemplary democracy has been driven by the contrast with communism.

These images of the Nicaraguan other are also crucial in the representation of an exclusive Costa Rican national identity, which, conversely, is defined as being middle-class, white, peaceful, and democratic. This crucial role of the Nicaraguan other does not suggest that it is the only reference of otherness in the Costa Rican imagined community. Indeed peasants and blacks have played similar roles, but another crucial feature of the Nicaraguan other remains in its location: it is situated externally as a threatening regime but also as a threat within, as a wave that swamps the nation, in one common media representation. Being inside and outside gives their presence a permanent salience.

During the 1980s the Sandinista government was represented as a communist threat in the region. Images similar to those created in the context of the strike of 1934 and the civil war of 1948 were reactivated. Nicaraguans were again portrayed as a "riotous" people, one whose violent character might go beyond a penchant for criminal offenses and turn to social protest. Sandinista governments were defeated in the Nicaraguan general elections of 1990 and 1996, while, in the international arena, the collapse of political regimes in Eastern Europe reconfigured the opposition between democracy and communism. These local and global political changes rendered meaningless the identification of the Nicaraguan other as a communist. Cold war ideologies have been replaced by a reinvigorated racialized politics, in which the Nicaraguan nationality as a whole has been categorized either in biological or cultural terms as a crucial other. The nica has replaced the Sandinista.

The media have played a key role in this transition. Nicaraguans are not a big political threat, but they are represented as problematic through diverse metaphors that relate body and nation in persuasive ways. Moreover, as shown in chapter 2, media representations have erased links between counterrevolutionary groups that received large-scale support from U.S. governments during the 1980s and bands that committed diverse robberies and kidnappings during the 1990s, making nationality, instead of political affiliation, the identifying characteristic of the culpable. Similarly, criminal acts in the northern region of Nicaragua have no relation to those committed in the south. Thus the lack of temporal and spatial links allowed the media to withdraw their support of the Contras and avoid any responsibility in the rise of kidnappings and other forms of criminality during the 1990s. In other words, framing is constructed through the fragmentation of temporal and spatial references.

The media have addressed this racialized politics as crime news, which is a journalistic genre without the salience of economics or politics but with a wider and more diverse readership that can easily identify the archetypal characters (e.g., heroes, helpers, victims, villains) that are present in the stories. Crime news items portray a very restricted range of offenses, especially those committed by disempowered people. Conversely, when a prosperous entrepreneur, for example, is suspected of fiscal evasion, such a crime is considered an item of economic news. Thus crime news items frame consistent distinctions between order and disorder which are deeply embedded in class-based divisions, generally taken for granted by the objectivity claimed by both the legal system and the institution of journalism. What is particularly relevant in this context is the misrecognition of crime news as a key form of constructing hegemony. Whereas there are frequent arguments about the "coverage" of political events, crime news is relegated to the shadows of a devalued job within the hierarchy of media institutions and academic research. Another major implication of media discourse has been to frame the Nicaraguan community in Costa Rica as a national problem. This practice has had a considerable impact on the views of those students who participated in the research, whose stories frequently associated Nicaraguans with violence. They reported that their principal source of information was the media rather than personal experience. That does not mean that during the 1990s the public has always accepted the media's views uncritically, but what is hardly disputable is that the Nicaraguan has been represented as an other.

Criminal news issues have not only constructed a racialized and criminalized representation of the Nicaraguan other, they have also facilitated the creation of an important sense of national belonging. A representation of Costa Rican national identity emerged under supposed diverse threats posed by immigration. This sense of national belonging is usually constructed as a collective actor, identified as the "we." *La Nación* has consistently considered itself able to define, "on behalf of the nation," the major problems posed by conflicts with Nicaraguan governments and by "immigrants." Notably in editorials, *La Nación* represents itself as a collective actor, which sometimes not only portrays the newspaper's views but also pretends to become *the* voice of the nation. Overall, it illustrates an assertion of this project, which argues that in the process of constructing the "other," a sense of national belonging, the "we," is also constituted.

The media combine criminalization with claims about the amount of money spent in public services for the Nicaraguan community. This emphasis on the exhaustion of public services, especially health, education, and housing, can be interpreted in the context of the decline of public investment in infrastructure and public services during the last two decades of the twentieth century in Costa Rica. The fieldwork reported in chapter 4 shows indeed that students whose families are vulnerable to this threat of decline are among those who are most hostile toward Nicaraguans. Especially students who belong to the lower middle classes represent the Nicaraguan other through metaphors of defilement, and such images seem to be more frequent among male students, though some female students also wrote racialized images. These images are activated under certain circumstances, especially when there is a sense of exclusion from a representation that identifies Costa Rica as a middle-class nation.

However, racialized images are not a simple working-class problem either. Certain pieces, written by students who belong, for example, to the upper class, identified the Nicaraguan community in Costa Rica as a plague. They do not feel economically threatened by Nicaraguans, but the latter are identified again with images of abjection (pollution, dirtiness, disease) that the bourgeoisie have historically attempted to expel materially and symbolically from their surroundings. Conversely, students who live in shantytowns, such as the community of La Carpio, where about half of the population is Nicaraguan, did not show great hostility toward Nicaraguans. As Les Back (1996, 71) has noted in the case of two of London's council estates, shared localities seem to offer an alternative identity to divisive and exclusive notions of nationality.

The stories written by students also showed an emergent new national identification, which represents Costa Rica as an "ecodemocracy." It combines landscape images and political values such as democracy, equality, and peace. The concept of ecodemocracy seems to rework old images of Costa Rica as the Switzerland of Central America, as depicted by travelers in the nineteenth century. The new context is characterized by the presence of tourism. As in the nineteenth century, the gaze of a desired other, the tourist, becomes a crucial way of favorably representing the nation. In contrast to the representations of the Nicaraguan community in Costa Rica, which have been dominated by overestimates of its numbers, there are no voices claiming that the number of tourists is too high, even though they rose to one million in 1999. Images of ecodemocracy seem to be the result of diverse discourses. They combine images present in some of the textbooks employed in formal education and images included in advertising campaigns that promote Costa Rica's attractions. These discourses, originating in diverse institutions, intersect and, in turn, are read in particular ways by students.

Interestingly, those students who considered tourism to be an important issue also expressed the most hostility toward the Nicaraguan community in Costa Rica. Tourists expect to find a clean and "ecological" country, and Nicaraguans—they argued—threaten both. This association seems to indicate two important consequences. First, ecological views might reinforce the exclusion and racialization of peoples by associating them with fears of pollution. Second, the opposition between tourists and immigrants confirms the shifting character of the "other." Both Nicaraguans and tourists are represented along the lines of racialized and class-based criteria: the Nicaraguan other is defined by dark skin and poverty, and the tourist is identified by whiteness and economic solvency. On the other hand, they are located in different ways; whereas tourists are desirable others, Nicaraguans are outside the core of national values.

This ambivalent other has been present in Costa Rica since the nineteenth century. The identification with idyllic views of Europe and lately with the "American" way of life augments the sense of difference from the rest of Central America. The attraction of European immigration was a permanent concern among politicians during the transition between the nineteenth and twentieth centuries. This identification with Europe and "America" has been worked out through the sense of difference regarding Nicaragua. For example, German traveler Wilhelm Marr, who introduced the metaphor of Costa Rica as the Switzerland of Central America, portrayed Nicaraguans as the "lost race."

On the other hand, to conceptualize Nicaraguans as others does not regard them as passive victims without agency. Indeed, the Nicaraguan community in Costa Rica has contested these racialized discourses. They live an intense internal tension between their own self-representation and racialized images circulating in the media. They know about their own contribution to Costa Rican society and recognize stigmatized discourses that claim that they are a burden to the Costa Rican economy. Although only a few Nicaraguans—most of them male and formerly engaged in the military conflict during the 1980s—have committed crimes, the Nicaraguan community as a whole is blamed for the rise of criminality and the spread of diseases such as cholera. Nicaraguan women are sometimes associated with prostitution. The testimonials explored these internal tensions between their own self-image and hegemonic versions that represent them as undesired others. Their writing illustrates precisely how these tensions are lived and how diverse informal networks of solidarity have been forged. The testimonials also showed the anxieties produced through being continuously addressed by the media without having any opportunity to express dissent. The chance to be an author offered the possibility of externalizing painful experiences and recognizing that other Nicaraguans live similar troubles. Writing was thought of as a way of reconciling deconstruction of racialized discourses and agency, creating a sense of community and exploring ways of self-organization.

Nonetheless, there are diverse topics that require further analysis. Future projects could look longitudinally at changes and continuities in the patterns identified in this project. Of special relevance would be an analysis of the emergence of the more inclusive representations of nationhood by students in the study who stressed that Costa Ricans and Nicaraguans possess human rights regardless of their nationality. This image is especially relevant, since neither the media nor the schools emphasize it. Equally important is to follow the discontent experienced by students from state schools, who fear being excluded from higher education and, in consequence, raise doubts about the "unique" attributes associated with the Costa Rican national identity.

A last topic that requires further study is the new identities that have been emerging in the context of daily interactions, especially between new generations of Nicaraguans and Costa Ricans. These new identities arise above all among youths, who have grown up in two countries and have to perennially negotiate their cultural backgrounds. These new generations are exposed to discourses that combine racialization and criminalization of Nicaraguans but simultaneously share experiences with them. This results in tension between generally narrow media imageries and lived experiences with peer groups especially in the neighborhood and the school. These youths, who share *the local* but are divided by public discourses regarding *the national,* might find common ground for instance through music—ska or reggae, for example—which might be considered a more *global* reference that sometimes overcomes the national divide and is "glocalized" in certain cultural spaces and practices. Rather than hybrid identities—a concept that sometimes underestimates that cultures interact under unequal power relations—these new identities express conflicts and modes of contestation in this landscape of displacement that characterizes Central America.

On Being Reflexive

There are at least three key sites of reflexivity that need to be addressed (see chapter 1). First is the social location of the researcher; another is the institutional domain in which the project is carried out. A last, but by no means less important, dimension consists of those concepts through which the research questions have been formulated. Researching Central American national identities in Britain might seem a contradiction in terms. However, this geographical distancing allowed me a sort of cultural and linguistic detachment from the mutual animosities between governments and the media on both sides of the Nicaraguan–Costa Rican border. The latter location has implied a permanent challenge, given my less-than-perfect English, but has also served as a point of reflection about the centrality of Spanish as an ethnic marker in the representation of the "other." Linguistic distancing made evident that what is called standard Spanish is merely another accent that never recognizes itself as such. This linguistic centralization seems to be a crucial device for the hegemonic constitution of a sense of nationhood.

Being in Britain has also enabled me to experience the rich tension between the lived experience of racialized boundaries that are still present in British society and academic debates on racism and nationalism. It has meant a permanent resistance to (post)colonial images that locate Britain as a world center that attracts tourists and celebrities. Indeed a multicultural Britain is far from the image promoted by the advertising and tourist industries and is scarcely recognized in mainstream academia.[1] My research in Britain has been a productive intellectual exercise in the recognition of racialized boundaries not only in Britain but, perhaps more important, in Costa Rica, where "race" is not a matter of debate as much as gender and even class are. This physical and intellectual detachment has precipitated, in turn, a new form of involvement in Central America—looking at those patterns of exclusion based on racialized boundaries which are crucial to the representation of an exclusive sense of nationhood in Costa Rica. In short, detachment enabled me to be surprised (Willis 1980) not by empathy but by difference and contrast.

I have lived involvement and detachment (Elias 1987a) in an effort to enrich the project with critical views, but at the same time I have attempted to keep my feet on the ground. In this sense, the institutional location of this research has sought to avoid the dichotomy between academic research and participatory action research. While the former is generally identified with university projects and sometimes criticized for its lack of engagement with local subjects, action research is carried out mostly by nongovernmental organizations and is called into question by academics for its voluntaristic views of social change. Perhaps the most damaging outcome of the separation between academic research and action research has been that this dichotomy has been taken for granted, for instance in the view that academic research does not require a situated engagement with particular social subjects. This project has addressed general questions regarding national belonging and difference but at the same time has sought to work dialogically with some of the subjects throughout the research project. The work with students in formal education as well as with members of the Nicaraguan community in Costa Rica endeavored to avoid precisely this dichotomy. Prescriptive claims on the politics of research, based frequently on vague experiences, are sometimes unable to translate general aims into particular research projects. Instead, located projects might show ways in which research can address current debates more convincingly without losing ground in local politics. The possibility of publishing in English adds another, more global, dimension which attempts to intervene in the field of Latin American studies, which is animated mainly by northern academia, with few possibilities of dialogue with those who practice social sciences and humanities in "América latina."

A third site of reflexivity involves the objectification of those concepts under which the research problem is thought and explored empirically. Throughout the last six years, most of my initial views have been modified. In particular, three displacements have had important repercussions. First, the relation self/other was assumed to be a binary opposition but later was reformulated as a mutually constitutive formation. Thus, the other is not external to the self/national representation but is inside the self and is indispensable, since the ideal self is feasible only through the expulsion of these undesired attributes. The self/other has been a useful category throughout this project but requires being situated both socially and historically. Only a permanent dialogue between conceptual debates and situated research problems can avoid the reification of theory. In particular, this transition has allowed me the conceptualization of the Nicaraguan other as indispensable for the representation of Costa Rican uniqueness.

Another important development has been the conceptualization of the links between racism and national identities, the relationship of which was not explicitly clarified in the first drafts of this project. A very important insight was provided by the consideration that difference is a powerful way of constructing commonalities. In particular, the distinction between the "true nationals" and the "immigrants"—Nicaraguans—is represented through racialization. Concepts such as class or gender have a currency in social sciences in Central America, whereas racialization, for example, has—as far as I know—no translation in Spanish. This absence shows the extent to which racism has frequently been missing from the agenda of the social sciences in the region. A third transition started with the awareness that part of the importance of national identities lies in their ability to articulate other identities under the heading of nationhood. Thus the sense of difference is produced by the recognition or misrecognition of images in which "race," class, sexuality, and gender are interrelated in diverse ways. Images of transgression shift frequently, seeing "others" now as criminals, now as prostitutes, now as diseased, or a combination of any of these. These articulations make national identities especially persuasive, since they can address wide sectors of the population in diverse ways but under similar themes. Yet they are continuously reworked and contested. In turn, these transitions have distanced this project from the perspectives considered initially as starting points, such as "migration studies," which have paid little attention to the fact that nations are not preconstituted formations "affected" by the arrival of "immigrants," who seek to be "integrated" in a new culture. Costa Rica—as many other nations—has been constituted by the permanent movement and displacement of people. Nations are diasporas continually made and remade under particular power relations. Another detachment took place in relation to interpretations of nationalism, either primordialist or modernist, that generally do not explore how national identities recognize or misrecognize other identities (see Smith 1998). Without these links, a sense of national belonging would hardly win support in everyday life. In particular, the reception of the concept of imagined communities in Central America has sometimes been characterized by looking at those aspects that have contributed to the formation of nationhood but have not always explored how such "communities" have also involved the exclusion of those who do not "fit" into the desired nation.

Although academic research findings seem to support the antiessentialist character of national identities, this antiessentialist view is not a dominant one in public debates on nationhood. For instance, the imagery of uniqueness is still pervasive in Costa Rica. A further task is to look at possible ways of decentering national identities, not only as an academic debate but also in terms of public understanding and policymaking.

Decentering the Nation?

National belonging constitutes a crucial identity not only because it is activated or mobilized by the media or the state but also because it is taken for granted most of the time in everyday life. Perhaps the most illustrative example of this naturalized sense of nationhood is the common question, Where do you come from? which is uttered in many languages and in many contexts. Interestingly, the question, Why does one need to belong to a nation? is scarcely asked. Although nations are recent and contingent forms of political and chronotopic organization, they have become naturalized, "timeless" entities.

Discourses on "immigration," for instance, seem to suppose that there are some people who are not immigrants (the citizens), whose ancestors have presumably belonged to the same nation since "primordial" times, as if no one in earlier times ever moved or changed their way of life. *Immigration* has become a "commonsense" word that requires critical debate; it illustrates what Pierre Bourdieu calls "unthought categories of thought which delimit the thinkable and predetermine thought" (1990, 56–57).[2] National identities are produced from the tension between centripetal and centrifugal forces. The former entails exclusivity; the latter calls for the obliteration of boundaries. Discourses on immigration, for example, illustrate centripetal forces emphasizing a sense of belonging.

Centrifugal versions call for more inclusive ways of life but, perhaps more important, for a permanent decentering of national belonging. The concept of decentering is used here following Mikhail Bakhtin's (1981) insights. Discussing the characteristics of the novel, Bakhtin argued that whereas poetry and epic narratives are characterized by the monologic presence of the author's views, the novel—especially those written by Dostoevsky—is characterized by heteroglossia: there is no single voice or dominant set of values. In *Crime and Punishment,* for example, Dostoevsky neither blames nor justifies Raskolnikov's decision. What is experienced in the novel can be translated into the analysis of nationhood: there are no founding fathers or idyllic past; any nation must obliterate its centeredness if it endeavors to historically explore its own formation.[3]

This decentering of national identities implies being able to imagine "oneself as another for oneself" not only in individual terms but also in a more collective mode. Decentering demands a permanent collective reflexivity, able to call into question received notions of national uniqueness. It is important in the case of Costa Rica but also more generally, since narratives of uniqueness are one of the most common features of nationhood. Bakhtin argued that national mythologies are organically fused with language. Decentering a nation comprises the decentralizing of the verbal ideological world; it means not only the recognition of diversity but also the awareness that there is no such thing as a center. Borrowing Bakhtin's interpretation of language (1981, 367), it means the loss of a sense of identity as a myth, that is, as an absolute form of thought. In short, the main concern of decentering is becoming rather than belonging. Between 1935 and 1936, long before the "linguistic turn," Bakhtin wrote, "This verbal-ideological decentering will occur only when a national culture loses its sealed-off and self-sufficient character, when it becomes conscious of itself as only one among *other* cultures and languages" (1981, 370; emphasis in original).

In particular, the autobiographies offer the possibility of perceiving that the Costa Rican nation is just one among others. Originally they were thought of as a means of exploring ways in which racialized discourses have addressed the Nicaraguan community in Costa Rica, but above all they provide an exceptional path toward decentering, being another than oneself through the gaze of an impoverished other.

Nicaraguans' autobiographies offer an opportunity—a third space—for the recognition of racialized and authoritarian elements present in the formation of nationhood. Although the Nicaraguan community in Costa Rica may not be completely aware of it, one of its major contributions has been to offer an opportunity for a more critical appraisal of the ways in which a sense of national belonging has been constituted in Costa Rica. This could be a singular opportunity for a more self-reflexive society, able to decenter itself and to stop taking icons and myths for granted. It would cause one's own sense of belonging to become strange. Thus the testimonials put Costa Ricans face to face with their own ways of stigmatization. As Bakhtin argues, "Our real exterior can be seen and understood only by other people, because they are located outside us in space and because they are others" (Bakhtin 1982, 352). Said provides a wider picture of this process:

> No one today is purely *one* thing. . . . Imperialism consolidated the mixture of cultures and identities on a global scale. But its worst and most paradoxical gift was to allow people to believe that they were only, mainly, exclusively, white or black, or Western, or Oriental. Yet just as human beings make their own history, they also make their cultures and ethnic identities. No one can deny the persisting continuities of long traditions, sustained habitations, national languages, and cultural geographies, but there seems no reason except fear and prejudice to keep insisting on their separation and distinctiveness, as if that was all human life was about. (1993, 407; emphasis in original)

Reflexive accounts such as this are supposed to be a key feature of modernity. However, as Peter Wagner (1994, 4) has argued, it is not clear whether such reflexivity is a desirable normative principle or a verifiable characteristic of modern institutions. The media, for instance, probably the key institutions in modern societies, are frequently defined by monologic views and the absence of self-criticism. Instead of calling for dialogue, media institutions usually fuel nationalistic and racialized conflicts (see chapter 2).

Despite the current predominance of antiessentialist perspectives in human and social sciences, nationalist and racialized discourses continue to deny that a nation is one among others, that each has no special uniqueness. In this sense, it is important to insist that a more contingent approach to national identities does not imply a more decentered representation of nationhood in public discourses. Calls for tolerance and multiculturalism, for example, might leave untouched the motives that reinforce racism and exclusion. As Hage has noted, "When those who are intolerant are asked to be tolerant, their power to be intolerant is not taken away from them. . . . the advocacy of tolerance left people *empowered* to be intolerant" (1998, 85, 86; emphasis in original). Similarly, liberal multiculturalism is deployed under the assumption that there is a "core" national identity and other "ethnic groups." Indeed, *ethnic majorities* is not a common expression (Wade 1997, 19). Statements such as "We are integrating the Nicaraguans into our culture" work under the assumption that the center of Costa Rican nationality is already constituted and the "others" are being added to it. Governmental decisions conferring citizens' rights (as in the amnesty analyzed in chapter 5) are a positive step but they do not guarantee a "practical nationality or citizenship" (Lister 1998). As Hage stresses, there is a "crucial difference between the multiculturalism of being and the multiculturalism of having" (1998, 140). Neither do promises of "globalization," "regional integration," and "postnational societies" guarantee more inclusive societies. A case in point is Europe, where old racisms do not seem to be challenged by integrationist policies (Gabriel 1994, 168).

Racialized representations will not disappear through the exposition of positive images of Nicaraguans, such as insisting that they are good workers. Neither would an economic regeneration of Central America guarantee an automatic decrease in racialization. Despite the multiple links between economic and cultural processes, the latter is not just a reflection of the former. Although more inclusive representations of national identity are always welcome, they might in turn become exclusive ones. In this sense, rather than just new inclusive elements, what seems to be required is a permanent self-critical detachment from the sense of nationhood. Decentering national identities is not only a discursive contestation; it also embraces power relations, since calling national identities into question also highlights racialized, class-based, and gendered inequalities. This is especially difficult in Costa Rica due to the lack of a culture of public debate. Nevertheless, this is an exceptional opportunity to discuss the historical formation of the sense of nationhood. If national identity were to become a subject of debate, it might be possible not just to challenge the racialization of the "other" by calling it the result of "prejudice" or "discrimination" but to decenter Costa Rican "uniqueness" entirely.

Appendix 1

Framing in News about Nicaraguans in Costa Rica, La Nación *and* La República, *1995–96*

La Nación 1995

Framing	Jan	Feb	Mar	Apr	May	Jun	Jul	Aug	Sep	Oct	Nov	Dec	Total
Immigration	7	1	1	-	-	-	1	-	-	-	-	-	10
Unidentified	-	-	-	-	-	-	-	-	-	-	-	-	-
Illegal Nicaraguans	3	-	1	-	-	-	1	-	-	-	-	-	5
Social services	-	-	-	-	-	-	-	-	-	-	-	-	-
Disease	-	-	-	-	-	-	-	-	-	-	-	-	-
Economic impact	-	-	-	-	-	-	-	-	-	-	-	-	-
Human rights violations	-	-	-	-	-	-	-	-	-	-	-	-	-
Governmental actions	3	1	-	-	-	-	-	-	-	-	-	-	4
Other	1	-	-	-	-	-	-	-	-	-	-	-	1
Crime News	4	16	3	1	2	-	5	3	2	-	-	5	41
Kidnapping	-	2	-	-	2	-	-	-	-	-	-	-	4
Robbery	1	2	-	-	-	-	1	-	-	-	-	-	4
Rape	-	-	-	-	-	-	-	-	1	-	-	-	1
Murder	2	11	2	1	-	-	4	-	1	-	-	5	26
Nicaraguan victim	1	1	-	1	-	-	-	-	1	-	-	-	4
Nicaraguan suspect	-	8	1	-	-	-	4	-	-	-	-	1	14
Nic. victim and suspect	1	2	1	-	-	-	-	-	-	-	-	4	8
Other	1	1	1	-	-	-	-	3	-	-	-	-	6
Borders	-	1	15	-	-	-	2	-	-	1	-	-	19
Limits	-	-	-	-	-	-	2	-	-	-	-	-	2
Duties	-	-	-	-	-	-	-	-	-	-	-	-	-
Incidents	-	-	15	-	-	-	-	-	-	-	-	-	15
Landmines	-	1	-	-	-	-	-	-	-	-	-	-	1
Other	-	-	-	-	-	-	-	-	-	1	-	-	1
Miscellaneous	-	-	-	-	-	-	-	-	-	-	-	-	-
Total	11	18	19	1	2	-	8	3	2	1	-	5	70

La Nación 1996

Framing	Jan	Feb	Mar	Apr	May	Jun	Jul	Aug	Sep	Oct	Nov	Dec	Total
Immigration	-	-	-	-	-	-	-	4	-	2	-	-	6
Unidentified	-	-	-	-	-	-	-	-	-	-	-	-	-
Illegal Nicaraguans	-	-	-	-	-	-	-	-	-	-	-	-	-
Social services	-	-	-	-	-	-	-	-	-	-	-	-	-
Disease	-	-	-	-	-	-	-	-	-	1	-	-	1
Economic impact	-	-	-	-	-	-	-	-	-	-	-	-	-
Human rights violations	-	-	-	-	-	-	-	2	-	-	-	-	2
Governmental actions	-	-	-	-	-	-	-	2	-	1	-	-	3
Other	-	-	-	-	-	-	-	-	-	-	-	-	-
Crime News	76	24	43	21	6	9	5	27	34	15	-	-	260
Kidnapping	74	24	43	20	5	6	5	24	34	12	-	-	247
Robbery	-	-	-	-	-	-	-	-	-	3	-	-	3
Rape	-	-	-	-	-	1	-	2	-	-	-	-	3
Murder	1	-	-	1	1	2	-	1	-	-	-	-	6
Nicaraguan victim	-	-	-	1	-	-	-	-	-	-	-	-	1
Nicaraguan suspect	-	-	-	-	-	-	-	-	-	-	-	-	-
Nic. victim and suspect	1	-	-	-	1	2	-	1	-	-	-	-	5
Other	1	-	-	-	-	-	-	-	-	-	-	-	1
Borders	-	-	-	-	-	1	-	-	-	1	-	1	3
Limits	-	-	-	-	-	-	-	-	-	-	-	-	-
Duties	-	-	-	-	-	-	-	-	-	-	-	-	-
Incidents	-	-	-	-	-	-	-	-	-	-	-	-	-
Landmines	-	-	-	-	-	1	-	-	-	1	-	1	3
Other	-	-	-	-	-	-	-	-	-	-	-	-	-
Miscellaneous	-	-	-	-	-	-	-	-	-	-	-	-	-
Total	76	24	43	21	6	10	5	31	34	18	-	1	269

La República 1995

Framing	Jan	Feb	Mar	Apr	May	Jun	Jul	Aug	Sep	Oct	Nov	Dec	Total
Immigration	6	5	-	-	1	1	1	-	5	1	2	-	22
Unidentified	-	-	-	-	-	-	-	-	-	-	-	-	-
Illegal Nicaraguans	4	1	-	-	-	-	1	-	2	-	1	-	9
Social services	-	-	-	-	-	-	-	-	-	-	-	-	-
Disease	-	1	-	-	-	1	-	-	1	1	-	-	4
Economic impact	-	-	-	-	-	-	-	-	-	-	-	-	-
Human rights violations	1	2	-	-	-	-	-	-	-	-	-	-	3
Governmental actions	1	1	-	-	-	-	-	-	2	-	1	-	5
Other	-	-	-	-	-	-	-	-	-	-	-	-	-
Crime News	1	-	2	-	-	1	4	1	-	1	2	1	13
Kidnapping	-	-	-	-	-	-	1	-	-	-	-	-	1
Robbery	-	-	-	-	-	-	1	-	-	1	-	-	2
Rape	-	-	-	-	-	-	-	-	-	-	-	-	-
Murder	1	-	2	-	-	1	2	1	-	-	-	1	8
Nicaraguan victim	-	-	-	-	-	1	-	-	-	-	-	-	1
Nicaraguan suspect	-	-	-	-	-	-	2	1	-	-	-	1	4
Nic. victim and suspect	1	-	2	-	-	-	-	-	-	-	-	-	3
Other	-	-	-	-	-	-	-	-	-	-	2	-	2
Borders	-	-	7	-	-	-	-	-	-	2	-	-	9
Limits	-	-	-	-	-	-	-	-	-	-	-	-	-
Duties	-	-	-	-	-	-	-	-	-	-	-	-	-
Incidents	-	-	7	-	-	-	-	-	-	2	-	-	9
Landmines	-	-	-	-	-	-	-	-	-	-	-	-	-
Other	-	-	-	-	-	-	-	-	-	-	-	-	-
Miscellaneous	-	1	-	-	-	-	-	1	-	-	-	-	2
Total	7	6	9	-	1	2	5	2	5	4	4	1	46

La República 1996

Framing	Jan	Feb	Mar	Apr	May	Jun	Jul	Aug	Sep	Oct	Nov	Dec	Tota
Immigration	3	3	1	-	-	-	1	1	1	3	-	1	14
Unidentified	3	-	-	-	-	-	-	-	-	-	-	-	3
Illegal Nicaraguans	-	-	-	-	-	-	-	-	1	-	-	1	2
Social services	-	1	1	-	-	-	-	-	-	-	-	-	2
Disease	-	-	-	-	-	-	1	-	-	-	-	-	1
Economic impact	-	1	-	-	-	-	-	-	-	-	-	-	1
Human rights violations	-	-	-	-	-	-	-	1	-	1	-	-	2
Governmental actions	-	-	-	-	-	-	-	-	-	-	-	-	-
Other	-	1	-	-	-	-	-	-	-	2	-	-	3
Crime News	52	5	21	11	5	3	2	20	23	-	-	-	142
Kidnapping	48	4	21	8	5	2	2	19	19	-	-	-	128
Robbery	-	1	-	2	-	-	-	-	2	-	-	-	5
Rape	1	-	-	-	-	-	-	-	1	-	-	-	2
Murder	1	-	-	1	-	-	-	-	1	-	-	-	3
Nicaraguan victim	-	-	-	-	-	-	-	-	-	-	-	-	-
Nicaraguan suspect	1	-	-	1	-	-	-	-	-	-	-	-	2
Nic. victim and suspect	-	-	-	-	-	-	-	-	1	-	-	-	1
Other	2	-	-	-	-	1	-	1	-	-	-	-	4
Borders	-	-	-	-	-	-	-	1	-	-	-	-	1
Limits	-	-	-	-	-	-	-	-	-	-	-	-	-
Duties	-	-	-	-	-	-	-	-	-	-	-	-	-
Incidents	-	-	-	-	-	-	-	1	-	-	-	-	1
Landmines	-	-	-	-	-	-	-	-	-	-	-	-	-
Other	-												
Miscellaneous	-	1	-	-	-	-	-	-	-	-	-	-	1
Total	55	9	22	11	5	3	3	22	24	3	-	1	158

Appendix 2

Toward a Network of Crimes Committed by Former Contras, 1991–96

1991

January 21

Romualdo Otárola was kidnapped in Pital, San Carlos (*LN* 5/4/94).

March 13

Víctor Cerdas Espinoza was kidnapped by former Contras (*LN* 5/4/94).

July 5

Four children and their father were murdered by former Contra Vicente Salmerón and Costa Rican Guillermo Aguilera in the community of Pocosol. During the eighties Salmerón and Aguilera were suspected of having committed several kidnappings and other crimes (*LN* 2/16/95).

Aguilera was murdered by members of the Sandinista Popular Army when he tried to escape persecution. Salmerón was killed by another former Contra, Santos Gómez, who was found guilty of six murders, robberies, and serious injury to two citizens (*LN* 2/16/95).

August 15

A merchant was assaulted (*LN* 5/4/94).

1993

Members of the Nicaraguan embassy in San José were kidnapped. This event started a series of kidnappings committed by former Contras. In 1996 it was revealed that José M. Urbina L., Guillermo Oporta, Dervin García, René Gaitán, and Julio Vega committed that kidnapping. García, Gaitán, and Vega took part in other kidnappings and assaults (*LN* 5/5/96, 6/4/96).

February 9

Juan R. Durán R. was assaulted by Teodoro Amador, who initially was considered responsible for the kidnapping in Boca Tapada [see 1996] (*LR* 1/8/96).

September 14

Agustín Aguilera M. was sentenced to twenty years in prison. He committed three murders (*LN* 7/27/94).

September 20

Joaquín Arauz A., Marco Zeledón A., and Juan G. Rodríguez kidnapped eleven Costa Ricans. Arauz and Zeledón were sentenced to seventeen years in prison (*LN* 4/7/94).

1994

April 10

Alfonso Altamirano threatened the elected Costa Rican President-elect José M. Figueres in San Carlos, Costa Rica. Altamirano admitted he had received military instruction from U.S. soldiers and mercenaries (*LN* 4/12/94).

May 1

Jairo Marín and Domingo Bermúdez, executives of the company Cabo Marzo, located in the northern region of Costa Rica, were kidnapped (*LN* 5/6/94).

Enrique Mendoza S., Dervin García R., and Ricardo Granados were found guilty of this crime. García also took part in the kidnapping in the Nicaraguan embassy (*LN* 3/15/96).

Mendoza and Granados, with other ex-Contras, committed robbery against the following businesses:

June 2

La Subasta Ganadera de Santa Ana (*LN* 8/18/94)

July 16

Olí Rent-a-Car (*LN* 8/18/94)

August 12

The Supermercados Periféricos in Hatillo and Pavas [not confirmed] (*LN* 8/18/94)

August 14

Mendoza and Granados also assaulted members of the Judicial Police and attempted to kidnap former Costa Rican MP Carlos Monge H. (*LN* 8/18/94).

November 1

A supermarket located in the community of Guatuso was presumably robbed by former Contras (*LR* 11/4/94).

1995

April 6

Gilberth F. Venegas was murdered. The principal suspect is René Gaitán, who participated in the kidnapping at the Nicaraguan embassy (*LN* 12/14/95).

Gaitán is also suspected of robbing the Banco de Costa Rica in Guápiles County and the gas station La Bomba, in Sarapiquí County.

1996

January 1

Two women are kidnapped in the community of Boca Tapada by Armando Aragón O., José F. Rodríguez M., Absalón Rodríguez M., Pedro A. Wong M., and Julio Vega. The kidnappers belonged to Contra groups—the South Front of the National Opposition Union (UNO) and the Democratic Revolutionary Alliance (ARDE)—that were operating on the border between Costa Rica and Nicaragua during the eighties (*LN* 6/30/96, 7/31/96, ?/7/96)

There was also an attempt to kidnap the Costa Rican ambassador to Nicaragua. The kidnappers wanted to exchange him for Julio Vega, leader of the Boca Tapada kidnapping. As mentioned above, Vega took part in the kidnapping at the Nicaraguan embassy in San José and in the kidnapping at Boca Tapada (*LN* 6/28/96).

August 24

Two Dutch citizens were kidnapped by Esteban Paiz L., Apolinar Requenes O., Justo Requenes O., Lucas Vivas López, Efrén Vivas L., Eugenio Sequeira M., and José de Jesús Reyes. The kidnappers were former members of the National Resistance, another Contra group (*LT* 10/5/96).

Paiz et al. robbed several shops in Chontales, Nicaragua, before that kidnapping (*LR* 9/21/96; *ND* 10/4/96).

Sources: La Nación, La Tribuna, La República, El Nuevo Diario.

Appendix 3

International News about Nicaragua, La Nación, *1994–96*

TOPIC	1994	1995	1996	TOTAL
POLITICAL ISSUES	37	109	66	212
Division within FSLN	17	4	-	21
Conflict between Chamorro's government and EPS	10	4	3	17
Constitution	3	67	-	70
1996 elections	2	11	35	48
Denunciation of fraud	-	-	13	13
Demonstrations	-	3	-	3
Strikes	3	6	1	10
Corruption	1	-	-	1
Confiscation	1	4	1	6
Polit. disenchantment	-	1	-	1
San André's dispute with Colombia	-	9	-	9
Clandestine graves	-	-	4	4
Pope's visit	-	-	9	9
CRIME NEWS	7	12	14	33
Robbery	4	6	7	17
Kidnapping	2	3	4	9
Criminality	1	1	-	2
Drug dealing	-	2	3	5
DEVELOPMENT	7	11	6	24
Economy	3	3	4	10
Drought	4	-	-	4
Health	-	7	1	8
Ecology	-	1	1	2
OTHER	-	-	5	5
TOTAL	51	132	91	274

Source: La Nación, 1994, 1995, 1996.

Appendix 4

News Actors in Reports about Nicaraguan General Elections (1996)

ACTORS IN ELECTIONS	FREQUENCY
A. Alemán	32
D. Ortega	20
V. Chamorro	11
Electoral council	9
S. Ramírez	4
A. Lacayo	4
B. Obando	6
Other candidates	2
Civil society	4
Observers	6
Media	5
U.S. government	3
FSLN	2
Parliament	4
Other	2
TOTAL	114

Source: La Nación, 1996.

Appendix 5

Stories by Primary and Secondary Students about Costa Rica as a Nation

Topic	Lincoln		S. Clare		Conbi		Poás		San Carlos		V. Calvo		D. Alighieri		Pavas	
	F	M	F	M	F	M	F	M	F	M	F	M	F	M	F	M
Home	6	-	-	2	-	-	-	-	1	1	-	-	-	-	-	-
Treasury	3	1	-	1	-	-	3	3	-	-	-	-	-	-	3	1
Cent. Am. Switzerland	-	-	-	-	-	-	1	1	-	-	-	-	-	-	-	-
Natural attributes	6	4	5	3	1	1	4	-	4	2	2	1	4	4	1	2
Political values	2	10	3	2	1	2	5	1	1	1	-	-	-	-	-	2
Nature + political values	-	-	3	2	-	4	2	-	-	-	-	-	2	4	-	-
God's creation	-	-	1	-	-	-	-	-	-	-	-	-	-	-	-	-
Technological progress	-	-	2	-	-	-	-	-	-	-	-	-	1	-	-	-
Diversity + contrasts	-	-	2	-	-	-	1	-	-	-	-	2	-	-	-	-
Hospitality	-	-	-	-	-	-	-	-	-	-	-	-	-	-	-	-
Tradition	-	-	-	-	-	-	-	-	-	-	-	1	-	1	-	-
Nature + antivalues	-	-	-	-	2	1	-	-	4	2	-	-	-	1	-	-
Values + deforestation	-	-	-	-	1	-	-	-	-	-	-	-	-	-	-	-
Values + antivalues	-	-	-	1	-	-	1	-	2	1	-	-	-	-	-	-
Values + criminality	-	-	-	-	-	-	-	-	1	-	-	-	-	1	-	-
Deforest. + antivalues	-	-	1	-	-	-	-	-	-	-	2	-	-	-	-	-
Criminality	-	-	-	-	-	-	-	-	1	-	-	-	2	4	-	-
Power/wealth concent.	-	-	2	1	-	-	-	-	-	1	1	1	1	-	3	1
Antipolitical values	-	-	-	-	-	-	-	-	-	-	2	1	-	-	1	-
Loss of identity	-	-	-	-	-	-	1	-	3	5	3	2	-	-	2	1
Deforestation	-	-	-	-	2	4	-	-	1	1	-	-	2	3	1	-
Conformism	-	-	-	1	-	-	1	-	-	1	-	-	-	-	-	-
Other	1	-	1	-	-	-	-	1	-	-	-	-	-	-	-	-
Total	18	15	20	13	7	12	19	6	18	15	10	8	12	18	11	7

Appendix 5 (continued)

TOPIC	SIQUIRRES		SARAPIQUÍ		LOS SITIOS		RINCÓN GRANDE		LA CARPIO*				TOTAL	
	F	M	F	M	F	M	F	M	F/N	M/N	F/CR	M/CR	F	M
Home	-	1	-	-	1	-	-	-	-	-	-	-	8	4
Treasury	-	-	-	-	-	-	-	-	-	-	-	-	9	6
Cent. Am. Switzerland	-	-	-	-	-	-	-	-	-	-	-	-	1	1
Natural attributes	1	2	2	3	2	1	2	2	2	6	4	4	40	35
Political values	1	3	3	2	4	4	6	1	-	-	-	1	26	29
Nature + political values	-	-	-	-	4	-	-	1	-	2	4	1	15	14
God's creation	-	-	-	-	-	-	-	-	-	-	-	-	1	-
Technological progress	-	-	-	-	-	-	-	-	-	1	-	-	3	1
Diversity + contrasts	-	1	-	1	-	-	-	-	-	-	-	-	3	4
Hospitality	-	-	1	-	-	-	-	-	-	-	-	-	1	-
Tradition	-	-	1	1	-	-	-	-	-	-	-	-	1	3
Nature + antivalues	-	-	-	-	-	-	-	-	-	-	-	-	6	4
Values + deforestation	-	-	-	-	-	-	-	-	-	-	-	-	1	-
Values + antivalues	-	-	-	1	2	-	-	-	1	-	-	-	6	3
Values + criminality	-	-	-	-	-	-	-	-	-	-	-	-	1	1
Deforest. + antivalues	-	-	-	-	-	-	-	-	-	-	-	1	3	1
Criminality	-	-	-	-	1	-	-	-	-	-	-	1	4	5
Power/wealth concent.	4	-	-	-	-	-	1	-	-	-	-	-	12	4
Antipolitical values	-	-	-	-	-	1	-	-	-	-	-	-	3	2
Loss of identity	-	-	-	-	-	-	-	-	-	-	-	-	9	8
Deforestation	-	-	-	-	-	1	-	-	-	-	-	1	6	10
Conformism	-	-	-	-	-	-	-	-	-	-	-	-	1	2
Other	-	-	-	-	1	-	-	-	1	-	-	-	4	1
TOTAL	6	7	7	8	15	7	9	4	4	9	8	9	164	138

*La Carpio students are grouped into four categories: female Nicaraguans (F/N), male Nicaraguans (M/N), female Costa Ricans (F/CR), and male Costa Ricans (M/CR).

Appendix 6

Portrayal of Nicaraguans in Costa Rica in Stories by Primary and Secondary Students

Portrayal	Lincoln		S. Clare		Conbi		Poás		V. Calvo		D. Alighieri		Pavas	
	F	M	F	M	F	M	F	M	F	M	F	M	F	M
Seeking opportunities	11	8	10	3	-	-	1	2	-	-	2	4	1	-
Good workers	4	2	2	6	1	4	3	-	1	1	2	-	-	2
Equal rights	-	-	-	-	1	-	3	1	1	2	-	-	-	2
Diversity	-	1	1	1	-	-	-	-	1	2	-	-	-	-
Discriminated against	-	2	3	-	-	3	5	1	1	-	1	2	-	1
Poor/ humbled/sad	-	-	-	-	-	-	1	-	-	-	-	-	-	-
Friendly	-	-	-	-	-	-	-	-	-	-	-	-	-	-
God's children	-	-	-	-	-	-	-	-	1	-	-	-	-	-
Good workers/ criminals	-	-	2	-	2	3	3	1	2	1	2	3	4	1
Criminals	-	-	-	-	-	-	-	-	1	-	-	2	1	-
Must leave Costa Rica	-	-	1	-	2	1	1	-	-	-	-	1	-	-
Too many	-	-	-	-	-	-	-	-	1	1	-	1	2	-
Take Costa Ricans' jobs	-	-	-	-	-	-	-	-	-	-	4	4	1	-
Water-related tropes	-	-	-	-	1	1	2	1	1	1	-	-	1	-
Plague	-	2	1	3	-	-	-	-	-	-	-	-	-	-
Dirty/ugly/ bad habits	-	-	-	-	-	-	-	-	1	-	1	-	-	-
Different culture	-	-	-	-	-	-	-	-	-	-	-	-	-	-
Must be happy to be in CR	-	-	-	-	-	-	-	-	-	-	-	-	1	1
Total	15	15	20	13	7	12	19	6	11	8	12	17	11	7

Appendix 6 *(continued)*

Portrayal	Siquirres		Sarapiquí		Los Sitios		Rincón Grande		La Carpio*				Total	
	F	M	F	M	F	M	F	M	F/N	M/N	F/CR	M/CR	F	M
Seeking opportunities	-	3	-	-	-	1	-	-	-	5	1	1	26	27
Good workers	1	-	-	-	2	2	-	3	-	1	2	1	18	22
Equal rights	-	1	3	-	3	1	1	-	4	1	2	2	18	10
Diversity	-	1	3	-	-	-	-	-	-	-	-	-	5	5
Discriminated against	-	-	-	-	-	-	-	-	-	-	-	-	10	9
Poor/ humbled/sad	-	-	-	-	-	-	4	1	-	2	1	-	6	3
Friendly	-	-	-	-	2	-	-	-	-	-	-	-	2	-
God's children	-	-	-	-	-	-	1	-	-	-	-	-	2	-
Good workers/ criminals	3	1	-	1	4	2	-	-	-	-	-	2	22	15
Criminals	1	1	1	3	1	-	-	-	-	-	-	1	5	7
Must leave Costa Rica	-	-	-	-	-	-	-	-	-	-	1	1	5	3
Too many	-	-	-	-	-	-	-	-	-	1	-	1	3	4
Take Costa Ricans' jobs	-	-	-	-	-	-	-	-	-	-	-	-	5	4
Water-related tropes	-	-	-	2	1	-	-	-	-	-	-	-	6	5
Plague	1	-	-	-	-	-	-	-	-	-	-	-	2	5
Dirty/ugly/ bad habits	-	-	-	-	-	-	1	-	-	-	-	-	3	-
Different culture	-	-	-	-	1	-	-	-	-	-	-	-	1	-
Must be happy to be in CR	-	-	-	-	-	-	-	-	-	-	1	-	2	1
Total	6	7	7	6	14	6	7	4	4	10	8	9	141	120

*La Carpio students are grouped into four categories: female Nicaraguans (F/N), male Nicaraguans (M/N), female Costa Ricans (F/CR), and male Costa Ricans (M/CR).

Notes

Introduction

1. In all, about three million Central American citizens, 10 percent of the total population (Román 1998), have left their countries during the violence and economic strangulation of the last two decades. The Salvadoran community in the United States, for instance, numbers about two million people (Cañas 2001, 40). The high concentration of Salvadoran and Mexican citizens in Los Angeles makes it the second most likely place for Salvadorans and the third most likely for Mexicans to live (Hondagnue-Sotelo 2001, 8; García Canclini 1999, 52).

2. In other Central American nations, nonparticipation has been traditionally high: 54 percent in Guatemala (1995), 55 in El Salvador (1995), 35 in Honduras (1993), 20 in Nicaragua (1996), and 26.3 percent in Panama (1995) (*LT* 12/2/95; *LN* 10/23/96, 2/3/98).

3. Interestingly, *America* is used to refer to the United States, whereas other regions need to be specified; for instance, Latin America (for a notable exception, see Gabriel 1998, 196). In turn, Latin America is usually identified with South America, leaving the Caribbean, Central America, and Mexico as "unnamed" regions.

4. A reflection about class origins seems to be a paradoxical process. As Lynne Pearce observes, "Only once one has been given middle-class citizenship can one take pride in one's roots and not be ashamed because 'what I was is not what I now am'" (in Skeggs 1997, 97).

5. A recent collection of essays has addressed issues regarding testimonial and translation in the "Unitedstatesian" academia (Kearney 1991, 54). In the introduction, Georg Gugelberger notes, "Obviously the euphoric 'moment' of the testimonio has passed, and it is now time to assess in a more self- and metacritical spirit its reception by the critical and academic disciplines" (1996, 1). In a solid critique of the founding statement published by the Latin American subaltern studies, Gareth Williams identifies several challenges that derive from "a disciplinary practice that automatically positions the subaltern as 'peripheral' to our theoretical site of 'centrality'" (1996, 229).

Chapter 1

1. Latin America as a region as well as several Latin American nations in particular have been defined as unique in literature and other forms of representation (Brunner 1993; Larraín 1996, 171). Chile has been considered a unique country, with more economic initiative than its neighbors (Larmer 1998, 20); Colombia is also unique, since it is "both the Latin America's oldest democracy and the western hemisphere's most violent country" (Villaceves, in Marcus 1998, 22); the Sandinista revolution was described by its "uniqueness" (Olivares 1993, 7). Perhaps the most profound notion of uniqueness was constructed in Mexico after the revolution of 1910, indeed "there is no other [country] like Mexico!" (Knight 1996, 1). The multicultural constitutions of Canada and Australia have also been defined as "unique" (Mackey 1996, 144, 167; Hage 1998). Englishness is an example of uniqueness par excellence—England hardly recognizes itself as just another nation (Hall 1991b, 21). The decline of the British Empire has been replaced by the "American way of life," another form of uniqueness "in which the dominant localizes and naturalizes itself and associates with it a variety of other forms" (Hall 1991a, 67).

2. Many studies have looked at racialization in Latin America. Since it is almost impossible to read all of them, I focused on those books and articles that have critically explored the concept of mestizaje: Graham 1990b; Stepan 1991; Wade 1993, 1997; Bourgois 1994; Palmer 1995, 1996; Radcliffe and Westwood 1996; and Gould 1997.

3. These key dimensions have been of abiding interest in social and cultural theory. Peter Berger and Thomas Luckmann (1966), for instance, provided an interesting formulation long ago: *objectivation* of social reality in the form of representations, *internalization* of intersubjective relations, and *externalization* of such relations in terms of institutions and social order are considered key processes in the social construction of reality. What seems to be missing in this formulation, as well as in other interactionist and phenomenological perspectives, is how these dimensions are configured, internalized, and eventually resisted and contested in specific sets of historical power relations.

4. Such preferences not only result from theoretical positions, but also express processes of institutionalization of academic agents. Ethnography and fieldwork in general are sometimes perceived as a job for beginners but not suitable for consolidated agents in the academic field. Theory, on the other hand, is a valuable resource in the process of acquiring academic power. Sometimes the more theoretical, general, or abstract academic work is, the

greater is its recognition and the easier its marketing. In the field of cultural studies, as David Morley (1992, 3) notes, theory travels and sells best (see also Johnson 1993b, 101–2; Willis 1997, 187–88).

5. I will not inquire into the perennial debates about the authorship of the "disputed books." For a discussion of the orthodox Marxist interpretations of language during the 1920s, specially Marr's and Stalin's perspectives, see Radics and Keleman (1983). Charles Woolfson (1976) and Stuart Hall (1986) offer differing approaches to Voloshinov within cultural studies. Billig (1997) explores the relevance of Bakhtin's contributions for the future of cultural studies.

6. Michael Gardiner (1992) and Craig Brandist (1996) offer interesting contrasts between Gramsci and the Bakhtin Circle. Beyond their differences, both perspectives share a considerable interest in exploring dimensions such as common sense and everyday genres.

7. Bakhtin identified three crucial chronotopes among a wide range of literature. The first is especially associated with the ordeal novel, in which the hero is tested through a succession of troubles that are finally resolved. Such testing does not appear to leave traces, since the hero does not experience changes throughout the plot (1981, 106). A second type of chronotope is the adventure novel, where unusual events take place. The individual becomes other than what he was (115). A third conception of chronotope is described as the connection of the hero with his or her time and space. "Life is historicized," maintains Bakhtin (167, 177, 209). Biographical writing has played an important role in this transition toward an open-ended narrative since issues considered private began to be the subject of public genres (123).

8. Testimonial literature has been a frequent experience in Latin America. Although most of the publications have suffered from a restricted cultural circulation, they have become an important encounter between deconstruction of meanings and political agency. Women working in sweatshops on the U.S.-Mexican border (Iglesias 1985), peasants in Costa Rica (UNA 1981; ASEPROLA 1997), and relatives of "missing" people in Chile (Rojas et al., 1987) are among the lesser known experiences.

Chapter 2

1. Nicaraguans have a relatively lower opinion of the media. In a 1995 survey done by the Centro de Investigaciones en Communicación (Center for Communication Research), 49 percent of those consulted in Managua felt newspapers did not offer an accurate perspective on current affairs. Under

such conditions, the media could seldom act as interlocutors between citizens and the political elite.

2. *Barricada* was closed in February 1998 during the crisis experienced by the Sandinista National Liberation Front (FSLN).

3. In English, as in Spanish, "to cover" could mean either "to attend to" or "to hide." Sometimes, *coverage* seems to indicate the latter meaning!

4. Leoncia seems to be addressing not only a local racialized politics but also an extended "global racism." For example, Jean-Marie Le Pen, the leader of the French National Front, stated, "I prefer my daughters to my nieces, my nieces to my cousins, my cousins to my neighbors, my neighbors to my fellow citizens, my fellow citizens to foreigners. What's wrong with that?" (in Gabriel 1994, 169).

5. Uli Linke (1999, 138) notes important similarities between the fantasies of members and officers of the Freikorps (militias that fought the German working class after World War I) and discourses on immigration published in German newspapers during the 1980s and 1990s. Again both seem to be threatened by "floods" that undermine boundaries. In a similar vein, Jorg Haider, the leader of the far right in Austria, claimed that the inclusion of Eastern countries in the European Union "would swamp the country with impoverished Slav immigrants" ([London] *Daily Telegraph,* 2/9/00).

6. The denunciation by *Nuevo Diario* was presented as a nationalist claim framed within the style of tabloid journalism. One of the headlines was "Migra [immigration authorities] Worse than Nazis" (*ND* 2/23/95).

7. In this conjuncture, members of the Nicaraguan Resistance (Contras) threatened the Nicaraguan consul in the Costa Rican community of Los Chiles, Alajuela Province. They were motivated by her lack of interest in the face of the human rights violations (*LN* 8/25/96; *LP* 8/26/96).

8. The interpretation offered about the Costa Rican example by this editorial is similar to those historical interpretations and fictional writings that identify Costa Rica with rural democracy and uniqueness and will be discussed in chapter 3.

9. The analysis of autobiographies written by members of the Nicaraguan community in the context of this project (see chapter 5) expands on how these racialized discourses have been contested by Nicaraguans themselves.

10. In 1996 there were about three hundred thousand cases of cholera in Latin America. U.S. environmental authorities estimated that $200 billion will have to be spent on new water and sewage systems in order to prevent further epidemics in the region (Nathan 1996, 370).

11. Stuart Hall, speaking of the BBC in Britain, offers a balance that can be employed in the case of *La Nación:* "It produced the nation which it ad-

dressed: it constructed its audience by the ways in which it represented them" (in Morley and Robins 1994, 196).

Chapter 3

1. In a study by the Universidad Nacional in Costa Rica peasants from different regions of the country were invited to write their lived experience. The organizers received 815 pieces, representing over a third of people initially registered. The university published twenty-seven contributions in five volumes; five by women and twenty-two by men. Unfortunately, there are few references on the ways in which women represent and contest narratives of nationhood (UNA 1981).

2. It might be suggested that the neutrality of Switzerland during World War II inspired a step further in this comparison and that the natural similarities were enlarged with political commonalities since both nations share a peaceful destiny (Manuel López, in Cersósimo 1978, 51). Thus, the Switzerland of Central America combined both natural and political attributes.

3. In turn, as Douglas Tompson notes, for English and North American travelers the contact with the ways of life of Central American peoples "served to validate these travelers' inflated sense of their native countries' importance as wellsprings of 'civilization,' 'industry' and 'progress'" (1998, 8).

4. As early as the 1930s, Mario Sancho (1980, 132) advanced a bold critique. He noted that in a context of economic crisis, idyllic versions of the past became a way of making sense of the decline.

5. The image of the Switzerland of Central America was a matter of public discussion in 1998 in letters to the editor published by *La Nación* online. While some readers attempted to demonstrate the truth of the comparison, others denied the analogy, arguing that Costa Rica does not have, for instance, the "cleanliness of the Swiss." However, none of them inquired into the origins of such a naturalized representation of the Costa Rican national identity. In other words, the past is present. This debate coincided with several xenophobic and racist letters to the editor in which some readers claimed that the number of Nicaraguans had increased dramatically. Thus identification with "significant others," such as the Swiss, and negative feelings projected onto Nicaraguans, seem to be dimensions of the same process. Identity and difference are complementary ways in which the "true nationals" are represented. Both significant others and "outsiders" are indispensable.

6. Arnoldo Mora considers *El costarricense* "a masterpiece of the national literature that has had wide acceptance among the national audience and

tourists" (1997, 122, 135, 139). By 1994, *El costarricense* had seen eight reprints.

7. This "natural" source of identity has had strong appeal. The Costa Rican ambassador to Nicaragua delivered a lecture at a Nicaraguan university in 1996 in which he reworked this link between nature and nation: "This lack of vocation for international relations is a consequence of Costa Rican history, which began in the mountains, where people are shy and distrustful; the plainsman on the other hand is open, uninhibited, and confident. . . . These are two completely different attitudes that have influenced foreign policy. Costa Rica was born looking inward. . . . Nicaragua, on the other hand, since Rubén Darío's literature, has had an outward perspective. Nicaragua was born asking itself, What is beyond the lake?" (*LP* 9/11/96).

8. Costa Rican "national" literature emerged in the last decades of the nineteenth century (A. Quesada 1988, 1998). The first period is identified with the liberal epoch between 1870 and 1914, a period characterized by debates between nationalist perspectives and cosmopolitan claims. Tradition and modernity disputed the hegemony of representing nationhood, though both shared an exclusionary representation of the nation (Ovares et al. 1993; Quesada 1998, 37). A new formation arises in the context of the liberal crisis and international developments such as the Russian Revolution, World War I, and the U.S. interventions in Latin America. The interpretation of these events meant a rupture with the liberal conception of nation, and plebeian characters, which had been considered external to the "national" narrative, became subjects of novels during this period (Quesada 1988, 198; Quesada 1990). A third period could be identified with the emergence of social or radical literature in the 1940s. New geographical locations, new characters, and new problems appear within a context defined by realistic aesthetics and political commitments (Quesada 1998, 128).

9. The colonial elite were not a harmonious group either. There were frequent conflicts between the Spanish governors and the local elite, and the control of commercial activities was a source of dispute between them (J. Fernández 1998, 74).

10. In 1848, Costa Rica was declared a republic by the then chief of state, José María Castro. In 1998, Castro's great-great-grandson, Miguel Angel Rodríguez, president of the republic, celebrated the 150-year-old decision of his ancestor. Interestingly, contemporary news reports turned this family heritage into an exemplary tradition (*LN* 8/31/98). An alternative interpretation might argue that the conquistadors' dynasty is still alive. This event replaced an eventual debate of the fiftieth anniversary of the civil war of 1948 that I will discuss later in this chapter.

11. In the second edition, published in 1979, Rodríguez acknowledged that

if this new impression had any relevance, it was to show how much social sciences had changed since he wrote this essay at the beginning of the 1950s.

12. *Concho* is a derivation of Concepción, a common name in rural areas of Costa Rica until, perhaps, the first decades of the twentieth century. Concepción probably comes from the "conception" of the Virgin Mary (Láscaris 1994, 116).

13. *La Patada*'s producer, Parmenio Medina, was murdered in July 2001; two years later no information was available about those responsible for his death.

14. Similar images of peasants have been depicted in other Latin American societies. The gaucho in Argentina and the charro in Mexico illustrate also how peasants are represented as national icons but at the same time as objects of derision among the urban "learned society."

15. *Pachuco,* according to Simon Webb (1998), is a nickname given to those Mexican men who arrived in the United States in the 1920s and sought to dress in an elegant manner, seeking to be "accepted" there. Probably, the word *pachuco* arrived in Costa Rica in the 1950s or 1960s with Mexican films, which became very popular then.

16. Homi Bhabha (1994, 145, 148) notes that national identities are constructed through a double narrative, in which people are "object" and "subject." They are the object of a nationalist pedagogy, based on a pregiven historical origin, but they are also subjects of a performative discourse in which they appear as contemporaneity, "as a sign of the present through which national life is redeemed as a reproductive process." Thus a sense of nationhood can be produced only through narration, which makes possible the mixing of these pedagogic and performative versions.

17. When I started teaching at the university, a colleague commented that the style of my jeans "reflected" my plebeian background. I do not know if I have overcome my shame, but at least I know where *his* authority comes from.

18. The poem was dramatized in the final ceremony of the autobiographies' project. Most of the authors and their families had, probably for the first time, the opportunity of seeing a representation of their lives, written and performed by peasants (UNA 1981, 272).

19. Costa Rican literature from the 1940s became a key political reference when I was at secondary school. It has been disquieting to come across violent images of indigenous or foreign people that I did not perceive when I read these works more than twenty years ago.

20. This scene of a little girl being surprised by the "discovery" of a black child is close to Franz Fanon's experience, in which a little girl says about him: "Look at the nigger! . . . Mama, a Negro" (1986, 113). Being kissed by the little girl is a singular event in Cocorí's life since it implies physical contact

with a "white" child. Pieterse also notes how "washing" blacks has been a popular motif in soap advertising. "In Dutch," he argues, "in the eighteenth century and after, the saying 'washing the Moor' simply meant to undertake something impossible" (1991, 195). Interestingly, a picture postcard published in the Netherlands in 1932 illustrates precisely a little white child "scrubbing off" a black child (196).

21. Even today the inhabitants of Nicoya are sometimes called *nicas regalados* (unwanted Nicaraguans) since their Costa Ricanness is under "suspicion."

22. Similar developments took place in 1998, when fourteen Nicaraguan border communities announced their intention to become part of Costa Rica as a consequence of their lack of basic public services such as electricity, roads, and water supply. Interestingly, new right governments had just come to power in both countries and this conflict "on behalf of the motherland" and against "an external threat" became a national crusade that contributed to the forging of political alliances on both sides of the border. Nicaraguan newspapers denounced a possible "pact" between the right-wing government and the FSLN (*LT* 8/19/98). In fact, most of the Sandinista members of the parliament and Alemán's government, formerly bitter rivals, agreed that the nation was under threat. It was reported that the Costa Rican government suffered a similar lack of popularity . This conflict even included religious authorities since the Nicaraguan cardinal and the Costa Rican archbishop had a violent disagreement, which meant a singular "clerical" intervention in a so-called secular problem.

23. In March 1903 the U.S. Congress approved the construction of the canal across the isthmus of Panama (which at that time belonged to Colombia). The move was a consequence of Nicaragua's refusal to cede the civil jurisdiction of a portion of land along the canal to the United States (Kinloch 1994, 53, 55).

24. In the 1840s and 1850s, the filibusters were used "to invade or aid in a revolution in another country in order to gain money and power. The American government did little to stop these people" <http://www.vanderbilt.edu/register/Mar11_02/story8.html>

25. The identification of Nicaraguans with rubber tapping and violence is still present among the population of Costa Rica's northern region, as Alvaro Chaverri, a reporter at a local radio station, noted (interview, 2/24/99). Such an identification might have been reactivated in the context of border conflicts and kidnappings that took place in the region in the last two decades of the twentieth century (see chapter 2).

26. Darío's poetry is the most distinguished literature of the liberal period in Central America. In Nicaragua his poetry also became an arena of dispute

among different ideologies. Darío has been interpreted by Pablo Antonio Cuadra, one of his most persuasive supporters, as "a universal Nicaraguan, the best synthesis of the Nicaraguan mestizaje" (P. Cuadra 1987, 72). Literary critic Julio Valle argues that "Nicaragua is a republic of poets . . . a republic invented by poetry" (1993, 41). As María Pérez (1998) has shown, Darío has been a cohesive figure in diverse nation-building projects in Nicaragua.

27. According to the description provided by Joaquín Gutiérrez (1976), this social movement could be the strike of 1934, mentioned above.

28. The key role of characters from the national bourgeoisie in *Puerto Limón* might be related to the Communist Party's views on Latin America. They argued that the national bourgeoisie could become an anti-imperialist subject around which the working classes—which are considered too weak to undertake the leadership—could achieve social reforms. It could be a contextual element in this discussion, but I am by no means reducing fiction writing to political imperatives.

29. This image is similar to one analyzed by Franz Fanon, in which spending a night with a white woman is interpreted as a desire to be white: "By loving me she proves that I am worthy of white love. I am loved like a white man" (1986, 63).

30. Women are also often associated with negative roles. Diana and Elvira, characters in *Puerto Limón,* are related to materialistic values. In *Gentes y gentecillas,* an abortion is considered a woman's fault, whereas the baby's father is not criminalized. Also in the novel, a Panamanian woman who was working in a cabaret cheated and abandoned her husband in an interesting combination of gender and nationality markers (Fallas 1986, 274). In *Bananos,* Quintana (1962, 54–57) also represents women as agents of immoral acts.

31. The civil war took place in the context of U.S. interventions and local political contradictions between Conservatives and Liberals. After the end of the U.S. intervention that took place between 1912 and 1925, President Díaz asked for a new intervention, which was justified by the Liberal opposition to his Conservative government. The Liberal protest soon became also an anti-imperialist resistance against this new U.S. intervention. Among the liberals was Augusto César Sandino, who in 1927 would organize the Ejército Defensor de la Soberanía Nacional (EDSN, Army for the Defense of National Sovereignty). In 1934 the EDSN and the government signed a peace treaty, but Sandino was murdered a year later by the National Guard (Wünderich 1995).

32. After this strike the tradition of resistance among black workers, consolidated in the strikes of 1913 and 1918, was eroded. Meanwhile, the Communist Party did not address issues of ethnicity as part of its politics (Echeverri-Gent 1992, 296–97).

33. I came across this collection of letters for the first time in 2000 and two years later I reread them. The loss of my father was the main event in my life between these two readings and it might have made me more aware of the intensity of Rosa's worries since I was also abroad during my father's illness.

Chapter 4

1. In Costa Rica primary and secondary education lasts six and five years respectively. Access to the institutions was negotiated with the principals, who in turn made contact with a teacher, under whose coordination the activity was carried out. Most institutions showed interest in this initiative.

2. The Organization of Central American States (ODECA) published another collection in the 1960s. It was a regional initiative that aimed to offer reading materials to Central American children in areas such as mathematics, Spanish, social studies, and the natural sciences. Up to 1973, over three and a half million copies had been published. Costa Rican academics criticized this collection for undermining the core of Costa Rican nationality, since the books were written in El Salvador without much knowledge of Costa Rica's history (Ovares 1978, 75, 86). In the 1980s the Ministry of Education published a collection of books titled *Toward the Light;* it was the first state initiative after the ODECA's collection.

3. There were some institutional disputes between Santillana and the University of Costa Rica about the simultaneous publication of two collections in a relatively small market. While Santillana argued that it was unfair competition, the university emphasized the expertise of its faculty in research and publication. Unfortunately, there were no debates about the different conceptualizations of nation present in the collections.

4. Women have only recently been recognized as citizens, as indicated by the struggle for female suffrage. The Feminist League presented projects to the parliament in 1931, 1934, and 1939 that advocated allowing "literate" women to vote, but they were not approved (Eugenia Rodríguez 1998, 18). As early as 1941, Gonzalo Facio, several times deputy and minister, "reasoned" against women's right to vote in Costa Rica because, he said, such a decision would multiply the nation's problems, since women did not have "positive values" (in Solís 1992, 162, 305). Women would not get the vote until 1953.

5. Paradoxically, in 1874 the Atlantic Railroad Company, which was in charge of the construction of the railway, "sold" the Chinese workers who had gone on strike for better job conditions. Fourteen of them were "acquired" by Guardia (Edelman 1998, 377).

6. In 1936, Rafael Calderón Guardia and Teodoro Picado Michalski, at the time deputies and later presidents, suggested banning the distribution of Communist literature through the post offices. In 1942 the government banned the Communist Party's newspaper from public libraries. The PC was the most suppressed organization during the political ferment of the 1940s in Costa Rica (Solís 1992, 121, 305).

7. Hartmann and Husband in Britain found a similar conclusion early in the 1970s. They determined that racist attitudes were more evident among those children who lived in areas where they have little direct contact with the black population (in Morley 1999, 145). Furthermore, the far right in Britain has done better in areas (e.g., East London) where the immigrant presence has not been so high. What seems to inspire these allegiances is the threat associated with the newcomers, especially in areas that have experienced a long-term industrial decline (Gabriel 1998, 158).

8. An unintentional implication of autobiographical writing is its intrinsic selective character, since only those having spare time and literacy would send their contributions. However, this project taught me how these limitations could be overcome for many of the participants.

9. Similarly, Homi Bhabha suggests that any interpretation is never simply an act of communication between the self (I) and the other (you): "The production of meaning requires that these two places be mobilized in the passage through a Third space" (1994, 36). This third space is the space of enunciation, which "makes the structure of meaning and reference an ambivalent process" (37).

10. The interpretations regarding domestic work provided by Stallybrass and White (1986) and McClintock (1995) follow the pioneering contributions made by historian Leonore Davidoff (1995), published originally in the 1970s.

11. In the context of Hurricane Mitch, the government was negotiating an aid package for $37 million with the U.S. authorities in order to cope with state spending on immigration (*LN* 8/30/99).

12. Leoncia addressed me as an inscribed reader, though we had not met each other yet. She knew about the testimonials from listening to a radio program. In a more general perspective, Sommer points out that testimonials address the reader "by the immediate appeal to 'you'": "When the narrator talks about her*self* to *you,* she implies both the existing relationship to other representatives selves in the community and potential relationships that extend her community through the text" (Sommer 1988, 118; emphasis in original).

13. Interestingly, this critical religious common sense is not present in a testimonial written by Martín, who has been heavily involved in a Pentecostal church. For him, any success or failure is the result of God's will.

Chapter 5

1. A notable exception to this confrontational conjuncture was a humorous and critical radio program, *La Patada* (The kick). One of the characters, Rugama, expected to do good business with the money provided to the Contras by Reagan. Meanwhile, his wife, Milda, constantly blamed him for his laziness. The Contras were portrayed in carnivalistic terms. To what extent this critical view was shared by the audience has been left unexplored.

2. The MCRL began its activities in 1962 in response to the Cuban Revolution, and the peak of its activities occurred in 1974, when it resisted extending diplomatic relations to the former Soviet Union (Sandoval 1985a, 7–8).

3. As early as 1982 the government withdrew the monthly magazine *Aportes* from post offices in response to criticism from the Monge administration.

4. I interviewed one of them for the first time in 1984 as part of a journalistic project (Sandoval 1985a). I suppressed their names in order to preserve the anonymity of their claims.

5. Little attention has been paid to the number of Nicaraguan financial groups operating in Costa Rica. According to figures published by the financial authorities, nine out of twenty of these investment groups are Costa Rican, four are Nicaraguan, and the rest of the capital comes from Panama, El Salvador, Guatemala, Mexico, the United States, Canada, and Taiwan (PNUD 2000, 157).

6. This was one of the few cases in the news reports in which Nicaraguans were considered agents. Moreover, the reports were not typified as crime news but appeared in the national news section; the stories were framed differently, by journalists with different professional experience.

7. The voices of the government and the newspaper are fused. The latter takes over the official discourse about Nicaraguans as its own. Such assimilation might be the consequence of a close political relationship between *La República* and Liberación Nacional, the political party in office during the presidential term of 1994–98.

8. Nicaraguans maintain, another liberal intellectual states, "a dubious loyalty and weak identification with the national symbols and institutions" (Vega-Carballo, quoted in Alvarenga Venutolo 1998, 69).

9. These and other examples suggest that the emergence of interactive media and a "virtual society" are by no means a guarantee of dialogic narratives.

10. Name withheld, e-mail to the author.

11. Such responses were similar to those obtained in Nicaragua, where two-thirds of those polled supported the possibility of being governed by a "strong leader" (Delgado 1995, 59). There are similar cases in South Amer-

ica, and Brook Larmer argues that "the frustration with crime and corruption has led Latin Americans to increasingly favor hard-line politicians" (1998, 19), like Gen. Hugo Banzer in Bolivia, Hugo Chaves in Venezuela, Alberto Fujimori in Peru, and Gen. Harold Bedoya in Colombia.

12. Adorno et al. (1950, 711) suggest that in an unresolved relationship with the father, the subject seeks to be on the side of his father's authority. This could explain the genesis of authoritarianism, conventionalism, and conservatism. In turn, the hatred against the father is projected onto certain groups through ethnocentrism. The opposite takes place when there is no recognition of limits or authority. Thus the subject feels himself able to commit any crime against others. While in the former case there is a strong superego that acknowledges authority as an invariable reference and subordination as the most pleasurable condition, in the latter there is no resolution of the Oedipal complex, and narcissism is therefore strong. The weak point of this typology seems to be its lack of historical references.

13. Holding outsiders responsible for crimes is a common pattern. Despite statistics, rape, for instance, is frequently associated with "strangers" and not with relatives and acquaintances of the victim, who are most often the perpetrators of rapes (Rohr 1995).

14. The U.S. case shows how the decline in incomes in the industrial sector is not principally generated by newcomers but is a consequence of the decline of the U.S. economy in the world market. The urgency of cutting costs has meant, for instance, moving some plants to Mexico (Borjas, in Orozco 1997, 28).

15. I inquired at the clinics of San Carlos, Siquirres, and Sarapiquí Counties, close to plantations and farms that offer jobs to Nicaraguan workers, to find out whether they registered information about spending on Nicaraguan patients. None had such information, although in 1999 they were starting to document it. Some members of the staff had been surprised when the national health authorities published estimated health spending for Nicaraguans, because they, in their local clinics, did not have such accounts! (See *LN* 8/7/99.)

16. José Gabriel Román (1998, 10–11) estimates that including 3,080 Nicaraguan families in the Family Housing Bonus—$5,000 given to each family to build a home—would require an increase in expenditures of nearly $16 million, which is equal to about twenty percent of public spending on the housing bonus for 1997.

17. Building a house can consume one's whole life. Almost every day for about two years, a mason took one block from the construction project on which he was working, hiding it in his bag. These blocks helped him construct his own house. Ironically, masons and carpenters build houses but they seldom have the means to assemble their own.

18. Indeed, a son of the last Somoza announced his political projects in Nicaragua. "His" new party, the Nationalist Democratic Force, promised that "lost prosperity" would return to Nicaragua (*DE* 2/13/99).

Conclusion

1. For example, the increasing acceptance of British cultural studies in Latin America does not seem to take into account the centrality of debates on racism in the constitution of the field; cultural studies is read, rather, as another theory.

2. Immigration is not just a consequence of globalization, Hobsbawm notes: "There is relatively less international migration today than a century ago" (1998a, 5). However, the "retreat of social sciences into the present" (Elias 1987a) makes it difficult to approach long-term perspectives.

3. Decentering and other contributions of Bakhtin later became familiar concepts within poststructuralism. See Zavala (1991) and Emerson (1997) for critical views on these developments. A recent collection of essays has highlighted the centrality of Bakhtin's concerns for the understanding of national identities. Galin Tihanov, for example, suggests that "Bakhtin's theory of the novel can be seen to function as a latent theory of nation and nationalism" (2000, 55). However, this optimism regarding the novel as a cultural form has to be examined carefully. Said (1994, 82, 84–85), for example, has shown how English novels without overt political connotations are unthinkable without capitalist and imperial expansion. Further research might look at the implications of these diverse interpretations.

Bibliography

Autobiographies

Authors are identified by their initials. A few of the autobiographies were published by EUNA under the title *Autobiografías campesinas* (5 vols.). The rest are available from the Department of Social Promotion, Universidad Nacional, Heredia, Costa Rica.

A. P. C. 1979. "Autobiografía de Angelita." Vol. 1. Heredia, Costa Rica: EUNA.

E. S. C. 1979. "Autobiografía de El Compositor Cariareño." Vol. 2. Heredia, Costa Rica: EUNA.

F. V. Z. 1979. "Autobiografía." Vol. 2. Heredia, Costa Rica: EUNA.

H. A. 1979. "Autobiografía." Vol. 1. Heredia, Costa Rica: EUNA.

H. S. Z. 1982. "Autobiografía." Vol. 3. Heredia, Costa Rica: EUNA.

L. E. S. 1981. "Autobiografía." Vol. 5. Heredia, Costa Rica: EUNA.

M. O. A. 1982. "Autobiografía." Vol. 4. Heredia, Costa Rica: EUNA.

Newspapers

COSTA RICA

Al Día (AD)
Diario Extra (DE)
La Gaceta (LG)
La Nación (LN)
El Norteño (EN)
El Pacífico (EP)
La Prensa Libre (LPL)
La República (LR)

NICARAGUA

Barricada (B)
El Nuevo Diario (ND)
La Prensa (LP)
La Tribuna (LT)

Books and Articles

Acuña, Marielos, and Doriam Chavarría. 1991. "El mestizaje: La sociedad multiracial en la ciudad de Cartago (1738–1821)." Licenciate thesis, Universidad de Costa Rica.

Acuña Ortega, Víctor Hugo. 1984. *La huelga bananera de 1934.* San José: CENAP/CEPAS.

———. 1986. "La transición del capitalismo en Costa Rica." In *El desarrollo económico de Costa Rica: De la colonia a la crisis de 1930,* by V. H. Acuña Ortega and I. Molina. San José: Editorial Alma Mater.

———. 1992–93. "Artesanos, obreros, y nación en Centroamérica en el período Liberal (1870–1930)." *Revista de historia* (Managua) 2.

———. 1995. "Historia del vocabulario político en Costa Rica: Estado, república, nación, y democracia." In *Identidades nacionales y estado moderno en Centroamérica,* ed. A. Taracena and J. Piel. San José: EUCR/FLACSO–El Salvador.

Adorno, Theodor, et al. 1950. *The Authoritarian Personality.* New York: Harper and Brothers.

Ahmad, Aijaz. 1992. *In Theory: Classes, Nations, Literatures.* London: Verso.

Allan, Stuart. 1994. "'When Discourse Is Torn from Reality': Bakhtin and the Principle of Chronotopicity." *Time and Society* 3 (2).

Alter, Peter. 1983. *Nationalism.* London: Edward Arnold.

Alvarenga Venutolo, Patricia. 1997. *Conflictiva convivencia: Nicaragüenses en Costa Rica.* Cuadernos de ciencias sociales, no. 101. San José: FLACSO.

———. 1998. "La identidad amenazada: Los costarricenses ante la inmigración nicaragüense." *In Memoria: Política, cultura, y sociedad en Centroamérica: Siglos XVIII–XX,* ed. M. Vannini and F. Kinloch. Managua: Instituto de Historia de Nicaragua y Centroamérica, UCA.

———. 1999. "La immigración extranjera y la nación costarricense." Photocopy.

Anderson, Benedict. 1983. *Imagined Communities.* London: Verso.

Araujo, Patricia. 1991. "El graffiti: Una comunicación alternativa." *Herencia* (San José) 3 (1–2).

ASEPROLA (Asociación Servicios de Promoción Laboral). 1997. *Historias de vida.* San José: EUNED.

ASTRADOMES (Asociación de Trabajadoras Domésticas de Costa Rica). 1997. *Situación del oficio doméstico: Estudio por muestra, Costa Rica.* San José: ASTRADOMES/CONALCTRAHO.

Avirgan, Tony, and Martha Honey. 1989. *John Hull: El finquero de la CIA.* San José: Varitec.

Azofeifa, Isaac. 1971. "La isla que somos." In *Ensayistas costarricenses,* ed. L. Ferrero. San José: Imprenta Lehmann.

Back, Les. 1996. *New Ethnicities and Urban Culture: Racisms and Multiculture in Young Lives.* London: UCL Press.

Bakhtin, Mikhail. 1981. *The Dialogic Imagination: Four Essays.* Ed. M. Holquist. Trans. C. Emerson and M. Holquist. Austin: University of Texas Press.

———. 1982. *Estética de la creación verbal.* Trans. T. Bubnova. Mexico City: Siglo XXI Editores.

Balibar, Etienne. 1991a. "Class Racism." In *Race, Nation, Class: Ambiguous Identities,* ed. E. Balibar and I. Wallerstein. Trans. C. Turner. London: Verso.

———. 1991b. "The Nation Form: History and Ideology." In *Race, Nation, Class,* ed. E. Balibar and I. Wallerstein. London: Verso.

———. 1991c. "Racism and Nationalism." In *Race, Nation, Class,* ed. E. Balibar and I. Wallerstein. London: Verso.

Barboza, Francisco. 1997. "La situación de la empleada doméstica nicaragüense en San José, Costa Rica." Master's thesis, Universidad de Costa Rica.

Barker, Martin. 1981. *The New Racism: Conservatives and the Ideology of the Tribe.* London: Junction Books.

———. 1989. *Comics, Power, and the Critics.* Manchester: Manchester University Press.

Barthes, Roland. 1972 [1957]. *Mythologies.* London: Cape.

Bennett, Tony. 1979. *Marxism and Formalism.* London: Methuen.

Berger, Peter, and Thomas Luckmann. 1966. *The Social Construction of Reality: A Treatise in the Sociology of Knowledge.* Harmondsworth: Penguin.

Bertaux, Daniel. 1988. "El enfoque biográfico: Su validez metodológica, sus potencialidades." In *Historia oral e historias de vida,* ed. V. H. Acuña Ortega. Cuadernos de ciencias sociales, no. 18. San José: FLACSO.

Bhabha, Homi. 1994. *The Location of Culture.* London: Routledge.

Billig, Michael. 1995. *Banal Nationalism.* London: Sage.

———. 1997. "From Codes to Utterances: Cultural Studies, Discourse, and Psychology." In *Cultural Studies in Question,* ed. M. Ferguson and P. Golding. London: Sage.

Bourdieu, Pierre. 1986. *Distinction.* Trans. R. Nice. London: Routledge.

———. 1990. *In Other Words: Essays toward a Reflexive Sociology.* Trans. M. Adamson. Cambridge: Polity Press.

———. 1993. *Sociology in Question.* Trans. R. Nice. London: Sage.

———. 1998. *On Television and Journalism.* Trans. P. Parkhurst Ferguson. London: Pluto.

———. 2000. *Pascalian Meditations.* Trans. R. Nice. Cambridge: Polity Press.

Bourdieu, Pierre, and Wacquant, Loïc. 1992. *An Invitation to Reflexive Sociology.* Chicago: University of Chicago Press.

Bourgois, Phillipe. 1994. *Banano, etnia, y lucha social en Centroamérica.* San José: DEI.

Bradley, Harriet. 1996. *Fractured Identities: Changing Patterns of Inequality.* Cambridge: Polity Press.

Brandist, Craig. 1996. "Gramsci, Bakhtin, and the Semiotics of Hegemony." *New Left Review* 216.

Braudel, Fernand. 1980. *On History.* Trans. S. Matthews. Chicago: University of Chicago Press.

Breuilly, John. 1982. *Nationalism and State.* Manchester: Manchester University Press.

Bromley, Roger. 1988. *Lost Narratives: Popular Fictions, Politics, and Recent History.* London: Routledge.

Brunner, José J. 1993. "Tradicionalismo y modernidad en la cultura latinoamericana." In *América Latina a fines de siglo,* ed. J. L. Reyna. Mexico City: FCE.

Cáceres, Rina. 1986. "Lo que se cuenta en Costa Rica: Un análisis del discurso histórico oficial en dos textos básicos de la historia de Costa Rica." Licenciate thesis, Universidad de Costa Rica.

———. 1996. "Negros, mulatos, esclavos, y libertos en la Costa Rica del siglo XVII." Ph.D. thesis, Universidad Iberoamericana, Mexico.

Cañas, Roberto. 2002. "Eleccíones á la vista y diplomacia activada." *Envío* (Managua) no. 242.

Carvajal, Amalia. 1997. *Características socioeconómicas y epidemiológicas de la población nicaragüense atendida en el servicio de obstetricia y las implicaciones financieras para el Hospital San Carlos de la Región Huetar Norte CCSS, 1997.* San José: Instituto Centroamericano de Administración Pública.

Carvajal Alvarado, Guillermo. 1994. *Costa Rica: Análisis demográfico de su población (1522–1988).* San José: Cuadernos para la Enseñanza de los Estudios Sociales, Escuela de Historia y Geografía, Universidad de Costa Rica.

Casanova, Rafael. 1995. "¿Héroes o bandidos? Los problemas de interpretación de los conflictos políticos y sociales entre 1845 y 1849 en Nicaragua." In *Nicaragua en busca de su identidad,* ed. F. Kinloch. Managua: Instituto de Historia de Nicaragua.

Casey Gaspar, Jeffrey. 1979. *Limón, 1880–1940: Un estudio de la industria bananera en Costa Rica.* San José: Editorial Costa Rica.

Castro, Carlos, and Abelardo Morales. 1998. *La inserción laboral de la fuerza de trabajo nicaragüense en el sector de la construcción, la producción bananera, y del servicio doméstico en Costa Rica.* San José: FLACSO.

CCCS (Centre for Contemporary Cultural Studies, University of Birmingham). 1980. "Recent Developments in English Studies at the Centre." In *Culture, Media, Language: Working Papers in Cultural Studies, 1972–79,* ed. S. Hall, D. Hobson, A. Lowe, and P. Willis. London: Routledge.

CCSS (Caja Costarricense de Seguro Social). 1999. *Relación Morosidad Cobro Administrativo vs Cobro Judicial.* San José: Departamento de Gestión de Cobros.

CENIDH (Comisión Nicaragüense de Derechos Humanos). 1998. *Derechos humanos en Nicaragua.* Managua: CENIDH.

Cerdas, Jaime. 1994. *La otra vanguardia.* San José: EUNED.

Cersósimo, Gaetano. 1978. *Los estereotipos del costarricense.* San José: EUCR.

Chaney, Elsa, and Mary García Castro, eds. 1993. *Muchacha, cachifa, criada, empleada, empregadinha, sirvienta y . . . más nada: Trabajadoras del hogar en América Latina y el Caribe.* Trans. C. Guayara Sánchez. Mexico City: Editorial Nueva Sociedad.

Chavez, Leo. 2000. *Covering Immigration: Popular Images and the Politics of the Nation.* Berkeley: University of California Press.

Clare, Mariette, and Richard Johnson. 1998. "Method in Our Madness? Identity and Power in a Memory Work Method." In *Memory and Method,* ed. S. Radstone. Oxford: Berg.

Clarke, John. 1991. *New Times and Old Enemies: Essays on Cultural Studies and America.* London: HarperCollins Academic.

Clifford, James, and George Marcus, eds. 1986. *Writing Culture: The Poetics and Politics of Ethnography.* Berkeley: University of California Press.

Cohen, Phil. 1980. "Subcultural Conflict and Working Class Community." In *Culture, Media, and Language,* ed. S. Hall, D. Hobson, A. Lowe, and P. Willis. London: Routledge/CCCS.

Colley, Linda. 1994. *Britons: Forging the Nation, 1707–1837.* London: Vintage.

Cordero, Luis Fernando. 1999. "Costarricenses cada vez más inseguros." *Presencia universitaria* (Universidad de Costa Rica) 66.

Córdova, Ricardo, and Michael Seligson. 1995. "Nicaragua 1991–1995: Una cultura política en transición." In *Cultura política y transición democrática en Nicaragua,* ed. R. Córdova and G. Maihold. Managua: Instituto de Estudios Nicaragüenses, Centro de Análisis Socio-Cultural, UCA.

Crang, Mike. 1998. *Cultural Geography.* London: Routledge.

Cuadra, Abelardo. 1977. *Hombre del Caribe.* Ed. S. Ramírez. San José: EDUCA.

Cuadra, Manolo. 1962. Prologue to *Bananos: La vida de los peones de la Yunai* by E. Quintana. San José: Ediciones Distribuidora Cultural.

Cuadra, Pablo Antonio. 1987. *El nicaragüense.* San José: Asociación Libro Libre.

Dadivoff, Leonore. 1995. *Worlds in Between: Historical Perspectives on Gender and Class.* Cambridge: Polity Press.

DaMatta, Roberto. 1991. *Carnivals, Rogues, and Heroes. An Interpretation of the Brazilian Dilemma.* Trans. J. Drury. Notre Dame, Ind.: University of Notre Dame Press.

Davies, Charlotte. 1999. *Reflexive Ethnography.* London: Routledge.

Delgado, Rodolfo. 1995. "Gobernabilidad, cultural política, y opinión pública." In *Cultura política y transición democrática en Nicaragua,* ed. R. Córdoba and G. Maihold. Managua: Instituto de Estudios Nicaragüenses, Centro de Análisis Socio-Cultural UCA.

Dijkstra, A. 1999. "Technocracy Questioned: Assessing Economic Stabilisation in Nicaragua." *Bulletin of Latin American Research* 18 (3).

Dobles, Fabián. 1979 [1947]. *El sitio de las abras.* San José: Editorial Costa Rica.

Douglas, Mary. 1966. *Purity and Danger.* London: Routledge.

Dyer, Richard. 1997. *White.* London: Routledge.

Echeverri-Gent, Elisavinda. 1992. "Forgotten Workers: British West Indians and the Early Days of the Banana Industry in Costa Rica and Honduras." *Journal of Latin American Studies* 24 (1).

Echeverría, Aquileo. 1976 [1905]. *Concherías.* San José: Imprenta Lehmann.

Edelman, Marc. 1998. "A Central American Genocide: Rubber, Slavery, Nationalism, and the Destruction of the Guatuso-Malekus." *Comparative Studies in History and Society* 40.

Elias, Norbert. 1978. *What Is Sociology?* London: Blackwell.

———. 1982. *The History of Manners.* Vol. 1 of *The Civilising Process.* Trans. E. Jephcott. London: Blackwell.

———. 1987a. *Involvement and Detachment.* London: Blackwell.

———. 1987b. "The Retreat of Sociology into the Present." *Theory, Culture, and Society* 4:223–47.

———. 1994. Introduction to *The Established and the Outsiders* by N. Elias and J. Scotson. 2d ed. London: Sage.

———. 1996. *The Germans: Power Struggles and the Development of Habitus in the Nineteenth and Twentieth Centuries.* Ed. M. Schroter. Trans. E. Dunning and S. Mennell. Cambridge: Polity Press.

Emerson, Caryl. 1997. *The First Hundred Years of Mikhail Bakhtin.* Princeton, N.J.: Princeton University Press.

Epstein, Debbie, and Richard Johnson. 1997. *Schooling Sexualities.* Buckingham: Open University.

Erdheim, Mario. 1995. "Lo propio y lo ajeno." In *Etnopsicoanálisis y hermeneútica profunda en la investigación social: Reflexiones sobre el rascismo.* Trans. Jorge Sanabria. Actualidades en psicología, vol. 11, no. 87. San José: Instituto de Investigaciones Psicológicas, Universidad de Costa Rica.

Facio, Rodrigo. 1975 [1942]. *Estudio sobre la economía costarricense.* San José: EUCR.

Fairclough, Norman. 1995. *Media discourse.* London: E. Arnold.

Fallas, Carlos Luis. 1981 [1947]. *Gentes y gentecillas.* San José: Editorial Costa Rica.

———. 1986 [1941]. *Mamita Yunai.* San José: Editorial Costa Rica.

Fanon, Franz. 1986. *Black Skin, White Masks.* London: Pluto.

Fernández, José Antonio. 1998. "La competencia por la hegemonía entre representaciones metropolitanas y élites locales. Espacios y mecanismos de confrontación en Costa Rica a finales de la colonia 'clásica.'" In *Cultura, política, y sociedad en Centroamérica: Siglos XVIII–XX,* ed. M. Vannini and F. Kinloch. Managua: Instituto de Historia de Nicaragua y Centroamérica, UCA.

Fernández Guardia, Ricardo. 1970 [1929]. *Costa Rica en el siglo XIX.* San José: Editorial Costa Rica.

———. 1984 [1909]. *La cartilla histórica de Costa Rica.* San José: ECR.

Ferrero, Luis, ed. 1971. *Ensayistas costarricenses.* San José: Editorial Costa Rica.

Ferreto, Adela, and Carlos Luis Sáenz. 1980. *Leer y escribir: Tercer grado.* San José: Editorial Costa Rica.

———. 1981. *Mi pequeño mundo 2.* San José: Editorial Costa Rica.

Ferreto, Adela, and Carlos Meléndez. 1981. *Nueva historia de Costa Rica.* San José: Editorial Costa Rica.

Fiske, John. 1996. *Media Matters: Race and Gender in U.S. Politics.* Rev. ed. Minneapolis: University of Minnesota Press.

Fletcher, Jonathan. 1997. *Violence and Civilization: An Introduction to the Work of Norbert Elias.* Cambridge: Polity Press.

Fonseca, Elizabeth, et al. 1996. *Estudios sociales* 6. San José: Hacia el Siglo XXI/EUCR.

Fonseca, María E. 1999. "Educación: Medicina preventiva." *Presencia universitaria* (Universidad de Costa Rica) 60 (May).

Foro Emaús. 1996. *Diagnóstico de la situación de los migrantes de la diócesis de Limón, Costa Rica.* Limón: Pastoral Social Diócesis de Limón–Foro Emaús.

Foucault, Michel. 1980. *Power/Knowledge.* New York: Pantheon.

Fuentes, Raúl. 1990. *Un campo cargado de futuro: El estudio de la comunicación en América Latina.* Mexico City: FELAFACS.

Fumero, Patricia. 1995. "De la iniciativa individual a la cultura oficial: El caso del General José Dolores Estrada, década de 1870." In *Nicaragua en busca de su identidad,* ed. F. Kinloch. Managua: Instituto de Historia de Nicaragua–PNUD.

Gabriel, John. 1994. *Racism, Culture, Markets.* London: Routledge.

———. 1998. *Whitewash: Racialized Politics and the Media.* London: Routledge.

García, Alfonso, and Gilberth Guzmán. 1998. "Estudio de las condiciones de vida de los migrantes nicaragüenses en las fincas bananeras para orientar políticas de salud." Master's thesis, Universidad de Costa Rica.

García Canclini, Néstor. 1999. *La globalización imaginada.* Buenos Aires: Paidós.

Gardiner, Michael. 1992. *The Dialogics of Critique: M. M. Bakhtin and the Theory of Ideology.* London: Routledge.

Garita, Nora. 1999. *Ni ciudadanos ni consumidores.* San José: PNUD.

Gellner, Ernest. 1983. *Nations and Nationalism.* Oxford: Blackwell.

Giddens, Anthony. 1986. *The Constitution of Society.* Berkeley: University of California Press.

———. 1991. *Modernity and Self-identity: Self and Society in the Late Modern Age.* Cambridge: Polity Press.

Giglioli, Giovanna. 1996. "¿Mito o idiosincracia? Un análisis crítico de la literatura sobre el carácter nacional." In *Identidades y producciones culturales en América Latina,* ed. S. Ortiz. San José: Editorial Universidad de Costa Rica.

Gil, José. 1996. "Controlaron el espacio, hombres, mujeres, y almas." Paper presented at Tercer Congreso Centroamericano de Historia, San José.

Gilman, Sander. 1985. *Difference and Pathology: Stereotypes of Sexuality, Race and Madness.* Ithaca: Cornell University Press.

———. 1988. *Disease and Representation.* Ithaca: Cornell University Press.

Gilroy, Paul. 1987. *There Ain't No Black in the Union Jack.* London: Routledge.

———. 1993. *The Black Atlantic.* London: Verso.

Gitlin, Todd. 1980. *The Whole World Is Watching: Mass Media in the Making and Unmaking of the New Left.* Berkeley: University of California Press.

Gómez, Gloriana, et al. 1999. *La Carpio 2: Un barrio urbano marginal del cantón Central de San José con mayoría migrante.* San José: Sociology Department, University of Costa Rica.

Gould, Jeffrey. 1997. *El mito de "la Nicaragua mestiza" y la resistencia indígena, 1880–1980.* San José: EUCR/Instituto de Historia de Nicaragua.

Graham, Richard. 1990a. Introduction to *The Idea of Race in Latin America,* ed. R. Graham. Austin: University of Texas Press.

———, ed. 1990b. *The Idea of Race in Latin America.* Austin: University of Texas Press.

Gramsci, Antonio. 1973. *Selections from the Prison Notebooks.* Trans. and ed. Q. Hoare and G. Nowell-Smith. London: Lawrence and Wishart.

Granados, Carlos. 1995. "Etnicidad, parentesco, localidad, y construcción nacional en Costa Rica." In *Identidades nacionales y estado moderno en Centroamérica,* ed. A. Taracena and J. Piel. San José: EUCR/FLACSO–El Salvador.

Gray, Ann. 1997. "Learning from Experience: Cultural Studies and Feminism." In *Cultural Methodologies,* ed. J. McGuigan. London: Sage.

Green, Michael. 1997. "Working Practices." In *Cultural Methodologies,* ed. J. McGuigan. London: Sage.

Grigsby, Arturo. 2002. Nuevo gobierno: ¿Nueva economía? *Envío* (Managua) nos. 238–39.

Gudmundson, Lowell. 1978. *Estratificación socio-racial y económica de Costa Rica.* San José: EUNED.

Gugelberger, Georg. 1996. "Institutionalization of Transgression: Testimonial Discourse and Beyond." Introduction to *The Real Thing: Testimonial Discourse and Latin America,* ed. G. Gugelberger. Durham: Duke University Press.

Gupta, Akhil. 1997. "The Song of the Nonaligned World: Transnational Identities and the Reinscription of Space in Late Capitalism." In *Culture, Power, Place,* ed. A. Gupta and J. Ferguson. Durham: Duke University Press.

Gutiérrez, Joaquín. 1976 [1950]. *Puerto Limón.* San José: Editorial Costa Rica.

———. 1977a [1948]. *Cocorí.* San José: Editorial Costa Rica.

———. 1977b. *Murámonos Federico.* San José: Editorial Costa Rica.

Hage, Ghassan. 1998. *White Fantasies.* Sidney: Pluto Press.

Hajdukowski-Ahmed, Maoussia. 1998. "Bakhtin without Borders: Participatory Action Research in the Social Sciences." In *Bakhtin/"Bakhtin." Studies in Archive and Social Sciences and Beyond. The South Atlantic Quarterly,* ed. P. Hitchcock. Durham: Duke University Press.

Halbwachs, Maurice. 1992. *On Collective Memory.* Ed. and trans. L. Coser. Chicago: University of Chicago Press.

Hale, Charles. 1987. "Inter-ethnic Relations and Class Structure in Nicaragua's Atlantic Coast." In *Ethnic Groups and the Nation-State: The Atlantic Coast of Nicaragua.* Stockholm: CIDCA/Development Study Unit, Department of Anthropology, University of Stockholm.

Hall, Stuart. 1980a. "Cultural Studies and the Centre: Some Problematics and Problems." In *Culture, Media, Language: Working Papers in Cultural Studies, 1972–79,* ed. S. Hall, D. Hobson, A. Lowe, and P. Willis. London: Routledge.

———. 1980b. "Encoding/Decoding." In *Culture, Media, Language: Working Papers in Cultural Studies, 1972–79,* ed. S. Hall, D. Hobson, A. Lowe, and P. Willis. London: Routledge.

———. 1980c. "Race, Articulation and Societies Structured in Dominance." In *Sociological Theories: Race and Colonialism.* London: UNESCO.

———. 1986. "For Allon White: Metaphors of Transformation." In *Carnival, Hysteria, and Writing,* ed. A. White. Oxford: Clarendon Press.

———. 1988. *The Hard Road to Renewal: Thatcherism and the Crisis of the Left.* London: Verso.

———. 1990 [1981]. "The Whites in Their Eyes: Racist Ideologies and the Media." In *The Media Reader,* ed. M. Alvarado and J. Thompson London: British Film Institute.

———. 1991a. "The Local and the Global: Globalization and Ethnicity." In *Culture, Globalization and the World System,* ed. A. King. London: Macmillan.

———. 1991b. "Old and New Identities, Old and New Ethnicities." In *Culture, Globalization, and the World System.* London: Macmillan.

———. 1996. "Cultural Studies and Its Theoretical Legacies." In *Stuart Hall: Critical Dialogues in Cultural Studies,* ed. D. Morley and K. H. Chen. London: Routledge.

Hall, S., C. Critcher, T. Jefferson, J. Clarke, and B. Roberts. 1978. *Policing the Crisis: Mugging, the State, and Law and Order.* London: Macmillan.

Harvey, David. 1989. *The Condition of Postmodernity.* Oxford: Blackwell.

Herrera García, Adolfo. 1981 [1939]. *Juan Varela.* San José: Editorial Costa Rica.

Hobsbawm, E. J. 1983. Introduction to *The Invention of Tradition,* ed. E. J. Hobsbawm and T. Ranger. Cambridge: Cambridge University Press.

———. 1990. *Nations and Nationalism since 1780: Programme, Myth, Reality.* Cambridge: Cambridge University Press.

———. 1992. "Ethnicity and Nationalism in Europe Today." *Anthropology Today* 8 (1).

———. 1998a. "The Death of Neoliberalism." *Marxism Today,* November/December.

———. 1998b. *On History.* London: Abacus.

Holquist, Michael. 1990. *Dialogism: Bakhtin and His World.* London: Routledge.

Hondagneu-Sotelo, Pierrette. 2001. *Doméstica: Immigrant Workers Cleaning and Caring in the Shadows of Affluence.* Berkeley: University of California Press.

Honey, Martha, and Tony Avirgan. 1985. *La Penca: Reporte de una investigación.* Lima: Ediciones El Gallo Rojo.

Ibarra, Francisco. 1948. *La tragedia del Nicaragüense en Costa Rica.* San José: Imprenta Borrasé.

Iglesias, Norma. 1985. *La flor más bella dela maquila.* Mexico DF: SEP–Centro de Estudios Fronterizos del Norte de México.

INC (Instituto Nacional de Criminología). 1999. *Informe de población penitenciaria, 1994–1998.* San José: Ministerio de Justicia.

———. 1999. *Población penitenciaria extranjera al 31–2–98.* San José: Ministerio de Justicia.

INEC (Instituto Nacional de Estadísticas y Censos). 2001. *Noveno censo nacional de población y vivienda del 2000: Resultados generales.* San José: INEC.

Innes, C. L. 1994. "Virgin Territories and Motherlands: Colonial and Nationalist Representations of Africa and Ireland." *Feminist Review* 47.

Jauss, Hans Robert. 1982. "Literary History as a Challenge to Literary Theory." In *Toward an Aesthetic of Reception.* Trans. T. Bahti. London: Harvester Press.

Jervis, John. 1999. *Transgressing the Modern.* London: Blackwell.

Johnson, Richard. 1986. *What Is Cultural Studies Anyway?* Working Papers in Cultural Studies, no. 74. Birmingham: CCCS, University of Birmingham.

———. 1993a. "Everyday Life: National and Other Identities." In *Watching Europe: A Media and Cultural Reader,* ed. U. Bechdolf et al. Tübingen: Foundation and Tübinger Vereinigung für Volkskunde e.V.

———. 1993b. "Towards a Cultural Theory of the Nation, A British-Dutch Dialogue." In *Images of the Nation,* ed. A. Galema et al. Amsterdam: Rodopi.

———. 1997. "Contested Borders, Contingent Lives." In *Border Patrols: Policing the Boundaries of Heterosexuality,* ed. L. Steinberg, D. Epstein, and R. Johnson. London: Cassell.

Kearney, Michael. 1991. "Borders and Boundaries of State and Self at the End of Empire." *Journal of Historical Sociology* 4 (1).

Knight, Alan. 1996. "Pueblo, polítca, y nación, siglos XIX y XX." Paper presented at the Tercer Congreso Centroamericano de Historia, San José.

Kinloch, Frances. 1994. "El canal interoceánico en el imaginario nacional: Nicaragua, siglo XIX." *Cuadernos centroamericanos de historia* (Managua) 6.

———. 1995. "Civilización y barbarie: Mitos y símbolos en la formación de la identidad nacional." In *Nicaragua en busca de su identidad,* ed. F. Kinloch. Managua: Instituto de Historia de Nicaragua/PNUD.

———. 1996. "Geopolítica y nación: Nicaragua, 1838–1848." Paper presented at the Tercer Congreso Centroamericano de Historia, San José.

———. 1998. *Política, cultura, e identidad en la transición al Estado-nación (1838–1858).* Master's thesis, Universidad de Costa Rica.

Kristeva, Julia. 1991. *Strangers to Ourselves.* New York: Columbia University Press.

Laliotou, Ioanna. 1994. "Nationalism in the Era of the End of Ideology: Short Stories, Grand-Narratives, and Greek Mythologies." *Cultural Studies from Birmingham* (University of Birmingham) 3.

Lancaster, Roger. 1992. *Life Is Hard: Machismo, Danger, and the Intimacy of Power in Nicaragua.* Berkeley: University of California Press.

Langer, John. 1998. *Tabloid Television: Popular Journalism and the "Other News."* London: Routledge.

Larmer, Brook. 1998. "The Long Goodbye." *Newsweek,* March 16.

Larraín, Jorge. 1994. *Ideology and Cultural Identity: Modernity and the Third World Presence.* Cambridge: Polity Press.

———. 1996. *Modernidad, razón, e identidad en América Latina.* Santiago: Editorial Andrés Bello.

Láscaris, Constantino. 1994. *El costarricense.* San José: EDUCA.

Láscaris, Constantino, and Guillermo Malavassi. 1975. *La carreta típica.* San José: MCJD.

Lawrence, Errol. 1982. "Just Plain Common Sense: The 'Roots' of Racism." In *The Empire Strikes Back: Race and Racism in '70s Britain,* ed. CCCS. London: Routledge.

Lechner, Norbert. 1998. "Nuestros miedos." *Perfiles latinoamericanos* (Mexico City: FLACSO) 7 (13).

Lehoucq, Fabrice. 1995. "La dinámica política institutional y la construcción de un régimen democrático: Costa Rica en perspectiva Latinoamericana." In *Identidades nacionales y Estado Moderno en Centroamérica,* ed. A. Taracena and J. Piel. San José: EUCR/FLACSO–El Salvador.

León, Patricia, and Isabel Ovares. 1983. "La prensa llama a la guerra." *Revista de ciencias sociales* (Universidad de Costa Rica) 26.

Linke, Uli. 1999. *German Bodies: Race and Representation after Hitler.* New York: Routledge.

Linkogle, Stephanie. 1996. *Gender, Practice, and Faith in Nicaragua.* London: Avebury.

Lister, Ruth. 1998. "Citizenship and Difference: Towards a Differentiated Universalism." *European Journal of Social Theory* 1 (1).

Lobo, Tatiana. 1997. "La vida cotidiana." In *Negros y blancos: Todo mezclado,* ed. T. Lobo and M. Meléndez. San José: EUCR.

López, José Roberto. 1989. *El ajuste estructural en Centroamérica: Un enfoque comparativo.* Cuadernos de ciencias sociales, no. 26. San José: FLACSO.

Lyra, Carmen. 1988 [1931]. "Bananos y hombres." In *Los otros cuentos de Carmen Lyra.* San José: Editorial Costa Rica.

Mackey, Eva. 1996. "Managing and Imagining Diversity: Multiculturalism and the Construction of National Identity in Canada." Ph.D. dissertation, University of Sussex.

Marcus, George. 1998. *Ethnography through Thick and Thin.* Princeton, N.J.: Princeton University Press.

Martín Serrano, Manuel. 1986. *La producción social de la comunicación.* Madrid: Alianza Editorial.

McClintock, Anne. 1995. *Imperial Leather: Race, Gender, and Sexuality in the Colonial Contest.* London: Routledge.

McRobbie, Angela. 1982. "The Politics of Feminist Research." *Feminist Review* 12.

Medvedev, Pavel N. 1985. *The Formal Method in Literary Scholarship: A Critical Introduction to Sociological Poetics.* Trans. J. Wehrle. Cambridge, Mass.: Harvard University Press.

Meléndez, Carlos. 1981. "Aspectos sobre la inmigración jamaicana." In *El negro en Costa Rica* by C. Meléndez and Q. Duncan. San José: Editorial Costa Rica.

Miles, Robert. 1991. *Racism.* London: Routledge.

Molina, Felipe. 1850. *Cuestiones de límites entre Costa Rica y el estado de Nicaragua.* Madrid: Imprenta de la Viuda de Calero.

———. 1851. *Bosquejo de la república de Costa Rica.* New York: Imprenta de S. W. Benedict.

Molina, Iván. 1984. *El capital comercial en el valle de labriegos sencillos (1800–1824).* Master's thesis, Universidad de Costa Rica.

———. 1986. "Labriegos sencillos y comerciantes en el Valle Central: Una interpretación del legado colonial de Costa Rica." In *El desarrollo económico y social de Costa Rica: De la colonia a la crisis de 1930* by V. H. Acuña Ortega and I. Molina. San José: Editorial Alma Mater.

———. 1999. "Clase, género, y etnia van a la escuela: El analfabetismo en Costa Rica y Nicaragua." Photocopy.

———. 2002. *Costarricense, por dicha: Identidad y cambio cultural en Costa Rica durante los siglos XIX y XX.* San José: Editorial de la Universidad de Costa Rica.

Molina, Iván, and Patricia Fumero. 1997. *La sonora libertad del viento: Sociedad y cultura en Costa Rica y Nicaragua (1821–1914).* Mexico City: Instituto Panamericano de Historia.

Monge-Alfaro, Carlos. 1982 [1941]. *Historia de Costa Rica.* San José: Trejos.

Montero, Alberto, ed. 1995. *La polémica 1894–1902: El nacionalismo en la literatura.* San José: EUNED.

Mora, Arnoldo. 1997. *La identidad nacional en la filosofía costarricense.* San José: EDUCA.

Morales, Abelardo. 1997. *Los territorios del cuajipal: Frontera y sociedad entre Nicaragua y Costa Rica.* San José: FLACSO.

Morales, Elsa, et al. 1995a. *Estudios sociales 2.* San José: Santillana.

———. 1995b. *Estudios sociales 4.* San José: Santillana.

———. 1995c. *Estudios sociales 6.* San José: Santillana.

Morales, Sergio. 1997. "La creación de identidad nacional a través de los chistes." Unpublished paper, Escuela de Comunicación, Universidad de Costa Rica.

Morley, David. 1992. *Television Audiences and Cultural Studies.* London: Routledge.

———. 1997. "Theoretical Orthodoxies: Textualism, Constructivism, and 'New Ethnography' in Cultural Studies." In *Cultural Studies in Question,* ed. M. Ferguson and P. Golding. London: Sage.

———. 1999. "Finding Out about the World from Television: Some Difficulties." In *Television and Common Knowledge,* ed. Jostein Gripsrud. London: Routledge.

Morley, David, and Kevin Robins. 1994. *Spaces of Identity: Global Media, Electronic Landscapes, and Cultural Boundaries.* London: Routledge.

Morson, Gary, and Caryl Emerson. 1990. *Mikhail Bakhtin: Creation of a Prosaics.* Stanford: Stanford University Press.

MS (Ministerio de Salud). 1998. *Notificación semanal, cólera 1998.* San José: Sistema de Vigilancia Epidemiológica.

Nagel, Mónica. 1999. "Exposición de la señora Ministra de Justicia ante la Comisión de Asuntos Sociales de la Asamblea Legislativa." Photocopy, Ministerio de Justicia, San José.

Narayan, Uma. 1997. *Dislocating Cultures: Identities, Traditions, and Third World Feminism.* London: Routledge.

Nathan, Debbie. 1996. "*Love in the Time of Cholera:* Free Trade at the Border Line." In *Geography and Identity,* ed. D. Crow. Washington, D.C.: Maisonneuve Press.

Noelle, Elizabeth. 1993. *La espiral del silencio: Opinión pública.* Barcelona: Ediciones Paidós.

Obregón, Clotilde. 1993. *El Río San Juan en la lucha por las potencias (1821-1860).* San José: EUNED.

OIJ (Organismo de Investigación Judicial). 1997. *Annual Report.* San José: Departamento de Planificación, Sección de Estadística.

———. 1998. *Annual Report.* San José: Departamento de Planificación, Sección de Estadística.

———. 2000a. *Homicidios dolosos atendidos por el Organismo de Investigación Judicial durante el período, 1990–1999.* San José: Departamento de Planificación, Sección de Estadística.

———. 2000b. *Suicidios atendidos por el Organismo de Investigación Judicial durante el período 1990–1999.* San José: Departamento de Planificación, Sección de Estadística.

———. 2001. *Homicidios dolosos atendidos por el Organismo de Investigación Judicial durante el año 2000: Un análisis desde el punto de vista informativo.* San José: Departamento de Planificación, Sección de Estadística.

Olivares, Sheila. 1993. "A Double Transition to Democracy: Class, Gender, and Ethnicity in the Reconstruction of Political Mediations in Nicaragua, 1979–1993." Research proposal, sociology department, New School of Social Research.

Oreamuno, Yolanda. 1961. *A lo largo del corto camino.* San José. Editorial Costa Rica.

———. 1994 [1947]. *La ruta de su evasión.* San José: Editorial Costa Rica.

Orozco, Manuel. 1997. "La política immigratoria de los Estados Unidos: Implicaciones en las relaciones internacionales y al soberanía." In *Inmigración y remesas familiares,* ed. M. Orozco et al. Cuaderno de ciencias sociales, no. 98. San José: FLACSO.

Ovares, Flora. 1978. "Educación como integración ideológica: Lectura crítica de los textos ODECA-ROCAP." *Praxis* (Heredia, Costa Rica: Universidad Nacional) 8.

Ovares, Flora, et al. 1993. *La casa paterna: Escritura y nación en Costa Rica.* San José: EUCR.

Palmer, Steven. 1993. "Sociedad anónima, cultura oficial: Inventando la nación en Costa Rica (1848–1900)." In *Héroes al gustos y libros de moda: Sociedad y cambio cultural en Costa Rica (1750–1900),* ed. I. Molina and S. Palmer. San José: Editorial Porvenir.

———. 1995. "Hacia la auto-inmigración: El nacionalismo oficial en Costa Rica, 1870–1930." In *Identidades nacionales y estado moderno en Centroamérica,* ed. A. Taracena and J. Piel. San José: EUCR/FLACSO–El Salvador.

———. 1996. "Racismo intelectual en Costa Rica y Guatemala, 1870–1920." *Mesoamérica* (San José) 31.

Parker, Andrew, et al., eds. 1994. *Nationalisms and Sexualities.* London: Routledge.

Perceval, José. 1995. *Nacionalismos, xenofobia, y racismo en la comunicación: Una perspectiva crítica.* Papeles de la comunicación, no. 10. Barcelona: Paidós Ibérica.

Pérez, Héctor, et al. 1996. *Estudios sociales 3.* San José: Serie Hacia el Siglo XXI, Universidad de Costa Rica.

Pérez, María. 1998. "La imagen de Rubén Darío en dos momentos de la historia literaria nicaragüense: La generación de vanguardia y la generación de los sesenta." Paper presented at the Cuarto Congreso Centroamericano de Historia, Managua.

Pickering, Michael. 1997. *History, Experience, and Cultural Studies.* London: Macmillan.

Pieterse, Jan. 1992. *White on Black: Images of Africa and Blacks in Western Popular Culture.* New Haven: Yale University Press.

PNUD (Programa de Naciones para el Desarrollo). 1997. *El estado de la nación en desarrollo humano sostenible.* San José: PNUD.

———. 1998. *Estado de la nación en desarrollo humano sostenible.* San José: PNUD.

———. 1999. *Estado de la nación en desarrollo humano sostenible.* San José: PNUD.

———. 2000. *Informe del estado de la nación.* San José: PNUD.

Poulantzas, Nicos. 1980. *State, Power, Socialism.* London: Verso.

Propp, Vladimir. 1968. *Morphology of the Folktale.* Austin: University of Texas Press.

Quesada, Alvaro. 1988. *La voz desgrarrada: La crisis del discurso oligárquico y la narrativa costarricense (1917–1919).* San José: Editorial Universidad de Costa Rica.

———. 1998. *Uno y los otros.* San José: EUCR.

Quesada, Carlos. 1998. *Al sur del Río San Juan: Diagnóstico sobre la situación de los derechos humanos de los migrantes nicaragüenses en Costa Rica.* San José: CODEHUCA.

Quesada, Juan Rafael. 1988. "El nacimiento de la historiografía en Costa Rica." *Revista de historia* (Heredia) special number.

Quintana, Emilio. 1962. *Bananos: La vida de los peones de la Yunai.* San José: Ediciones Distribuidora Cultural.

Radcliffe, Sarah, and Sallie Westwood. 1996. *Remaking the Nation: Place, Identity, and Politics in Latin America.* London: Routledge.

Radics, Katalin, and János Keleman. 1983. "Linguistics." In *A Dictionary of Marxist Thought,* ed. T. Bottomore. London: Blackwell.

Raventós, Ciska. 1995. "The Construction of an Order: Structural Adjustment in Costa Rica, 1985–1995." Ph.D. dissertation, New School for Social Research, New York.

———. 1997. "De la imposición de los organismos internacionales al 'ajuste a la tica': Nacionalización de las políticas de ajuste en Costa Rica en la década de los años ochenta." *Revista de ciencias sociales* (Universidad de Costa Rica) 76.

Robertson, Roland. 1991. "Social Theory, Cultural Relativity, and the Problem of Globality." In *Culture, Globalization, and the World System,* ed. A. King. London: Macmillan.

Rocha, José Luis. 2002. "Microsalarios y megasalarios: Megadesigualdad y microdesarrollo." *Envío* (Managua) no. 240.

Rodríguez, Carlos, et al. 1998. *Modificaciones sociales en la estructura social costarricense a partir de la década de los 80s.* San José: Instituto de Investigaciones Sociales, Universidad de Costa Rica.

Rodríguez, Eugenia. 1998. "¿Por qué se aprobó el voto femenino hasta 1949?" Paper presented at the Cuarto Congreso Centroamericano de Historia, Managua.

Rodríguez, Eugenio. 1979 [1953]. *Apuntes para una sociología costarricense.* 3d ed. San José: EUNED.

Rohr, Elizabeth. 1995. "Etnopsicoanálisis y hermeneútica profunda en la investigación social: Reflexiones sobre el racismo." Trans. Jorge Sanabria. *Actualidades en psicología* 11 (87). San José: Instituto de Investigaciones Psicológicas, Universidad de Costa Rica.

Rojas, Rosario, et al. 1987. *Memorias contra el olvido.* Santiago: Amerinda Ediciones.

Román, José Gabriel. 1998. *La presencia migrante en los asentamientos humanos del Cantón Central de San José.* San José: CERCA.

Rosenthal, Doreen. 1987. "Ethnic Identity Development in Adolescents." In *Children's Ethnic Socialization,* ed. J. Phinney and M. Rotheram. Newbury Park, Calif.: Sage.

Rowe, William, and Vivian Schelling. 1991. *Memory and Modernity: Popular Culture in Latin America.* London: Verso.

Ruiz, Johnny. 1998. *Aporte a la investigación de las migraciones laborales en Costa Rica.* San José: Ministerio de Trabajo y Seguridad Social.

Rutherford, Jonathan, ed. 1990. *Identity, Community, Culture, Difference.* London: Lawrence and Wishart.

Said, Edward. 1994. *Culture and Imperialism.* London: Vintage.

Salazar, Carlos. 1978 [1947]. *Cuentos de angustias y paisajes.* San José: Editorial Costa Rica.

Samandú, Luis, and Ricardo Pereira. 1996. *Los nicaragüenses en Costa Rica.* San José: Consejería en Proyectos para Refugiados Latinoamericanos.

Samuel, Raphael. 1994. *Theatres of Memory.* London: Verso.

Sancho, Mario. 1980 [1936]. "Costa Rica, la Suiza centroamericana." In *Antología de comunicación y lenguaje.* San José: Editorial Fernández Arce.

Sandoval, Carlos. 1985a. "Una nueva historia se escribe en el sur." *Aportes* (San José) no. 25.

———. 1985b. "Qué piensa y qué hace la derecha en Costa Rica." *Aportes* (San José) no. 24.

———. 1985c. "Una voz ajena en Costa Rica." *Aportes* (San José) no. 23.

———. 1987. "Salud Nacional: Ardiendo en calentura." *Aportes* (San José) no. 39.

———. 1994. "Costa Rica: Muchos canales, poca televisión." *Contribuciones* (Instituto de Investigaciones Sociales, Universidad de Costa Rica) 21.

———. 1996. "Comunicación: De la *gran teoría* a aproximaciones cualitativas." *Revista de ciencias sociales* (Universidad de Costa Rica) 72.

———. 1997. *Sueños y sudores en la vida cotidiana: Trabajadores y trabajadoras de la maquila y la construcción en Costa Rica.* San José: EUCR.

———, ed. 2000. *¿Cómo me siento en Costa Rica? Autobiografías de nicaragüenses.* San José: Instituto de Investigaciones Sociales, Universidad de Costa Rica.

Sandywell, Barry. 1998. "The Shock of the Old: Mikhail Bakhtin's Contributions to the Theory of Time and Alterity." In *Bakhtin and the Human Sciences,* ed. M. Mayerfeld and M. Gardiner. London: Sage.

SC (Sala Constitucional). 1993. *Voto, 1786–93.* San José: SC.

Schlesinger, Philip. 1991. *Media, State, and Nation: Political Violence and Collective Identities.* London: Sage.

Schmidt, Anabelle. 1979. *Los extranjeros en Costa Rica.* San José: Comité Nacional de Población.

Scott, Joan. 1992. "Experience." In *Feminists Theorize the Political,* ed. J. Butler and J. Scott. London: Routledge.

Seidel, Gill. 1988. "Right-wing Discourse and Power: Exclusion and Resistance." In *The Nature of the Right: A Feminist Analysis of Order Patterns,* ed. G. Seidel. Philadelphia: J. Benjamins.

Selser, Gregorio. 1974. *Sandino, general de hombres libres.* 2d ed. San José: EDUCA.

Sibley, David. 1995. *Geographies of Exclusion.* London: Routledge.

SITAGAH/CODEHU (Sindicato de Trabajadores Agrícolas, Ganaderos, y

Anexos de Heredia/Comisión de Derechos Humanos). 1994. "Testimonios de la huelga en la Geest Caribbean 1994." Photocopy, San José.
Skeggs, Beverly. 1997. *Formations of Gender and Class.* London: Sage.
Skidmore, Thomas. 1990. "Racial Ideas and Social Policy in Brazil, 1870–1940." In *The Idea of Race in Latin America,* ed. R. Graham. Austin: University of Texas Press.
Smith, Anthony. 1995. *Nations and Nationalism in the Global Era.* Cambridge: Polity Press.
———. 1998. *Nationalism and Modernism.* London: Routledge.
Sojo, Carlos. 1991. "Fuerzas sociales y política exterior: Análisis de las relaciones Costa Rica–Nicaragua." Master's thesis, Universidad de Costa Rica.
Solís, Manuel. 1992. *Costa Rica: ¿Reformismo socialdemócrata o liberal?* San José: FLACSO.
———. 1995. "Sobre la cuestión de las soluciones a la tica." Photocopy.
Solís, Manuel, and Alfonso González. 1998. *La identidad mutilada.* San José: EUCR.
Sommer, Doris. 1988. "'Not Just a Personal Story': Women's *Testimonios* and the Plural Self." In *Life/Lines: Theorizing Women's Autobiography,* ed. B. Brodzki and C. Schenck. Ithaca: Cornell University Press.
———. 1991. "Rigoberta's Secrets." *Latin American Perspectives* (18) 3.
Sommers, Margaret. 1994. "The Narrative Constitution of Identity: A Relational and Network Approach." *Theory and Society* 23.
Soto Quirós, Ronald. 1998. "Inmigración e identidad nacional en Costa Rica, 1904–1942." Licenciate thesis, Universidad de Costa Rica.
Stallybrass, Peter, and Allon White. 1986. *The Politics and Poetics of Transgression.* Ithaca: Cornell University Press.
Steedman, Carolyn. 1986. *Landscape for a Good Woman.* London: Virago.
———. 1997. "Writing the Self: The End of the Scholarship Girl." In *Cultural Methodologies,* ed. J. McGuigan. London: Sage.
Stepan, Nancy. 1991. *"The Hour of Eugenics": Race, Gender, and Nation in Latin America.* Ithaca: Cornell University Press.
Stone, Samuel. 1985. *La dinastía de los conquistadores.* San José: EDUCA.
Summerfield, Penny. 1998. *Women's Wartime Lives.* Manchester: Manchester University Press.
Taracena, Arturo. 1995a. "Historia política de Centroamérica (1821–1930)." In *Encuentros con la historia,* ed. M. Vannini. Managua: Instituto de Historia de Nicaragua UCA.
———. 1995b. "Nación y república en Centroamérica (1821–1864)." In *Identidades nacionales y estado moderno en Centroamérica,* ed. A. Taracena and J. Piel. San José: EUCR/FLACSO–El Salvador.

Thompson, Edward. 1978. *The Poverty of the Theory and Other Essays.* London: Merlin.

Tihanov, Galin. 2000. "Cultural Emancipation and the Novelistic: Trubetzkoy, Savitzky, Bakhtin." *Bucknell Review* 43 (2).

Todorov, Tzvetan. 1984. *The Conquest of America: The Question of the Other.* New York: Harper.

———. 1991a. *Nosotros y los otros.* Trans. M. Mur Ubasart. Mexico City: Editorial Siglo XXI.

———. 1991b. *The Poetics of Prose.* Ithaca: Cornell University Press.

Tompson, Douglas. 1998. "'Civilization' or Savagery? The Construction of Oppositional Identities in Nineteenth-Century Central America." Paper presented at the Cuarto Centroamericano de Historia, Managua.

Tuchman, Gaye. 1978. *Making News: A Study in the Construction of Reality.* London: Free Press.

UCA (Universidad Centroamericana). 1999. "En el vórtice de otro huracán: La corrupción." *Envío* (Managua) no. 204.

———. 2002. "Alemán: Enriquecimiento." *Envío* (Managua) nos. 238–39.

Umaña, Imelda. 1989. "La política exterior de Costa Rica hacia Nicaragua durante las administraciones del Lic. R. Carazo (1978–1982) y de don Luis Alberto Monge (1982–1986)." Licenciate thesis, Universidad de Costa Rica.

UNA (Universidad Nacional). 1981. "Presentación e introducción al Concurso Nacional de Autobiografías Campesinas." In *Autobiografías campesinas,* vol. 5. Heredia, Costa Rica: EUNA.

Valle Castillo, Julio. 1993. *Poetas modernistas de Nicaragua.* Managua: ENN.

van Dijk, Teun. 1992. "Discourse and the Denial of Racism." *Discourse and Society* 3 (1).

———. 1994. *Prensa, racismo, y poder.* Cuadernos del postgrado en comunicación, no. 3. Mexico City: Universidad Iberoamericana.

Víquez, Pío. 1887. *Relación del viaje del señor presidente de Costa Rica a la república de Costa Rica.* San José: Imprenta Nacional.

Voloshinov, Valentin. 1973. *Marxism and the Philosophy of Language.* Trans. L. Matejka and I. R. Titunik. New York: Seminar Press.

Wade, Peter. 1993. *Blackness and Race Mixture: The Dynamics of Racial Identity in Colombia.* Baltimore: Johns Hopkins University Press.

———. 1997. *Race and Ethnicity in Latin America.* London: Pluto.

Wagner, Peter. 1994. *A Sociology of Modernity: Liberty and Discipline.* London: Routledge.

Wallerstein, Immanuel. 1991. "The Construction of Peoplehood: Racism, Nationalism, Ethnicity." In *Race, Nation, Class: Ambiguous Identities,* ed. E. Balibar and I. Wallerstein. Trans. C. Turner. London: Verso.

Westerman, William. 1994. "Central American Refugee Testimonies and Performed Life Histories in the Sanctuary Movement." In *Migration and Identity,* ed. R. Benmayor and A. Skotnes. International Yearbook of Oral History and Life Histories, vol. 3. Oxford: Oxford University Press.

Webb, Simon. 1998. "Masculinities at the Margins: Representations of the *Malandro* and the *Pachuco.*" In *Imagination beyond Nation: Latin American Popular Culture,* ed. E. Bueno and T. Caesar. Pittsburgh: University of Pittsburgh Press.

Williams, Brackette. 1989. "A Class Act: Anthropology and the Race to Nation across Ethnic Terrain." *Annual Review of Anthropology* 18.

Williams, Gareth. 1996. "The Fantasies of Cultural Exchange in Latin American Subaltern Studies." In *The Real Thing: Testimonial Discourse and Latin America,* ed. G. Gugelberger. Durham: Duke University Press.

Williams, Raymond. 1977. *Marxism and Literature.* Oxford: Oxford University Press.

Willis, Paul. 1980. "Notes on Method." In *Culture, Media, Language: Working Papers in Cultural Studies, 1972–79,* ed. S. Hall, D. Hobson, A. Lowe and P. Willis. London: Routledge/CCCS.

———. 1997. "Ties: Theoretically Informed Ethnography Study." In *Anthropology and Cultural Studies,* ed. S. Nugent and C. Shore. London: Pluto Press.

Winant, Howard. 2000. "Race and Race Theory." *Annual Review of Sociology* 26.

Wolf, Mauro. 1992. *La investigación de la comunicación de masas.* Mexico City: Paidós.

———. 1994. *Los efectos sociales de los media.* Mexico City: Paidós.

Wood, Ellen Meiksins. 1986. *The Retreat from Class: A New "True" Socialism.* London: Verso.

Woolfson, Charles. 1976. *The Semiotics of Working Class Speech.* Working Papers in Cultural Studies, no. 9. Birmingham: CCCS.

Wright, Patrick. 1986. *On Living in an Old Country.* London: Verso.

Wright, Sue. 1998. "The Politisation of Culture." *Anthropology Today* 14 (1).

Wright, Winthrop. 1990. *Café con leche. Race, Class, and National Image in Venezuela.* Austin: University of Texas Press.

Wünderich, Volker. 1995. *Sandino: Una biografía política.* Managua: Editorial Nueva Nicaragua.

Young, Lola. 1994. "National Selection, Ideology, Environmentalism, 'Race.'" *Cultural Studies from Birmingham,* no. 4.

Young, Robert. 1995. *Colonial Desire: Hybridity in Theory, Culture, and Race.* London: Routledge.

Yuval-Davis, Nira. 1997. *Gender and Nation.* London: Sage.

Zavala, Iris. 1991. *La postmodernidad y Mijail Bajtín: Una poética dialógica.* Madrid: Espasa-Calpe.

Index